I SAW A DOZEN FACES...

... AND I ROCKED THEM ALL.

THE DIARY OF A NEVER WAS
BY TIM LEE

The events and conversations in this book have been set down to the best of the author's ability and memory, although some names and details have been changed to protect the privacy of individuals. In some instances, time was compressed and conversations were recreated. Occasional truths have been stretched. Tall tales may have been told. If you remember things differently, please feel free to write your own book and correct the historical record. The author waits with bated breath.

I Saw a Dozen Faces … and I Rocked Them All:
The Diary of a Never Was
by Tim Lee

COOL DOG SOUND

All photos courtesy of the author's collection unless otherwise noted.

Cover and book design by Susan Bauer Lee

Cover photo from Amelia's, Iowa City, Iowa, 1986, by David Conklin
(from author's collection)

Bark back cover photo by Kyle Hislip

For Susan: Without you, there is no story.

I Saw A Dozen Faces...

CONTENTS

by Tim Lee

FOREWORD / FORWARD!

In 2011, our friend and collaborator Craig Schumacher was diagnosed with head-and-neck cancer. It was a tough time for him and his wife Karen Lustig, involving strenuous radiation and chemotherapy treatments. And this came just a few months after Karen had dealt with her own cancer scare.

I told Craig that when he incurred the inevitable total hair loss, I would shave my head as a show of support.

Not long afterward, my wife Susan and I were having drinks with friends during happy hour at a local bar when she got a text from Craig. He was several rounds of treatment in, and his head was now hairless.

We, on the other hand, were several rounds of drinks in, and our brains were a little hairy.

"You know what we've gotta do, don't you?" I said.

"Yep," Susan replied.

Within an hour, we were home, on our back deck, laboriously removing the hair from my own head with whatever crude tools we had at hand, fueled by alcohol and M&Ms.

It took a while, but we got it done.

I kept the shaved head for several months, in accordance with my vow to Craig. Of course, when you make such a drastic change to your appearance, your friends can't help but comment. Most reactions were of the "looks good on you" or "your head is the right shape; it works" variety. Nobody told me it looked bad; everybody was positive.

In time, Craig's hair grew back, so I stopped shaving mine. Eventually, it returned to its original aging-guy-thinning-but-kinda-still-there status.

Immediately, everyone's tune changed.

"Yeah, you shouldn't do that again."

"That didn't really work on you."

That kind of thing.

by Tim Lee

Why do I tell this story? The answer is simple: because many of those same people have told me over the years that I should write a book.

Now that I've taken their advice, we'll see if their song remains the same.

Perhaps they should have listened to my mother, who was quick to tell people "don't encourage him" when I was a kid.

I do appreciate the encouragement, though, and the thought of one day writing a book has long been appealing to me.

But how would I ever have the time to even start such an overwhelming project?

Turns out all I needed was a global pandemic to open up my social and musical calendar.

So here it is: the diary of a never was. My intention is not to present a straight memoir or autobiography, although there is plenty of that among these scribblings. Nor am I interested in axe-grinding or reliving old grudges. I'm too old for that crap. Besides, I never got cynical enough to lose sight of the joy in this racket.

There are volumes of volumes out there in the world, offering up the overplayed trope of sex, drugs, and rock and roll. This is simply a rock and roll book.

Specifically, this is my story as I remember it. More broadly, I'm sure there are many others' that parallel mine, either chronologically or in spirit. I'm certainly not the only kid that ever dove into rock and roll with an electric guitar and a dream. And I hope I'm not the last.

Really, I just wanted to explore this simple question: what makes a man start bands?

The long-hand version of that query is: what compels a person to climb in a van and drive around to play music, make records, and try to win folks over, well past their metaphorical (and chronological) sell-by date?

Spoiler alert: the answer is, because it's fun.

I'd like to think there's more to it than that, but who knows? I guess we'll see.

I Saw A Dozen Faces...

"It's Better To Be A Has Been (Than Be A Never Was)"
— Song title from a Doug and Rusty Kershaw single, 1954

This is where I'd planned to quote that Loudon Wainwright III song that refers to an older musician as a "has been," not a "never was." But tracking down permissions turned out to be a nigh-on impossible task, and one that most publishing gurus advise against as difficult and potentially expensive (song titles, however, are considered fair use). Anyway, that quote would've been cool, so Loudon, if you happen to read this, reach out and I'll buy you lunch or something.

Great song, by the way.

"There's nothing there, just rattle to that buzz
Somebody said something 'bout a never was.
But we never took the handoff, we never got the chance
To turn the handle on the organ and make the monkey dance."
— "Monkey Dance" by the Tim Lee 3

by Tim Lee   ix

I Saw A Dozen Faces...

PART I:
COUNTDOWN

I Saw A Dozen Faces...

I. WHO AM I?
AN INTRODUCTION

Who am I to tell these tales?

I'm a just-past-middle-aged punk rock kid, an old new waver who never caught the crest. A working stiff who lives for the beauty and madness of art. The manic burst of Barry Hannah's prose, the otherworldly drones of Junior Kimbrough and M'dou Moctar, the found objects turned to stunning visuals by folk artists such as Earl Wayne Simmons or Mose T, the poets, improvisers, painters, philosophers, preachers, teachers, rockers, composers, photographers, and rappers.

I love them all.

My heroes are Clay F. Lee and Dot Lee (my parents), Howlin' Wolf, Eudora Welty, Sputnik Monroe, Larry Brown, James Chaney, Michael Schwerner, Andrew Goodman, and Patti Smith. Give me Flannery O'Connor or give me death!

I make a lotta racket, but I don't identify as musician. I think of myself more as someone who likes to see cool stuff happen, even if I'm the one who has to put it into motion.

I've waded into the music business, but never above my knees. My friend RB Morris says, "There's no business like no business!" He's right, you know.

I'm a rock and roll dude by nature, and a power pop guy by association. Part of me is still that kid who cut his gigging teeth on Thin Lizzy riffs. I'm a singer-songwriter who can't find a thrift store suit that fits, a punk rocker who looks all wrong in the uniform. I'd be a blues man if I had it in me.

I'm just in this racket for the racket ... and the joy that comes with it.

It's been my good fortune to have been involved in a lot of cool stuff over the years, and these days it's no different. I get to play with Susan Bauer Lee, a badass drummer/singer/

by Tim Lee

3

songwriter (and excellent life partner) in a combo/duo called Bark.

One night, a couple of years ago, we were playing on a small stage somewhere in the Carolinas. One of those short, hollow platforms that telegraphs the bass drum through the floor to your feet and then up your legs. I felt every beat and marveled at the groove we created together. My heart swelled. I wanted to stop the song and tell Susan how much I loved the feeling, but she would've thought I was just drunk, crazy from the heat.

Truth was, I was crazy from the beat.

Maybe that's one thing that makes an otherwise seemingly sane person start bands. On the surface, there's no rational answer.

But I'm an artist. I don't look back. Except when it makes for a good story.

William Faulkner said the past isn't dead, that it isn't even past. Kurt Vonnegut's notion was that time isn't linear, that these are all just moments unstuck in time. My friend Dan Montgomery says there's no future in the past.

The goddess Patti said she doesn't fuck much with the past, but she fucks plenty with the future.

Me too. I just wanna know what happens next.

The past is a nice place to visit and all, but I wouldn't want to live there.

But, as I recall …

2. HISTORY OF THE WORLD PART I: MEET THE WINDBREAKERS

Bobby set his Budweiser on the end table and pulled himself up from the easy chair to put another record on the turntable, twisting the volume knob up a notch as a new song blasted through the speakers. Loud jangly guitars, yearning vocals, and a soaring chorus — the essential elements of the rock and roll we loved — converged in sonic bliss.

We nodded our heads in approval and had another sip of our beers.

Bobby Sutliff and I played in competing bands: he in the Oral Sox and me in the Occasions, but we'd met a few years earlier on the front row of an Alice Cooper concert during Suzi Quatro's opening set and we'd hung out together off and on since.

As Bobby tells it, he was talking about guitars when we first encountered one another, but I wasn't listening. I was busy staring at Suzi Quatro's black leather jumpsuit.

Sounds about right to me.

This was our Thursday ritual. Bobby's day off from work at BeBop Records, and me dodging work or school or whatever it is a 19-year-old kid avoids on a weekday afternoon in Jackson, Mississippi. Surrounded by massive stacks of vinyl courtesy of Bobby and his two housemates, Jimmy and Darrell, we hung out and listened to the living room stereo in their old rental house.

By now, Big Star, the Flamin' Groovies, Dwight Twilley Band, and Shoes were the staples of our weekly listening sessions. It was 1979, and power pop — a loud amalgam of

Beatles-esque melody and hard rock crunch — was relatively new to our record collections.

We were digging it deep.

Bobby pulled out some recent seven-inch records he'd picked up somewhere. An EP by a group simply called Sneakers and a single by Chris Stamey and the dB's caught my eye, if nothing else for their homemade appearance. These releases didn't involve glossy covers and high-budget photo shoots like the fancy-pants record sleeves I'd seen in the store. No, somebody had to do some actual work to make them happen.

And these guys were from North Carolina, actual Southerners, not coastal hipsters (despite their then-current Manhattan addresses). Hell, they even looked like people we might know.

The fact that these releases were seven-inch singles or EPs, as opposed to full-length twelve-inch albums, reinforced the notion that these works were likely produced on a shoestring budget. I was intrigued.

It was exciting stuff. I mean, if these guys could make these humble, yet very cool, recordings and get them out into the world, perhaps a couple of Magnolia State yahoos like us could do it too.

Within a year, Bobby and I, along with Jeff Lewis and Eric Arhelger, joined forces in a new band, the Windbreakers (a joke name that stuck around much too long), and set out to make some noise of our own.

And releasing one of those little records was a part of the plan from the get-go.

Coming of age in Jackson, it was a tough town for original music, which is ironic for an area once filled with independent record companies that produced some of the most influential blues sides of all time. There were remnants of that world still around in the late-1970s/early-1980s, but they trafficked in the era's modern African-American blues, r&b, and soul. They had their own thing, and our lily-white asses and ringing guitars were never going to fit in with it.

When we started the Windbreakers, there were no clubs that offered original music in our town. Our previous bands had thrown a few of our own songs into the mix, but to get gigs, by

God, you played cover songs. The Windbreakers' home base, the tastefully-named Skidmarks, tolerated originals, but still it would've been tough to fill that 9 p.m.-to-midnight shift with our handful of self-penned tunes. Either way, the partying types (and yes, I believe that the beginning of the end of modern civilization began with the adoption of "party" as a verb) wanted to hear us play Beatles and Stones songs.

So, for better or worse, we were a cover band playing three sets a night to drinkers and dancers.

The local music scene did produce a handful of great funk bands that made full-length albums during the late 1970s such as Freedom, Natural High, and Sho Nuf. The latter released their killer jam *From the Gut to the Butt* on Stax Records during that legendary Memphis label's death throes. Still, when you went to see those guys play, their sets were loaded with Commodores, Earth, Wind & Fire, and Ohio Players covers.

The Windbreakers' set list reflected our collective taste: a healthy dose of British Invasion, early punk, rockabilly and power pop. Rock snobs at heart, we were proud of our musical knowledge, old and new. Hell, we weren't even afraid to take on a few soul classics, although in retrospect I'm not sure who thought it was a good idea for *me* to sing James Brown's "I Go Crazy."

Bobby was the first person I knew who took writing songs seriously. He had two cassette decks he hooked together, adding overdubs to his demo recordings, and stacking tracks into an almost unidentifiable mountain of tape noise and hiss. It was glorious bedroom sonic wizardry at its finest. At least, *I* thought so.

I'd written a couple songs for the Occasions, including "That Girl" (which ended up on the first Windbreakers waxing), but Bobby was serious enough to capture his words and melodies on tape. His approach was inspiring; mine was barely a work in progress.

Outside our little deep South bubble, new wave and punk rock were burgeoning trends, laying the groundwork for an independent scene consisting of labels, clubs, and college radio stations that existed outside the influence of the dinosaur-like major label industry. Our little crowd of like-minded types was intent on dragging that scene kicking and screaming into the Magnolia State.

Not that we lived in a total musical and cultural hellhole.
Our hometown always had its share of oddballs, hipsters, and
record collectors, folks who had long been into underground
and obscure music. I had one friend who owned nine original
still-sealed copies of Radio City long before the Big Star
albums were reissued. Yes, there were obsessives among us.

By the early 1980s, a few local acts had released independent singles. The first one I remember was the late David Seay's infamous "Chrome Dildo" 45. While not necessarily punk or new wave, Seay definitely functioned outside the mainstream. His live shows often included an inspired takeoff on King Crimson's "In the Court of the Crimson King" renamed "In the Court of the Dairy Queen," in which his re-written lyrics told the tale of a bunch of hippies who live together in a big house, sending their women out to work at DQ everyday while the men stayed home to do hippie stuff. It remains, to this day, one of the funniest things I've witnessed live.

The Oral Sox put out a 45 in 1980, which included an early version of Bobby's "Make A Fool Out of Me." The Drapes, a self-described "Mod-a-billy" band from down the road in Hattiesburg, released an excellent seven-inch EP on their own Sharp Circle Records label that same year.

Though not actually a band, Jacksonian Ed Inman released an early punk single under the name Ed Nasty & the Dopeds that is highly sought after by collectors today.

In the surrounding areas, Alabama's Jim Bob and the Leisure Suits and Louisiana's Bas Clas put out their own seven-inch records. Even the notorious Shit Dogs from Baton Rouge released the *History of Cheese* EP (name a better record title; I dare you).

So there was some precedent when we started planning the first Windbreakers release in 1981.

We had no idea how we'd finance this project, but things have a funny way of working out sometimes. That winter, we were offered a New Year's Eve gig at the Port Gibson Country Club in the southwest corner of the state. I'm pretty sure they waited until the last minute to book a band and we were the only act available at such a late hour. Playing three sets for the well-heeled offspring of the Confederacy didn't sound like much fun, but the cabbage was plenty green, so we agreed and the die was cast. We booked studio time and contacted a pressing plant.

Come December 31, we suffered through the show, introducing every song (including our own) as a Bad Company number while the landed gentry danced and drank the night away.

I have almost no memory of that evening otherwise, but it certainly served as a means to an end. Less than a week later, we were in a recording studio for the first of three evenings at Trace, a joint that catered mostly to gospel musicians in Jackson's northern suburbs. Let's just say it was a learning experience. We didn't have a clue as to what we were doing, and I don't think the engineer knew much more than us about capturing the sound of rock and roll on magnetic tape.

Now that I think about it, "learning experience" is an overstatement. All we learned was that there had to be cooler ways to make records.

Song-wise, Jeff brought in "Young Republicans," which we all thought was great. He'd actually written a political song that we didn't think sucked. Neither Bobby nor I had that in us at the time. Hell, I'm not sure I could've spelled "politics" at that age.

Being the most prolific among us at the time, Bobby contributed two songs: "The Girl For Me" (in dropped D tuning no less) and "Black & White" (not to be confused with the dB's song of the same name), which pretty much set the template for Bobby's approach to songwriting moving forward.

The guy has written some amazing tunes over the years, with a style that he rarely strays from. It's a good formula, so if it ain't broke …

My sole contribution was "That Girl," with a title drolly borrowed from the 1960s sitcom starring Marlo Thomas. We were all suckers for retro-references. Despite my previous efforts to write songs, "That Girl" was the first (and probably only for quite some time) that passed muster as a complete song.

Listening back to that record now, it holds up pretty well for a first effort. Bobby's tunes already had the consistency of quality upon which he continued to build in the coming years. Jeff's song is different enough to foreshadow his impending departure from the band. Mine is decent, but I had a long way to go as a songwriter.

With the help of our pal and sound man George Kendrick, who hung out and helped us dial in sounds, we got four songs recorded. Step one completed.

The next lesson we learned was one that most bands encounter when releasing their first D.I.Y. record: artwork is always the holdup. You can write and record all the songs in the world, but until your artist buddy finishes the graphics, you're in hurry-up-and-wait mode. Let's face it, nobody's sense of urgency holds a candle to that of the band members.

I worked at a hip t-shirt printing shop and talked my boss, Paul Canzoneri, a local record collector guru who contributed much to my musical education, and our head artist Ed Millet, a local graphic/percussion arts weirdo who contributed much to my appreciation of the absurd, into putting together a present-able package. Jeff worked at a print shop that could reproduce the paper sleeves. Despite (or perhaps because of) these cost-cutting measures, it took several months to complete.

In the meantime, we sent the tapes off to be mastered and replicated at a pressing plant in Ville Platte, Louisiana. By early fall, hands still sticky from gluing sleeves together, at long last we held copies of our four-song EP, cheekily titled *Meet the Windbreakers*. We called our little record label Big Monkey Records in honor of our pal Richard Nolen's euphemism for the act of sex. Of course, the record was release number 007.

Meet the Windbreakers featured our picture on the cover, our names in the credits, and a smart-assed mention of the Port Gibson Country Club in the thank you list.

Dammit, we had a record.

Thrilled as we were to have our own little piece of vinyl, and despite the usual youthful expectations, nothing changed in our world. We were just another local band with a self-released record.

A potential fan could buy one from BeBop Records or I could dig one out of the back of my closet to give you. Thus was the extent of our distribution model.

On the naiveté scale, if the Minutemen were, as they once proclaimed, "corn dogs from (San) Pedro," we would've been lucky to aspire to the level of funnel cake on the fried carnival food pyramid.

But hey, I was now a recording artist, and the journey could officially begin.

3. GROWING UP

So, who *am* I to tell these tales?

No one, really. Just another rock-crazed white boy who grew up in the middle class of the deep South during a time of great change.

My earliest childhood memory involves a Sunday night when I joined the whole family in our den to watch the Beatles perform on the Ed Sullivan Show. Clad in my pajamas and sitting cross-legged on the floor mere inches from the television, I marveled at the girls screaming at those guys with the longish hair who played guitars and moved their mouths on the screen. I'm still not sure who made a bigger impression, the band or the screaming girls. Either way, Beatlemania was plenty intoxicating to a four-year-old's mind.

That's about all I remember. No great details have survived the passage of time. The fab mop tops from Liverpool may have played "She Loves You" or "I Want to Hold Your Hand" (yeah, I know I could find out easily enough via web search, but I prefer to keep a little bit of mystery to life). It really didn't matter, because the experience was enough to pave the way for full-blown rock and roll mania.

Eventually.

Ours was a pretty big family: mom, dad, five kids. I was next to youngest, which was an interesting spot, kind of an anonymous place that allowed me to observe the people around me and pick up behavioral clues on my own. I've since joked that, by the time I came along, babies weren't particularly novel and, besides, I was only the new one for a couple years before my little sister Kaye came along to steal the spotlight.

As a baby, I was known to poke out my bottom lip before unleashing an unholy wail, a propensity that is still joked about among family members. I like to think I was just practicing, getting my rock and roll chops together. Little Richard would've been proud.

I grew up in the 1960s, when the radio was the center of the universe, every bit as much as television and its whopping two (eventually three) channels of entertainment. Top 40 meant a myriad of genres — pop, soul, country, r&b, rock and roll — all mashed together in a way that made you want to know what was coming next.

Riding to the swimming pool in the summer, in the backseat with the windows down, my head leaned against the rear console with the sun in my face, I loved listening to that four-inch oval speaker whisper the truth about the world ahead of me.

The Animals said we gotta get outta this place. The Stones just wanted some satisfaction. Stevie Wonder was born to love her. Smokey Robinson cried the tears of a clown. The Who claimed the new boss was same as the old boss. And Johnny Cash's poor protagonist just lacked a gender-appropriate first name.

Sure, you suffered through Bobby Goldsboro and Bread (yeah, my nascent punk rock sensibilities developed pretty early on), but I believed there was always something cool about to happen in three minutes. As long as you stayed tuned in.

My father, Clay Lee, was a Methodist minister, so we moved pretty much every couple years, whether it was across town or to a different Mississippi community. I went to seven different schools in my 12 years of public education, so it didn't matter how long I was in one place, I was still the "new kid."

It wasn't always easy, but I learned to be comfortable with it. An existence just outside the mainstream eventually became the norm, and that was fine. Time spent alone was more time to discover music.

Of course, that doesn't really set you up to fit in everywhere you go. But I generally found the outside world more fascinating than my immediate surroundings. The places I read about in books and magazines or heard about in the songs on the radio held my imagination more than the next street over.

From an early age, I hoped one day to get out in the world and see those places.

I'm not sure my parents really knew what to make of my adolescent eccentricities. My mom would tell me I was too sensitive, and my dad would opine that I was too cynical. Often in the same day. All I could figure is that I wasn't enough of anything anybody wanted me to be. So I just kept my head down and

I Saw A Dozen Faces...

tried to make everybody happy, going about my business under everyone's radar, largely unnoticed, a ghost in my own home.

My brother Jack is five years older than me, but we shared a room until he moved out when I was probably 13. We had a record player in our room, and one day he had an album collection.

At least, that's the way I remember it. This oddly varied stack of vinyl seemingly appeared out of nowhere: a Bob Dylan's greatest hits collection (whichever one had the electric stuff), Jimi Hendrix's *Electric Ladyland* and *Smash Hits*, *The Best of Cream*, *Johnny Cash Live at San Quentin*, the Woodstock soundtrack, Sly and the Family Stone's *Stand*, some latter-day Beatles, and others.

Being a high schooler with a part-time job, a VW Beetle, and a girlfriend, Jack was rarely around. He had important teenage matters to attend to. So, in essence, his record collection became *my* record collection, a pretty good beginner's stash at that.

I spent hours listening to the sounds that emanated from the grooves while studying the album covers, marveling at the freaks with their long hair I wanted to emulate, the loud guitars, and crazy words they were spouting. Who the hell was "Napoleon in rags?" Who cares? I loved the wonderment and mystery that sprang from our crappy little speakers. The hows and whys didn't matter; the way the music took me to another place did. The way those sounds made me feel alive was everything.

I'd pick up the needle and move it back to hear Neil Young's intro to "Ohio" or George Harrison's bridge on Cream's "Badge," completely enthralled

Those two swaths of sound were what initially drew me to the guitar. I thought they were the coolest, most exotic things I'd ever heard. Years later, I learned that they were both comprised of simple three-chord progressions. Guitar lesson number one: never underestimate the power of simplicity.

Jackson had a great underground rock station, WJDX-FM, which I'd tune into when I got a chance, but there was something about playing albums that really captured my imagination. I loved how the songs flowed together, especially on the more thematic Beatles collections like *Abbey Road* and the *White*

by Tim Lee

Album. I felt like someone was trying to tell me a story that I didn't yet understand. It was a different feeling than that of the AM radio and its seemingly random song choices constantly punctuated by advertisements.

That might begin to explain my adult obsession with making records.

My fascination with song lyrics started early. Our family had a big console stereo and a small record collection that ran the gamut from early comedy (Bill Dana, Bill Cosby, and my favorite, Jonathan Winters) to some classical (of which I still know nothing) to the Mitch Miller sing-along albums you'd get from the Firestone Tire store.

Despite its variety, the family collection was short on rock and roll.

Digging through the shelves in that console one day, though, I discovered a compilation of recent pop music that included Simon and Garfunkel's "Homeward Bound." I was entranced by the story it told, so I pulled out a school notebook and started writing the words down. Eventually, on probably my twentieth raising of the stylus to reposition it and catch every nuance, the repetition became too much for my dad. I wasn't even aware he had entered the room but, in his usual calm manner, he let me know I could listen to the song one more time, then I needed to turn off the stereo.

I'm still a pretty slow transcriber.

The one full-length gem on the family's shelves that I recall, coincidentally, was Simon and Garfunkel's album *Bookends*. I can't imagine how that one ended up in the household record stash, but it did. Before my brother's collection materialized, I laid on the floor in the den and listened to that album a lot. I loved the production techniques and sound effects on songs like "Save the Life of My Child" and the story that unfolded in the verses of "America."

Years later, I would bond with the aforementioned Chris Stamey over our mutual appreciation of that album.

There was a lot of music in our house. Pretty much everyone in my immediate family is a good singer, myself excluded, which is funny since I'm the one who's sung quasi-professionally on a regular basis. My oldest sister Cissy played piano for high school and college choirs. Jack sang in a gospel quartet called the

Morning Star, who self-released an album. My mom, Dot, also played piano.

My dad has an amazing bass voice. We kids often joked that you could hear him over the entire congregation during the hymns. We weren't totally kidding; you really could.

When we traveled, the family sang along to 8-track soundtracks from the *Sound of Music* and *My Fair Lady*. Well, the rest of them did. By the time I reached my tween years, I spent all my time trying to slip a Foghat tape into the deck when no one was looking. A kid had to try, you know.

Music may not have come naturally to me, but rock and roll was an escape from the mundane worlds of school and church. As the preacher's family, you better believe we were on the premises every time the church doors opened. Sunday school, sermons, prayer meetings, youth group, choir practice, potluck dinners, all of it.

All the dressing up and sitting quietly never set right with me. It was too much restriction for a restless kid. Hell, still is. To this day, I get fidgety any time I attend a sit-down function. Concerts with assigned seating? Aargh! Gimme a crappy rock club, a bar stool, and the freedom to move around at-will any day. That's where I'm at home.

More often than not, my mother ran the show. She was a woman of steel who ruled with a velvet-gloved fist, who could whip five kids into shape enough to make a good showing during church services. While *he* never said anything about it, Dot ingrained into us that we were never, ever to do anything to embarrass our father, the minister.

My mom was a loving person, but stern, and appearances were important to her. She was prompt and fastidious; the house was always neat as a pin. One could write an entire book about her Dotness, as we refer to her collective personality traits. I figure half of me is just like her and the other half is the exact opposite. We butted heads well into my adult years, which was the last thing I wanted. I truly preferred to keep a low profile, but it seemed to take her a long time to accept that I wasn't going to be like everybody else, and despite my disinterest in conforming to her idea of normal, I was really okay.

Fortunately, we eventually found a middle ground and became close long before she passed unexpectedly in August of 2017.

by Tim Lee   15

Quieter and more contemplative, my father seemed content to let Dot drive the bus. He would absolutely rise to the occasion and take charge when needed, but I remember hearing "Ask your mother" a lot as a kid. He and I have become very close over the years as well.

Leavell Woods, the south Jackson neighborhood we settled into in 1967 after stints in Raymond, Quitman, midtown Jackson, and Philadelphia, was pretty idyllic in a late-1960s white-washed middle-class way. The adults looked after everybody else's kids. It was kind of a "Leave it to Beaver" existence (late in her life, I loved to remind my mom that she raised us like a psychotic June Cleaver).

A couple acres of woods stood at the end our block. Filled with trails, they provided the perfect path for biking down to Terry Road and Cook Center. Terry was the main thoroughfare in our part of Jackson and Cook Center was a classic old shopping center anchored by a Ben Franklin dime store, a Rexall drug store, and Bell's Speed Shop, where we constantly pestered the guys behind the counter for STP stickers with which to decorate our bicycles. Across the street was Dog n' Suds, a traditional hot dog and root beer joint that resembled a smaller version of the diner Arnold's from the "Happy Days" television show, and a Tote-Sum store, the regional equivalent of a 7-11.

That Ben Franklin store is where I bought my first Creedence Clearwater Revival 45 and where my older sister Lisa and I purchased our first album together. We scraped up our chore money to buy *ABC* by the Jackson 5, which we took turns keeping in our respective rooms.

The drug store sold single Black Diamond guitar strings from a display on the counter, which would eventually prove handy. It also had an extensive magazine rack that, over time, added much to my rock and roll education. By the time I reached junior high, I would visit the Rexall just to sit in the floor and thumb through issues of *Circus* and *Creem* until the manager ran me off.

Remembered through the hazy gauze of time, it was a near perfect little bubble in which to grow up.

Inevitably, though, things began to change.

By the late 1960s, our school district finally gave in to the mandates of *Brown v. the Board of Education* a decade-and-a-half after the fact.

Our schools undertook the overwhelming proposition of desegregation in 1970, when I was in the fourth grade. That year, we had our first Black teacher, Mrs. Hicks. During the second half of the school year, Black students were bused to our school and we experienced mixed-race classrooms for the first time.

Even that happened pretty smoothly where we lived. In our little world, segregation was only a big deal in the news (and with many of the adults, I suspect now). Other than seeing some of our neighborhood pals moved to private schools (usually the "Council" schools that appeared out of nowhere to allow white families an easy, though dubious, out from desegregation), to us kids, it didn't seem to be too big of a deal. We generally got along without any real issues. Regardless of color, our interests were pretty much the same: recess and games of dodge ball or kick soccer. Outside of school, we watched the same TV shows and heard the same songs on the radio.

Toward the end of the school year in May 1970, violent protests took place at Jackson State University, the historically Black college situated just west of downtown. Being on the evening news, the story eventually infiltrated our little fourth-grade bubble. The rumor went around that the Black Panthers were going to march on nearby Whitten Junior High, located just on the other side of Cook Center.

From there, it somehow made sense to a bunch of ten-year-olds that a roving gang of "dangerous radicals" (as the Panthers were portrayed) would then turn due west and descend on our little enclave at Sykes Elementary. Rioting with the grammar school kids, right?

We believed it.

Of course, based on what I know now, the only reason the Panthers would've marched on an elementary school would've been to serve free meals.

A few of my neighborhood friends and I got together to formulate a plan. Since I lived right across Mikell Street from the school, we intended to sneak out the side door and gather at my house. We'd be safe there, we figured.

Our Black classmates listened in to our conversations. Their concerns were no less than our own, so they asked if they could come with us.

by Tim Lee   17

We didn't hesitate. Of course. C'mon, we were all in this together. That was our innocent take on the deal: we planned to be one step ahead of the mayhem when the shit hit the fan.

Of course, we didn't know the real story. We didn't know that two people had actually been killed when police opened fire on the protesters at Jackson State.

We were just dumb kids. Well-meaning, mind you, but comfortably dumb.

The following year, a bunch of us sixth-graders from all over Jackson were bused downtown to Davis Elementary (heralded most recently for changing its name to Barack Obama Elementary) for an experimental year of education.

All in all, Davis was okay. The curriculum focused mostly on self-directed learning, some modern hokum that some of us learned to use to our advantage, cranking out our work quickly and mostly coasting through the school year.

With grammar school in the rear view mirror, we were ready for junior high school and some teenage news.

That's when things started getting interesting.

4. WELCOME TO THE CLUB

"Man, did you hear that new Mott the Hoople song on the radio last night? The one about violins? That was cool!"

With the move up to seventh grade, we returned to schooling in our own neighborhood at Whitten Junior High, which promised a change from my first six years of public education. As budding teens, we were expected to be a little more responsible and, in return, we had more freedom with some of our class choices.

That new schedule also gave me and my small group of friends time to loiter in front the building before classes and talk about the songs we'd heard on the radio the night before.

This was a new world, but some things didn't change. Rock music was still the center of my universe. WJDX-FM had transformed into WZZQ, and that station became a beacon, introducing a wider range of less commercial sounds into my world. No longer relying on my hand-me-down record collection, I was seeking out my own musical identity. Every morning before class, my pals and I compared notes about the songs we had heard the night before, deciding what we thought was cool and what was not. Based on our half-assed musical analyses, you'd have thought we were the little league staff of *Creem*.

Oh yeah, that Mott the Hoople song was "Violence," and it wasn't about violins. It definitely made the "cool" list.

In the early 1970s, school populations were still being mixed and expanded. In addition to our Leavell Woods neighbors and the Black students from other parts of town, our counterparts from the nearby, more hardscrabble, communities of Choctaw Village and Doodleville were added to our peculiar little south Jackson melting pot.

I fell in with a handful of kids who were into rock and roll. It was the only thing on my mind most of the time.

As we developed our own personalities, we also paid more attention to our clothing. I'd been wearing blue jeans since the fifth grade, having noticed that was what my older brother and his friends wore. By seventh grade, though, my pals and I were pretty much all denim, all the time. Bell-bottomed hip-huggers and a t-shirt covered by an unbuttoned "work" shirt generally completed our monochromatic ensembles.

With all that faded blue, we could've passed for Allman Brothers roadies in training.

I had a denim work shirt with a silk screen of Mickey Mouse emblazoned on the back. My prized possession at the time, I wore it until it fell apart on me, just like the Faces jersey my brother scored for me from his buddy who owned the screen-printing shop, or the Lou Reed shirt I bought from the bargain bin at a record store a couple years later. Cool clothes were hard to come by, so you wore them until they rotted.

Friday nights, after the networks news went off the air and the parents had gone to bed, were reserved for ABC's "In Concert" and "Midnight Special" on NBC. Between those two shows, you could take in non-stop popular music from 10:30 p.m. to 1 a.m. Everybody from Sparks to LaBelle to Uriah Heep (one of my gang's favorites) to Dan Fogelberg to Montrose to the Isley Brothers performed on those programs. The variety was staggering.

The Monday morning gathering in front of the school was reserved for discussion of the bands we had seen on those shows over the weekend.

Did you see Seals and Crofts? Meh.

What about Billy Preston? Cool!

Kiss? Hell yeah!

Ohio Players? Alright!

Wishbone Ash? Right on!

I can't stress enough what a musical education those programs provided.

For a rock and roll kid, it was prime time. WZZQ played T. Rex, the Allman Brothers Band, David Bowie, Pink Floyd, Mott the Hoople (my favorite), Lynyrd Skynyrd's first LP, Lou Reed, Led Zeppelin, Fleetwood Mac (the then-current Bob Welch material as well as the earlier Peter Green stuff), Little Feat,

Todd Rundgren, the Grateful Dead, Alice Cooper, Quicksilver Messenger Service, and more. Those TV shows rounded out that exposure with folkier and funkier fare. It was a lot to take in, and I was intent on absorbing as much as I could.

Seeing lesser-known acts like the New York Dolls, Sensational Alex Harvey Band, and Slade on the boob tube inspired me to search out their records in the bargain bins. Since that was the only place you could usually find them and the only place I could afford to buy records and tapes, the arrangement worked out just fine.

In the same way in which I'd been fascinated with the Dylan, Hendrix, and Simon and Garfunkel records around our house a couple years earlier, I was taken with the words that danced around the sounds and rhythms in the songs every bit as much as I was with the music. I loved the British quirkiness of Ian Hunter's lyrics with Mott, singing about an "automobeat on the street" and "screwdriver jivers" as much as I dug ZZ Top's wrangling and mangling of blues idioms such as "take home pay" and "my can of dinner and a bunch of fine." I was utterly fascinated with the proto-metal sci-fi of Blue Oyster Cult's *Secret Treaties* ("radiums of fear!") and the language Bowie used on the *Man Who Sold the World* album, with its *One Flew Over the Cuckoo's Nest* mental institution imagery. Oh by jingo, indeed.

Rock music was now a full-scale obsession. It was that thing that could take a Southern kid's mind to a thousand different places, each one more interesting and exotic than his immediate surroundings.

What I didn't know was that the next level was right around the corner.

During my eighth-grade year, a kid named Chad Johnson moved into our neighborhood from New Jersey. He was hip to cool music. Hell, his father had taken him to see the Rolling Stones at Madison Square Garden before he moved the family south.

Better than that, though, Chad had an electric guitar. A real electric guitar. Sure, it was the cheapest Teisco guitar-and-amp combo Montgomery Ward had to offer. But it was an electric guitar that made actual noise!

Chad mesmerized us with his single-string renditions of the "Smoke on the Water" and "School's Out" riffs. It was rudimentary, and pretty rough, but you could recognize the melodies. More than anything it was cool and noisy, so we had to get in on this!

We each started looking for an axe of our own. Fortunately for me, there was an old Kay hollow-body electric guitar in the back of my bedroom closet. A friend of the family had given it to Jack several years previously, thinking he'd get interested and learn to play, but he never took to it. It had three strings and no bridge, but otherwise it was mostly complete.

I pulled the dusty sunburst single cutaway instrument with the lone chrome pickup from the closet and tried to make a sound on it. Sadly, it was just too far gone in its current condition. It was going to take a little work to get me on the path I desired.

Once I expressed interest in guitar (very nonchalantly to the family, of course, while my inner Marc Bolan was dying to don some platform boots and get it on while banging a gong ... or something like that), my dad earned his sainthood credentials by carting me and that Kay down to Skeet's Guitar Shop over near the Western Plaza shopping center.

Skeets McWilliams was a celebrated jazz guitarist who'd grown up in Jackson before venturing out to make a name for himself in Chicago and elsewhere. By the 1970s, he'd settled back in town and opened his guitar shop.

The day my father and I came in with that sad old Kay, Skeets was behind the counter. In retrospect, he had to have noticed the gleam in my eye as I looked around his store, marveling at the guitars hanging on the walls, admiring their sleek outlines and splashy colors. He was kind enough to clean up my ragged old instrument, install a full set of six strings on it, and slide a wooden bridge under them for support. All for just a few bucks.

Thanks to Skeets and my dad, I had a guitar! I could start annoying my family members with my own single-string versions of the "Smoke on the Water" and "School's Out" riffs. And annoy them, I did. My sisters remind me to this day.

Watch out, world, I was ready to rock alongside my heroes on "In Concert!" Where do I report for the silver lamé suit fittings?

Of course, there was that sticky business of actually learning to play the guitar. I mean, I'd spent plenty of time on my moves, perfecting my air guitar technique in front of the full-length mirror in my bedroom, but getting some kind of sound out of an instrument was going to require a lot more work. Luckily, I had a little help right out of the gate, thanks to my two adult mentors: Mel Bay (the man who published the book of chords that had somehow survived with the old Kay) and one of our teachers at Whitten, Mr. Robinson.

The *Mel Bay Chord Book* is a time-honored tradition that has passed from generation to generation, illustrating finger positions for the various chords, starting with open "cowboy" chords and working through more complex barre versions and fingerings up and down the neck, illustrated with simple diagrams and photographs. I'm sure you can buy one today that has the same black-and-white pictures that the 1947 edition featured, with captions such as "This is how you hold a pick." An invaluable tool.

As for J.R. Robinson, our low-key instructor proved to be a godsend for aspiring axe wranglers.

Whitten had clubs that met every week on Thursday morning for various topics pertaining to students' interests. Each club was sponsored by one of the school's staff and (I assume) generally ran toward more mundane subjects as chess, bird watching, or stamp collecting.

I honestly don't remember what other clubs existed because, thanks to Mr. Robinson, we had a guitar club. That was the only one that mattered to us wannabe rockers.

We couldn't wait to join.

Guitar club met in the wood shop, and every Thursday, J.R. would bring an instrument from his collection. One week, he'd pass around an acoustic 12-string guitar or a banjo for us to get the feel of, the next week he'd let us crank up his Fender Princeton amp and hollow-body Gibson to get the rush of true volume.

He also provided us mimeographed sheets with the words and chords to the popular songs of the time, stuff like "Teach Your Children" by Crosby, Stills, and Nash or "Angie" by the Rolling Stones. Learning songs that we knew from the radio was infinitely more interesting to a bunch of young teens than standards like "Twinkle, Twinkle, Little Star" or "Mary Had a Little Lamb."

At the very least, it made me want to wrestle something recognizable as a song out of that old Kay.

One day, I was sitting on my bed, attempting to train my fingers to make the basic chords to Dylan's "Knocking on Heaven's Door," when my mom walked in the room.

"Play me a song," she said sweetly. I complied the best I could, pushing down on those strings with all my might and unevenly strumming the four chords in that particular song. (Random fansplaining: a lot of people think "Knocking on Heaven's Door" only has three chords, but that's because Guns & Roses butchered it. The third chord in the sequence, Am7, alternates with a C natural. There, that'll be $20 for the lesson.)

She mustered all the stamina she could to make it through maybe 30 seconds, then turned to leave my room, wincing and saying over her shoulder, "Maybe you need to tune your guitar," as she shut the door behind her.

Later in life, my mom and J.R. Robertson became close friends and collaborated on many church projects together.

It's a small world, sometimes to the point of claustrophobia, but mine was about to open up on several levels.

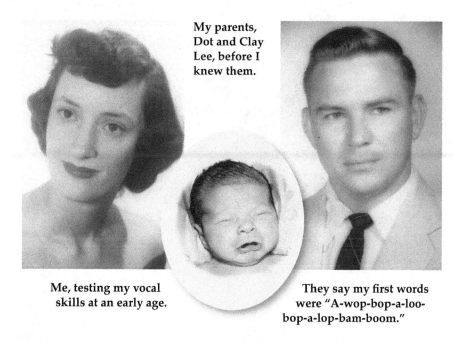

My parents, Dot and Clay Lee, before I knew them.

Me, testing my vocal skills at an early age.

They say my first words were "A-wop-bop-a-loo-bop-a-lop-bam-boom."

Family vacation, 1965 (left to right): Kaye, Dot, Cissy, Jack, Lisa, me. Kaye appears to be done with us already.

Me at 14: Faces jersey? Check.
Hip-hugger bell-bottoms? Check.
Teen scowl? Check.

Grade school me was a pretty
dapper little dude. Who would've
guessed?

I Saw A Dozen Faces...

Rockin' the auditorium, Murrah High School, circa '77 (left to right): Billy Beard, myself, Tom Gober, Tom's amp.

Me, *really* rockin' the auditorium.

I Saw A Dozen Faces...

PART 2: LIFTOFF

I Saw A Dozen Faces...

5. 12 BARS OF GLORY

"We're moving at the end of the school year."

Those were not unfamiliar words. So, in 1974, as my final eighth-grade semester wound down, we packed our stuff in boxes and started making our goodbyes.

We were only moving 60 miles south to the small town of Brookhaven, but to a 14-year-old kid it might as well have been another continent.

My classmate Beth McKee (look her up, she's a great singer/songwriter/keyboardist) threw me a farewell party. She and some friends chipped in to buy me the Duane Allman *Anthology* album as a parting gift. Pretty sophisticated choice for a bunch of 14-year-olds.

By mid-June, the family was settled in Brookhaven, where my dad had taken the job of district superintendent for the United Methodist Church's state conference. Jack and Cissy were off on their own at junior college, so it was just Kaye, Lisa, me, and our parents. I met a few of the kids in my neighborhood that summer, but mostly stayed in my room listening to music and hunkering down to learn that damn guitar. Nothing I've ever attempted has come naturally to me; everything has required a serious long-term effort to learn, let alone master. So I battled to overcome the blistered fingertips and aching hands, busted my ass to get a handle on that six-string beast all summer long. Honestly, I don't think I've ever worked at anything harder. I wanted this.

In those pre-cable days, our television's rabbit ears picked up a station out of New Orleans that showed Don Kirchner's "Rock Concert" on Saturday nights. I'd stay up late and watch, usually with my portable cassette player shoved up against the TV speaker to record the acts I really dug like the New York Dolls and Mott the Hoople. I played that Dolls tape over and over.

On weekends, I generally preferred to sleep on the couch in the living room, which was on the opposite end from the bedrooms in the ranch-style parsonage the district provided. There I'd lie in the dark with a transistor radio on my chest, long after everyone else was asleep, and try to dial in "Beaker Street," a rock show that traveled the late-night airwaves all the way from an AM radio station up in Little Rock, Arkansas. Amid the static, I could just make out songs by Robin Trower, ZZ Top, Procol Harum, and Blue Oyster Cult.

The sounds seemed to drift in from another universe. "Bridge of Sighs" never sounded more perfect than it did beaming in from the ether through that tiny speaker. The feeling was completely mysterious and thrilling.

By day, we could pick up ZZQ, which was starting to flirt with the standard format and programming that would eventually morph into what's now considered Classic Rock. Even as FM radio was becoming less adventurous, they still offered programs such as the "King Biscuit Flower Hour," where I heard bands like Roxy Music for the first time.

Music was constant discovery, which I loved then as I do now. There's never any shortage of music you've never heard (or, if you're as old as me, that you've forgotten and can come back to). Any place I could turn to add to my growing knowledge bank of music was welcomed: radio, television, magazines, books, whatever.

Rock and roll music was the perfect companion for a new kid in a small town with few acquaintances and nothing but time on his hands. Fortunately, all you had to do was put up your mind's antennae and receive the incoming sound waves from space.

I made it a point to seek the lesser-known sounds that weren't necessarily omnipresent on the commercial airwaves. Bands like Slade, the Runaways, the Dictators, and the Velvet Underground (I'd picked up an odd Verve edition of their first album with a wildlife painting on the cover for a couple bucks at the Green Stamp store, of all places) became "my bands." Nobody I knew listened to them, which suited me fine.

I loved the secret world I was able to inhabit through recorded music. Sure, I was cognizant of the popular bands of the day and was happy to talk about Aerosmith or Kiss all day long with other rock fans. But lesser known acts, I didn't have to share them with others.

This was my music, the perfect soundtrack for my teen angst.

Of course, I tried to convert a few folks, but my rantings about Mott the Hoople were generally met with, "Who the hell is Martha Cooper?"

As my sisters and I became acclimated to the small town, Lisa fell in with the popular crowd at her high school. A couple of the guys who played guitar found out her little brother played as well and invited me to jam.

Alongside David Bowling and Glenn White, I learned the valuable lesson of musical interaction, how even at its rawest and most basic, the vibe of playing live music with another human is an amazing thing.

That feeling is the kind of thing you can spend your whole life chasing. Trust me on this one.

During those developmental years, as I tried to find some kind of footing as a guitar player, there were a handful of influential confluences that set the tone (pun intended) for my future.

Number one, I came across a book in the Brookhaven Library entitled *Play Lead Guitar*. Similar to the Mel Bay chord book, this volume broke improvising guitar solos down into simple, easy-to-understand diagrams and photographs. Plus, it came with a seven-inch flexi-disc with some standard blues backings you could play over. That made for a very practical way in which to put the lessons from the book into practice.

Once I'd digested the main parts of *Play Lead Guitar*, I spent hours soloing over the three jams on the disc. As I recall, there was a slow blues in the key of G, an up-beat shuffle in A, and something else in a minor key. It didn't matter what they were, though, as I was soon running up and down those simple scales with wild abandon.

It sounded cool as hell ... at least to me. In retrospect, I suspect that, to anyone else's ears, it probably sounded like a dying cat behind my bedroom door. I would've been horrified at that prospect then. Now, I'd probably think it was pretty cool. As I continued this practice during nearly every waking hour, I got my fair share of complaints from the rest of the family.

While the book eventually returned to the stacks at the town library, let's just say the flexi-disc stayed with me along with the lessons gleaned from that thin volume.

> I've often joked that the secret to rock and roll lead guitar is simply a matter of learning Jeff Beck's melodic solo in the Yardbirds' "Heartful of Soul" and mastering any three Chuck Berry licks (your choice). From there, just mix and match. Anything else is just showing off. Also, put some stank on it. A purely technical term, "stank" refers to a certain looseness achieved most often through the use of a less-than-rigid right-hand technique and overly enthusiastic string bends to slur note definition.
>
> Oh yeah, and get a "stun" pedal, something you can kick in at solo time to make your notes jump out and grab people by the throat while promoting endless sustain and ear-piercing feedback. You'll thank me later.
>
> I'm really not joking.

One day, a friend of Lisa's told me, "You need to meet Barron Sartin. He's a Dylan freak."

"Barron what?" I said, while thinking to myself, "Hell yeah!" I did need to meet anyone who was as crazy about music as me.

In no time, I fell in with Barron, who was bemused when I told him how he'd been described to me. "Dylan freak?" he said with his adopted upper-Midwest nasal twang, looking up from his heavily hooded eyes. "Well, I don't know about that."

Despite his mild protestation, Barron had an acoustic guitar, a *Blonde-on-Blonde* approved white-boy afro, and the knowledge of many tunes penned by the bard Zimmerman.

Barron was a year or two older than me. Having recently lost his mother to cancer, he lived out in the country in a small house with his father, Junior Sartin. I spent a lot of time at their house with my guitar (thanks to Jack, I inherited an old Gibson ES-125 from his gospel group's breakup, which was quite an improvement over that old Kay) and the tiny amp I'd recently bought from a family friend for $25. Barron would strum "The Lonesome Death of Hattie Carroll" and I'd counter with "Jumpin' Jack Flash."

Barron's older brother, Laddie, lived in New York City and had a job building sets for an off-off-off Broadway theater group. I couldn't think of anything cooler or more exotic, so I was always excited when he'd come to visit. During his time back home with Barron and Junior, Laddie would sit around, smoking, listening, and offering encouragement as Barron and I tried to master the craft of singing and playing simultaneously.

One afternoon, I played David Bowie's "Moonage Daydream" for them. It was a big deal for me to actually sing and play a song for other humans. Laddie went crazy, slapping his knee and calling me "the King of Rock and roll." Hyperbole? Perhaps. He was only half-serious, but it was my first good review, so I took it.

Another day, Barron and I came across a used Fender Mustang at the local pawn shop, a sharp-looking solid-body in metallic blue with a white racing stripe, which Barron bought. So, like his hero, Barron also "went electric."

With the Mustang plugged in, Barron and I worked up a three-chord instrumental (neither one of us had the guts to sing in public yet) and enlisted one of his classmates to play piano. A kid named Ed in my class had a kit and could keep a beat, so he became the drummer for our one-song debut at the year-end talent show in the Brookhaven High School auditorium.

After practicing a few times in Ed's living room, we were ready. When our time came, we hit the stage rocking. Barron strummed his blue Fender and offered up a harmonica solo, the piano player (I have no memory of her name) took a verse, and then it came around to my turn.

I dug in and pulled out every trick I'd learned from *Play Lead Guitar* during my 12 bars of glory. The sensation of playing loud guitar in front of my classmates was exhilarating, and a bit nerve-wracking at first, but within moments became quite comfortable. I liked this feeling a lot. I'd learn to love it.

At the conclusion of the song, we did the traditional "big ending." Barron pointed his guitar neck to the sky, a la Rolling Thunder Dylan, and I jumped off my borrowed Peavy combo amp, a la **Born to Run** Springsteen, nearly skewering my chest on his upraised instrument's headstock.

As far as we were concerned, our schoolmates' polite applause may have been a massive roar. What a rush! This was another step beyond that initial kick of playing music with

by Tim Lee

others. We'd rocked out in front of a group of people who didn't seem to hate us. It was one of those moments of clarity that hit me like a ton of bricks: I wanted to do more of this!

> *I made my first attempt at songwriting around this time. Comprised of three simple barre chords, "A Flame Unto Every Passing Hand," was a cringe-worthy tribute to David Bowie's futurist rock a la **The Man Who Sold the World**. Fortunately, I had the good sense to never play it for anyone.*
>
> *I probably shouldn't have even mentioned it here. Forget I said anything. Really. Move along.*

When ranking events that influenced young Tim's guitar dreams, one particularly important instance was seeing ZZ Top on the *Tres Hombres* tour at the Mississippi Coliseum in Jackson. Folks who only know "The Top" as the MTV darlings with fancy duds, matching guitars, and long beards probably don't get the true essence of That Lil' Old Band from Texas.

Indulge me a bit of fansplaining, please.

At that point in time, ZZ Top were still building their audience. "LaGrange" was on the radio, but they were still working the road, spanking the planks, and playing hard and loud for anyone who would listen.

ZZ Top was popular in Jackson before most markets, mainly due to WZZQ, whose DJs played them as early as their debut album, the simply-titled *ZZ Top's First Album*. "Just Got Back from Baby's" and "Somebody Else Been Shakin' Your Tree" were staples on the station, as were "Just Got Paid" and "Francene" from their follow-up, *Rio Grande Mud*. Hell, the ZZQ DJs even assembled the first mashup I ever heard, which consisted of "Brown Sugar" from *First Album* and Jimi Hendrix's "Foxy Lady," dubbed "Brown Foxy Sugar Lady." You'd be surprised how seamlessly it worked. So Mississippi's capital city rock fans were primed and ready for the release of *Tres Hombres*.

The show I saw in 1974 was like a homecoming of sorts, and the 10,000-seat coliseum was packed to the rafters. Me and my friend David McRainey (who was a year older and had his driver's license) were there when the doors opened and grabbed a spot against the barriers in front of the stage and stayed there for the duration.

Opener Spooky Tooth was cool, but there was nothing like ZZ Top during that era. Sporting short haircuts, jeans, plain white western shirts, cowboy hats and boots, Billy Gibbons, Dusty Hill, and Frank Beard just looked like a trio of shit kickers when they emerged from the side of the stage and sauntered out in front of those stacks of Rio Grande amplifiers (six amps and cabinets on either side of the drums for those of you keeping score at home).

This didn't look like the rock bands we were accustomed to, but as Bo Diddley said, you can't judge a book by looking at the cover.

Gibbons strapped on his Gibson Les Paul, which hung nearly to his knees by an ultra-thin rhinestone-studded strap (the only hint of glamor on the stage), and turned his back to the audience. Raising his right hand, he leveled his forearm and ran it across the front of the control panels of the amps on his side, left to right, in a deft bit of stagecraft that made it look like he was turning every knob up as high as it would go.

With that, they dove into "Thunderbird" and pinned this little rocker's ears back.

Watching Gibbons weave his ear-splitting blues-rock spells was magical. He used every trick in his very deep bag — open harmonics, finger taps, pinch harmonics, insane bends, sustain, feedback — to great effect. In that sense, Gibbons, for me, was like Jimi Hendrix to the previous generation or Eddie Van Halen for the next. Witnessing his singular approach opened my young mind to the possibilities of making the twine whine in a particularly unhinged manner.

Gibbons' performance was life-affirming stuff. I left that show knowing that, whatever else lay ahead of me in life, I wanted to play electric guitar. Loud.

A year or so later, I learned another valuable lesson at that same location when I convinced McRainey that we needed to sneak in early to catch a Slade soundcheck. The British glam megastars were opening for headliners Aerosmith as they tried to make an impact on the American market, and I was excited to see one of my favorite bands in my hometown.

We showed up, found an open door, waltzed into the arena, and even did the stereotypical thing of hiding in the bathroom stall and standing on the toilets during the security sweep. When we heard Slade start getting their sounds, though, we rushed onto the coliseum floor. I ran to the front of the stage and managed to yell, "I've got all your records," to guitarist Dave Hill, who squinted, got a confused look on his face, and replied, "You do?," before McRaney and I were unceremoniously escorted out of the building.

After the show, we wandered around to the back of the venue, where we happened upon all four members of Slade, leaning on a station wagon and waiting for their ride back to the Holiday Inn. I asked them for their autographs, and they hung around and cheerfully chatted with us for a while until their driver showed up.

I was happy to learn that Noddy Holder, Dave Hill, Jim Lea, and Don Powell, these bigger-than-life characters I'd seen on television and read about in magazines, were cool guys who were happy to talk about guitars with some goofy kid in Mississippi. That taught me that, no matter their stature in the world, once they removed the glitter and the platform shoes, they put their guitar strings on one at a time, just like the rest of us. Well, they probably had somebody to change strings for them, but you get my drift.

6. UNCIVIL WARS

"We're moving at the end of the school year."

Sense a pattern here? This time, it came in 1976, at the end of my sophomore year. After two years in Brookhaven, we were moving back to Jackson, which was pretty exciting for me. Although I'd made some friends and progressed as a guitar player during our time away, I was ready to be back in the Bold New City, as the Magnolia State's capital billed itself at the time.

I was certainly ready for something bold and new.

I'd never really felt at home during our time in Brookhaven. I always felt just a little out of step with most of my schoolmates. Maybe it was just that awkward age; maybe I was just a weirdo who spent too much time in his own head (the soundtrack was definitely better up there). Whatever it was, that period offered solid boot camp training for the years to come. It taught me how to swim outside the mainstream and avoid the sharks.

Instead of settling back on Jackson's south side, where I'd spent most of my childhood, we landed on the ritzier north side of town. Swimming pools, movie stars, nice neighborhoods with manicured lawns … you get the picture.

My father had been appointed to the pulpit at Galloway United Methodist Church, the largest congregation the denomination had to offer in the state. So we settled into a new (to us) parsonage in the Eastover neighborhood, although technically we were on the west side of Eastover, affectionately known as Leftover. It was nice and all, but nothing compared to the opulence located just the other side of Ridgewood Road.

Ours was yet another low ranch-style home, this time in the center of an upper middle-class area. The best part was that I wound up with a bedroom that was more like an adjunct of the garage than a part of the overall floor plan. That arrangement allowed me to listen to my records and play my guitar at slightly higher volumes than would have been tolerated otherwise. And I obliged.

by Tim Lee   39

I entered 11th grade at John B. Murrah High, a large public school with a diverse population, but I actually knew a few of my classmates from our shared time at Davis Elementary in sixth grade. As with my previous schools, Black and White kids mixed easily through each day's various activities. There were even a couple of out gay guys and several recent Vietnamese immigrants who seemed just another piece of the social fabric that made up the diverse student body, one that would have been unheard-of just a few years earlier.

> *Please note that I, in no way, shape, or form, can even pretend to know or understand how my non-straight/non-white friends interpreted our school days together in the 1970s. I've often wondered about that, but all I have to offer are my own version of events. I humbly request you take my teenaged understanding of cultural differences, and their implications, with a grain of salt.*

I was a curious teen and read a lot. Like a lot of kids of that era, I devoured my share of Kurt Vonnegut Jr., Ken Kesey, and Hunter S. Thompson books, but I also scoured the stacks at the local library for anything that looked interesting. If Thompson mentioned a Horatio Alger rags-to-riches story, I checked out books by that author so I'd know what he was talking about.

Hey, it wasn't all just *Creem* and *Circus* for me.

I didn't really dig school, but got into my art and English classes, despite the fact that my painting and writing projects were generally pretty bad. I could muster an artistic temperament; I just didn't possess any raw talent or the concentration required to produce good work. My water color paintings featured shadows and light sources that came from the same direction; short story attempts were heavy-handed and clumsy. But it was more interesting than math and science.

To my mind, high school was just something to get through so I could get on to the next thing, whatever that was.

One weekend, my dad mentioned that he was going to be interviewed for a Public Broadcasting Service show after church on Sunday and asked if I'd like to hang out and watch. Sure. I was always up for something different.

I Saw A Dozen Faces...

Since then, I've wondered if he knew there was a history lesson I needed to learn. Was that why he asked me to attend, or was it just a random invitation? Either way, it turned out to be educational in a way that actual school rarely was.

The filmmaker conducting the interview was Andy King, a young New York University film student who had grown up in a prominent family in Philadelphia, Mississippi. We'd lived there in the mid-1960s, so we knew them.

Being an oblivious teenager, I hadn't bothered to ask what they'd want to talk to my dad about. But as they conducted the interview in his office — "60 Minutes" style in opposing chairs with the camera shooting over the shoulder — I listened to a story unwind of which I'd been blissfully ignorant as a child.

My father was assigned to Philadelphia's First Methodist Church in 1964, and I was four years old when we made the usual early-summer move just a few weeks before search crews discovered the bodies of James Chaney, Michael Schwerner, and Andrew Goodman, the three murdered civil rights workers, buried in an earthen dam.

Tensions were high in the small east Mississippi town, which only grew more insular as extra federal authorities were brought in to investigate the crime. So-called "outside agitators" were frowned upon, as were locals who associated with them. The Ku Klux Klan was a not-so-subtle presence in the community and had a hand in both local government and law enforcement.

My dad is an interesting guy. He worked within the framework of the United Methodist Church his entire adult life, from small pulpits to larger ones to administrative jobs and ultimately to the title of bishop, the highest position they offer. So he knows the workings of the church and is highly accomplished at all levels of its business and operation.

He is equally conversant with the spiritual side of Christianity and believes in the teachings of Jesus and what that means for a minister of the faith. He knows you have to walk it as well as you talk it, that you lead by example.

It was just natural that he went about his job in Philadelphia the way his faith dictated, the same as he had since he took on his first congregation at a little country church at the age of 19. He preached sermons of love and acceptance, of doing right according to the gospel.

He and my mom befriended a handful of federal agents and welcomed them into our home. In fact, a few of them were at our house playing cards with my folks the night before the arrests were made in the infamous civil rights case. Apparently, the subject never came up during the numerous hands of gin rummy.

As I heard my father recount the story for the film crew, some things began to make sense. The guy in the suit who hung around our house a lot, who I remembered as "Uncle Joe" or something like that, was actually an FBI agent who was just enjoying the comforts of a few friendly faces and the occasional home-cooked meal while stuck in a largely hostile community far from his own home.

Around the holidays late in 1964, my dad delivered a powerful sermon titled, "Is There Herod in Christmas?" His words were quoted in several national news outlets.

Without naming names, he'd basically laid out an indictment of the code of secrecy and the acceptance of hatred and criminal activity in our little town.

By that afternoon, angered parishioners were on the phone to the church's state headquarters, demanding "that communist" be removed from their pulpit. During the following week, my mom got random phone calls during the day, presumably from Klan members, telling her that her husband wouldn't be coming home alive that night.

Those were tense times for my folks.

The New York Times published a story just a few years ago about a theological scholar who was collecting civil rights era sermons to compile in book form. The main thrust of the story was how, of all the sermons my father wrote, "Is There Herod in Christmas?" is the only one for which the text disappeared, never to be found.

Both my dad and my meticulously organized mom searched high and low, but the original appears to be lost for all time.

The day after filming the interview, King and his crew arranged to come to Murrah for a couple hours to film me

I Saw A Dozen Faces...

walking the integrated hallways and sitting among racially-diverse classrooms.

To my knowledge, the program never aired in Mississippi, and I never saw it.

That PBS interview took place in the mid-1970s around the time that the murders of Chaney, Goodman, and Schwerner had reentered the limelight due to recent books on the subject, as well as the made-for-TV dramatization "Attack on Terror: the FBI vs. the Ku Klux Klan."

While watching that somewhat sensationalized mini-series, my folks added factual details. "That man is supposed to be Preacher Killen," my mom would say, referring to the notorious Klan henchman Edgar Lee Killen, giving a real name to the character whose "name was changed to protect the innocent." Hell, as far as I could tell, there wasn't an innocent bone in that bastard's body.

My parents' running dialogue provided a real-world context to the dramatized events in that television program.

The story became an obsession for me. I read everything I could find on the subject, trying to wrap my head around it. My knowledge of the event and my family's slight involvement has since been a major building block in the development of my world view.

It also presented my father in a different light than the one in which I'd previously considered him.

7. KICK OUT THE JAMS, Y'ALL

"You need to meet Benny. He's the best guitar player in school."

Despite my tendency toward a bookish loner's existence, as I grew more accustomed to life at Murrah, I sought out other guitar players, including Billy Beard, who'd gone to Davis Elementary when I did, and Tom Gober, a fellow Methodist preacher's son and longtime family friend.

Through those guys, I eventually met Benny Douglas, one of the most enigmatic and talented folks I've ever known. With hair that reached almost to his ass and innate musical skills, even as a teenager, Benny stood out in a crowd. Despite his appearance, he was a straight-laced cat who was an exemplary student and a leading member of the school choir.

And, boy, could he play guitar. The style didn't matter. He could finger-pick acoustic, Lindsey Buckingham-style, or full-on shred on the electric. Plus he was a good singer who had an encyclopedic knowledge of music.

Just the kind of guy I needed to know.

Over time, it became a habit for some combination of me, Benny, Tom, and Billy to bring our guitars and amps to whatever party was happening on any given weekend and jam out on any three chord songs we could all agree on.

I still remember the first time Benny and I played together. It was at a party in some recreation hall out near the Ross Barnett Reservoir, probably in 1976. There was a drummer on hand, but I'm not certain who. I just know that we played three songs and we went for an hour-and-a-half on that trio of tunes.

"Johnny B. Goode" was among them, I'm certain. Maybe "Jumpin' Jack Flash" or "Rocky Mountain Way." I'm not sure, but I can recall the feeling. I knew I was playing with somebody from whom I could learn a lot.

Soon, Benny and I became buds, hanging out at Pizza Hut, listening to records, and figuring out songs. We went to concerts at the Mississippi Coliseum together and talked our way in, underaged, to Town Creek Saloon to check out the professional hard rock cover bands who played their own unique club circuit: three sets a night, four or five nights a week.

By that summer, we'd pulled a few folks together to form a loose conglomeration, almost a band. Nuthin' Fancy usually consisted of me, Benny, and Tom, along with our classmate Lisa Goodman on vocals, Keith Treadwell on drums, and an older guy named Robert, who I worked with at my part-time job on the lumber yard, holding down the bass. Another classmate, David Weiss, was invited to sing with us on occasion since he was the only person we knew who owned a P.A. system, a Shure Vocal Master, of course.

We talked the owner of the local college dive bar Everybody's (formerly and later CS's) into letting us play Friday nights on the patio for free beer. Never mind that most of us were too young to be hanging out there, let alone drinking complimentary pitchers of Miller High Life.

Everybody's was a venerable neighborhood hangout located just across West Street from fraternity row at Millsaps College. A few of our friends would show up, along with a handful of summer school students, and the construction workers I knew from work who coasted easily from happy hour through the later hours, cheering us on while we figured out this whole band thing in public. We'd play two or three sets of Fleetwood Mac, Heart, Rolling Stones, and anything we could work out to perform for whoever was hanging around. If a song went particularly well, we played it twice.

I was in heaven. I had a gig, dammit! That alone made for a cool summer.

When the school year rolled around, I knew I was ready to be in a real band.

Okay, but how do you do that?

I gave the matter a lot of thought. One of the biggest lessons I'd learned from jamming with the older dudes in Brookhaven was that everybody wanted to talk about having a band, but nobody really knew how to make it happen. For some reason, it's not as simple as it seems.

My friends and I would plan it all out. We'd come up with a band name, we'd formulate an imaginary song list … hell, we'd even have a t-shirt design. We'd discuss it at great length. But months later, we were still just some guys playing an Allman

by Tim Lee

Brothers song for 20 minutes, not a cohesive musical group of any sort.

Somewhere in there, I made up my mind I was going to start a band. A real band. The kind that played places, had an actual set list, a logo maybe, all that stuff that bands have.

Eventually, we narrowed the lineup down to me, Benny, Lisa, and Keith, along with "Spooky George" Reid, the older brother of one of our Murrah classmates, who played bass. Tom stuck it out for a bit, but not long as I remember. We called ourselves Snowblind because Benny and I had seen a Hoyt Axton album called *Snowblind Friend* and we thought that sounded like a cool name for a rock band. We were completely oblivious to any other connotation.

Okay, step one complete: a steady lineup with a name and a growing setlist. Now, in order to be a real band, I figured we needed some kind of justification. You know, a gig. A real one, that paid money.

That's when it hit me. This whole band thing was never going to happen unless I got off my ass and just did it. That lightening-bolt moment defined my future: I was never going to sit back and wait for someone else to take the reins again, nor was I going to wait on things to happen on their own. And I rarely have.

Some people are born to lead, I suppose, but I've never felt like a natural anything. Regardless, I made it my goal to figure out this making-stuff-come-together business for myself, simply because I wanted cool things to happen, and somebody had to make them happen.

I called a cousin of mine who taught at a Catholic High School in town and, through her, was able to meet with the planning board for their fall homecoming dance. Against all odds, I convinced them that they needed to hire Snowblind.

And it paid $400. Hell yeah, we're professionals, baby!

From those humble beginnings, we managed to eke out a bit of a part-time teenage rock and roll career, playing three or four sets of popular rock songs for dances and clubs.

We would play anywhere in the area that would have us, including some roughneck joints around downtown Jackson that nice kids like us had no business being in. Snoopy's and the Wooden Nickel are a couple I recall that were particularly

*rough. But Benny and I would show up at these dives, ask for
the owner, and talk them into letting us play. We usually had
to wait for him to finish kicking some drunk guy's ass behind
the jukebox before he could talk to us, but we were patient.
Take your time, we'll wait over here.*

I saw some crazy shit in those places.

*Nothing fazed us, though. Not the reported knifings in the
parking lot, the occasional underpayment because we "shoulda
just played good stuff like Johnny B. Goode or some disco," not
the hard-asses who refused to pay the cover charge, certainly
not the woman at Snoopy's who compulsively displayed her
breasts to us. We just wanted to play, and we didn't care
where it was.*

By 1978, Keith moved on and Eric Arhelger took over on
drums. We kept that lineup for a year or so. Benny and Lisa had
graduated and were attending college, while Eric and I were
seniors in high school. Spooky George worked at a music store
and played bass at the First Baptist Church on Sunday mornings.

The band got a little more pro and landed shows around
the region. Dives like the Junkyard in Indianola, up in the
Delta (which did actually back up to a scrap parts yard), and
the Homestead in Hattiesburg (the only place I've ever seen a
condom dispenser on stage), fraternity parties in Louisiana and
Alabama, and more high school dances all over the place.

*For a while, we had a steady gig at the Shipwreck in Magnolia,
Mississippi, located just a few miles from the site of the
Lynyrd Skynyrd crash just a year earlier. One night, a guy
asked if we could play Free Bird for him. "It'd mean a lot to
me," he explained. "because I helped 'em pull the bodies outta
the plane."*

If there was a gig to be had, we were there to play it.

Among the wilder bookings we took was a one-nighter at
the Naughty Knight in Morgan City, Louisiana, located on the
coast where the oil rig roughnecks were stationed on their way
to and from the Gulf of Mexico. We played six sets from 10 p.m.
to 4 a.m., one of the most grueling gigs ever.

Somewhere about midway through the engagement, we introduced the last song of our fourth or fifth set and kicked into it. Lisa was singing, and when I turned around to add backing vocals, there was a tough-looking guy, dressed head to toe in leather and biker garb, about a foot from my microphone staring me down. And he wasn't smiling.

We reached the end of the tensest four minutes of my life up to that point, and I quickly moved to put my guitar in its case, hoping to get away from uninvited visitor to the stage.

I had barely gotten situated and was hurrying off the stage when he barked, "Hey you!"

Oh crap, I thought, here it comes. "Yeah?"

"I like the way y'all played that Heart song. That was real good."

With that, he toasted us with his beer bottle and returned to the bar.

In 1978, a typical Friday during my senior year at Murrah involved me sitting through morning classes with my Les Paul case next to my desk, awaiting the mid-day dismissal that released me out into the world and off on some grand cover band adventure for the weekend. For an awkward teen who was always "the new kid," that guitar was the conduit that not only connected me to the music I loved, but also gave me a bit of notoriety, a little notice. It was proof that I was different, that I had an interesting life outside our high school world.

On the Friday nights we weren't gigging, Snowblind usually practiced in Lisa's parents' living room while the rest of the Goodman family were at temple. There, we honed our setlist, adding anything we heard on the radio that featured electric guitars. From Heart's "Little Queen" to Tom Petty's "Breakdown" to the entire side three of Thin Lizzy's *Live and Dangerous* album, we covered a reasonable amount of rock ground.

Another of our more memorable gigs was for Lisa's younger brother Perry's Bar Mitzvah, which took place in the fellowship hall at Temple Beth Israel. Benny and I even dressed up and attended the service that morning.

At the party later that night, after the ceremony and reception, we were playing our first set, when we noticed a couple who were probably in their late 20s. They just looked out of place. These were obviously not your typical denizens of north Jackson.

During our break, we were introduced to the pair. She was none other than Nanette Workman, the Jackson-born session singer who'd appeared on numerous recordings, most notably the Rolling Stones' "Country Honk" (why do you think they changed the opening line to Jackson instead of Memphis?) and "You Can't Always Get What You Want." Her companion was Jim Ayoub, drummer with the Canadian hard rock band Mahogany Rush.

I was in awe. I'd never met rock royalty before. These were not the kind of acquaintances one usually made in my little world. These people beamed in from that other world I'd read about in rock 'zines, a place where they rubbed elbows with the likes of Mick Jagger, Keith Richards, and ... um, well, Frank Marino!

After picking my jaw up from the floor, I asked them both if they wanted to sit in. Nanette demurred and Jim tried ("I'd destroy that drum kit," he said), but I eventually wore him down and got him to kick off the second set with us on "Johnny B. Goode." Being a good little rock fan, I knew that Mahogany Rush had done that song on their live album so I was ready when he relented and said, "Okay, what do you want to play?"

That was the fastest version of the Chuck Berry classic I ever played.

One night, we were playing a homecoming dance in the ballroom at the Holiday Inn near where I lived. My parents had been out to dinner with friends and dropped by to stick their heads in and check out what their son was doing. They were there maybe ten or fifteen minutes.

The next morning, I asked my mom what she thought.

"You're going to hurt somebody's ears like that," she replied.

Like a lot of mothers of her generation, Dot was not particularly supportive of my musical endeavors. In fact, she often actively campaigned against them. Naturally, she pushed me to go to college to "have something to fall back on" and constantly pestered me to get my hair cut. "You just need to," was her rationale when challenged on either front.

Dot tended to do things her own way, but conformity was still important to her. Looking back, I realize that she probably felt she had to put in some extra work with me to try to make me fit in. The problem was that being a part of polite society didn't matter to me. I didn't picture myself so much as an outlaw as I just wanted to find my own world to inhabit, to make my own way.

Later in life, though, she and I agreed to a solid truce and became very close. Eventually, she even admitted that she admired the way Susan and I lived our lives on our own terms. Those was among the most important words anyone has ever spoken to me. I'll never know, but perhaps she recognized that, in some ways, we were not unlike her and my dad, who had stuck to their own guns all those years ago in Philadelphia.

Like most teen combos, Snowblind drifted apart in time. It was tough to keep it together with some of the band off at college and others still in high school. Before long, we all went our separate ways. Benny met Teresa, the love of his life, so he and I weren't hanging out as much. They're still married and living in the Pacific Northwest, where he's a doctor who posts YouTube videos of his classical guitar performances. Lisa moved on, and eventually became a successful businesswoman in Jackson and still performs around town with jazz combos.

Our high school hijinks taught me some important lessons, not the least of which was that nobody else was going to cut a trail for me if I was going to pursue this rock and roll racket.

As always, though, the ever-important next step wasn't so clear yet.

I Saw A Dozen Faces...

8. SPECIAL OCCASIONS: A PYRAMID SCHEME

Walking through the record department of Miller's in 1973, an album cover on display immediately caught my 13-year-old eye. In the photograph that filled the entire 12-inch square, a gaunt shirtless man leaned on a microphone stand with both hands and stared out into space, presumably at an audience. The singer oozed strange charisma with his platinum hair and dark lipstick. The photo showed enough of his torso to see that he was wearing silver lamé hip-hugger pants that barely hung on his thin frame.

It was one of the most intriguing things I'd ever seen. I couldn't believe that something so daring and oddly sexy could be blatantly displayed in a Mississippi department store in the early 1970s amid the infinitely tamer Doobie Brothers and Deep Purple artwork, as if it had been beamed there from outer space. I stared at the record, almost afraid to be seen in the presence of such outré material, like spending a few too many minutes in front of the soft-porn magazine rack at the convenience store.

Something about that image told my young mind that things had changed in the world, some seismic shift had occurred, and nothing was going to be the same.

This was not your grandmother's pop star. It was Iggy Pop, and the album was the Stooges' just-released *Raw Power*. I didn't have the money to buy it, and I doubt I would've bought it if I had. This was just too much. But I carried that image in my mind for years to come, ever curious as to what that recording must sound like.

Over the next few years, I read plenty about Iggy and the Stooges in my favorite magazines and even scored a copy of their first album in a bargain bin for a couple of bucks. But I

by Tim Lee   51

always wanted to hear *Raw Power*, because it felt emblematic of something I was missing out on.

By the time I was able to get a copy, the original had long been out of print, and I had to pay an import price for an overseas reissue. Also, that "something" that I'd felt that record represented had begun to come to fruition in the form of punk rock and its milder cousin, new wave.

In my ongoing quest to find the music I could call my own, in the late 1970s I finally discovered that sound, and it was a direct descendent of *Raw Power*. Even more than the oddball glam bands of which I'd been enamored in my early teens, punk rock spoke directly to me.

Although I'd spent my high school years playing music I thought people wanted to hear, most of my listening time was dedicated to the new sounds of punk rock and new wave. Patti Smith's *Horses* blew my mind all over again, just like Dylan's songs had done in the previous decade and Mott the Hoople's just a few years earlier. I loved her New York compatriots Television, the Ramones, Richard Hell, and Blondie as well. A cutout copy of Eddie & the Hot Rods' *Life on the Line* opened me to the thin line that barely separated British pub rock from punk, while exposure to the Sex Pistols, the Clash, the Jam, and Siouxie & the Banshees furthered my education.

For me, much of the initial allure of punk rock was that it is was of a different place. It came from distant planets like New York and London, thus it felt pretty exotic compared to the Southern and Midwestern boogie rock that occupied much of the airwaves. Beyond that, it was the antithesis of the bloated prog rock of the day that made it to our FM radios in the form of theatrical reinterpretations of classical music (Emerson, Lake, and Palmer), or literature (Jeff Wayne's rock opera interpretation of *War of the Worlds* and the Allen Parsons Project's take on the works of Edgar Allen Poe were huge on ZZQ). Not that there's anything wrong with any of those things, but they certainly didn't create scenarios that made a kid believe they might have a place in the rock world. I don't know too many young rockers who have access to orchestras.

More than anything, though, the message I took from this music was that there were no rules. You didn't have to sound like anybody else. "Do anything you wanna do," exhorted the Eddie & the Hot Rods song.

The Beatles may have inspired me to want to make music initially, but the Ramones convinced me I not only could, but that I could do it on my own terms.

At the risk of sounding like an old man yelling at kids to get off his new wave lawn, there was something special about those days. It took a lot of effort to be a fan of non-mainstream music, especially in places like where I grew up. We never heard much early punk or new wave on the radio. Even Jackson's fairly progressive FM rock station barely acknowledged this new music. Sure, they'd play a little Elvis Costello or Pretenders, but not much else. I'm talking pre-internet and streaming services here. There was no way to listen to bands like the Ramones without buying their records. No instant gratification. A lot of the albums I wanted to hear were only available as imports, which were generally twice as expensive as domestic releases, and I was on a bargain-bin budget. I still liked a lot of hard rock, as well as some of the newer singer-songwriter types like Warren Zevon and Tom Waits. I was almost overwhelmed by all of this different music that was coming into my world.

Thanks to *Rock Scene,* I had known about the Ramones since before their first album. Published photographs showed them to be an odd-looking lot, and the first review I read of their self-titled debut compared the LP to a "licorice pop tart." I was intrigued, but due to financial constraints, I didn't purchase anything of theirs until their third release, **Rocket to Russia**.

I still remember peeling the shrink wrap back from that stark black-and-white cover with the shocking bright pink lettering. I've rarely been so excited about the possibilities of a new record. Once the black wax was on the turntable, it delivered everything I'd hoped it would. Based on my previous experience, it was strange to hear a rock and roll record with no guitar solos, but everything else about their sound was undeniable: the energy, the power, and the catchy melodies sung over buzz-saw guitars played exclusively in downstrokes. Pure rock and roll nirvana.

My other teen obsession was Bruce Springsteen. I'd seen him on the **Born to Run** tour in 1976, and his brand of literate rock and roll struck a chord with my teenaged heart. His tour came through Jackson right about the time he was on the cover of *Time* and *Newsweek.* The folks at BeBop Productions booked him into the Mississippi Coliseum, a round orange-and-yellow 10,000-seat enormo-dome, on a Wednesday night in 1976.

by Tim Lee   53

Although WZZQ had played **Born to Run** tracks constantly, even the lengthy ones like "Jungleland," fewer than 2,000 ticket-buyers showed up. Basically, everybody was on the front row and Springsteen and his E-Street Band played nearly four hours. They laid into it like their lives depended on it, no matter how many empty seats there were at the back of the hall.

That dedication to playing to who shows up had a lasting affect on me.

During the summer of 1979, I visited a girl I knew in Birmingham and we went out to a music venue called Brothers Music Hall, where we saw the Brains, an early new wave band from Atlanta that was signed to Mercury Records.

Fronted by synthesizer-player/singer Tom Gray, the Brains had great hooky songs (their song "Money Changes Everything" was eventually a giant hit for Cyndi Lauper), loud guitars courtesy of future Georgia Satellite Rick Price, and a pounding rhythm section in drummer Charles Wolff and bassist Brian Smithwick.

I immediately loved them and bought their debut album. That they actually lived within driving distance of my home-town and I could read about them in *Trouser Press* had a huge impact on me. Being exposed to a Southern band who recorded cool music for a big label impressed on me that anything was possible, if I could just figure out how to pull the pieces together.

Toward the end of 1979, Eric and I landed a temporary gig backing soul singer Peggy Scott, who'd had a string of minor hits in the late 1960s with her singing partner Jo Jo Benson, including "Lover's Holiday," "Soul Shake," and "Pickin' Wild Mountain Berries."

Peggy had management in Jackson with the Frascogna family, whose Frasco Booking Agency pretty much ran things locally. With their backing, she'd developed an annual routine that consisted of a series of shows for a month or two around the holidays before disappearing again until the next winter. (Years later, Peggy had another R&B/Blues hit with "Bill," a song about a woman whose husband has eyes for another man.)

Greg Frascogna contacted me about the gig, which included a few weekends of corporate Christmas parties around the state and a couple of weeks at the Boll Weevil Lounge in the downtown Jackson Holiday Inn. Among the one-nighters was a Friday at Mae's Cabaret, Jackson's famous long-running gay bar. That one was memorable, not just because it was a fun show, but also because it was the first time I was ever treated like a professional musician by the staff of a club. These folks were glad to have us there, which was not the reception I was accustomed to in the dive bars where I usually plied my trade.

I figured out how to fake it as a bass player in order to get the gig, which paid $300 a week, a fortune for a teenager in the late 1970s. I was riding high for a few weeks. The rest of the band were a little older than Eric and I, so we largely kept to ourselves.

I loved Peggy. She was the real deal, a killer soul stylist who'd toured with Ben E. King, survived the chitlin' circuit, and opened for the Jackson 5 at Madison Square Garden. I listened to all of her stories about life and the realities of the music biz. She was something else.

By the time that gig ended, though, I was aging out of my teen years, just months away from bailing on my first attempt at college, and itching to be part of this new wave punk rock thing with which I was obsessed. I had rock and roll in my soul, but I was just another kid with a head full of big ideas and no clue how to put them into action. Oh yeah, and a lot of pointless and misdirected anger.

I was miserable. Nothing was going my way. I'd ask girls out to no avail. I worked a day job that next summer and went out at night, drinking and getting "belignorant" (as my pal David "Fuzzy" Nelson describes that sort of misbehavior). I got thrown out of bars I wouldn't even enter today. As hard as I tried, I couldn't make anything positive happen, couldn't find anywhere I fit in.

About that time, though, a couple of slightly older guys I knew, Bert Wallace and Mike Walters, asked me and Eric if we wanted to start a band to play old rock and soul as well as current new wave songs. Of course, we did, and the Occasions was born.

I don't remember how long that band lasted, a year or so maybe, but we had a regular gig at the infamous Pyramid, a former hotel lounge in a ... you guessed it ... pyramid-shaped building on the I-55 frontage road in Jackson. The Occasions played there two weekends a month, Thursday through

Saturday. The Oral Sox played one weekend a month, and the Drapes usually covered the fourth weekend.

The Sox were a long-running Jackson institution led by John Thomas, a dynamic front man and singer who we all knew as J.T. They were arguably at their best during this period. With Chuck Ripperton and Bobby Sutliff, they had a great Keith Richards/Mick Taylor-like guitar tandem. Bassist Larry Taylor, who went by Leroy, held down the bottom end along with Jeff Lewis on the drums. Bobby's brother, Robin Sutliff, blew a mean sax, adding color to their sound and expanding their lineup of soloists.

A great rock and roll band with a deep Chuck Berry/Rolling Stones groove who were equally adept at covering the Beatles or the Sex Pistols, the Sox were our (usually) friendly rivals during the Pyramid era. They had more charisma and were probably the more popular between our two bands, but we both worked hard to keep folks coming back to pay the meager cover charge and fill the dance floor.

Compared to the rest of us, the Drapes were a little more rootsy, and definitely more professional. In retrospect, they were the band we all wanted to be in. At least, I did.

Comprised of future roots-rock royalty, the Drapes were John McMurry, better known to the world these days as Webb Wilder, along with the amazing Suzy Elkins (who went on to form the Commandos in Austin and released a killer solo record called *Glass Slippers Just Hurt My Feet*), famed producer/songwriter R.S. Field, Rick "Casper" Rawls (later of the Leroi Bros. and Planet Casper) and future Omar & the Howlers rhythm section Gene Brandon (rest in peace) and Mark Hagg. The Drapes were a great band, way ahead of their time, eventually falling apart before the "great roots rock scare" of the mid-1980s, as R.S. called it. But that's how it worked in Mississippi back then.

At the end of the band's run, their final show was billed as "It's Curtains for the Drapes."

At our best, the Occasions were an energetic mess of madness. Bert was a monster talent, with a voice that was equal parts Paul McCartney and Wilson Pickett. He wrote better songs than any of the rest of us and, as a long-time record store employee, had an encyclopedic knowledge of cool music. For all of his talent, though, Bert possessed an equal or greater amount of slacker attitude and never pursued original music too seriously.

Mike was a great guitar player, but at times his own worst enemy. Able to play most anything, he often fell victim to thinking too much about what he was doing. And drinking even more. He could be charmingly cheerful or maddeningly moody. You just never knew.

Eric was probably at his best during this period, a good friend and a solid drummer. Over time, he became more immersed in college and the world of musical education, which eventually took him farther away from our little world of rock and roll, both mentally and geographically. For now, though, he was into it.

I was just happy to be doing anything, throwing myself into even the crappiest gigs as if *my* life depended on it. In some ways, I suppose it did.

Despite our personality differences, the four of us could be as exciting as any band around at the time. We played constantly. Our deal was that we were compact and portable, used small amplifiers and an easily transportable P.A. system, so we could take gigs cheaper than most anyone else and still go home with cash in our pockets.

This was a time when the most well-known cover bands traveled with big trucks loaded with sound equipment and light shows, putting on frat party spectacles that rivaled the shows of many major label touring acts, and paydays that were probably better than most second-tier major label acts.

We, on the other hand, could fit the four of us and our gear in Mike's short wheelbase cargo van that, depending on the day, might have a broken accelerator cable. Our remedy? Just remove the housing that covered the engine and shove a World War II bayonet into the carburetor linkage to create a hand throttle. As long as you kept the windows open to disperse the fumes, everything was cool.

We traveled around the South, primarily playing frat parties, where the students cut loose and reveled in post-*Animal House* debauchery, which we gladly encouraged as long as their checks cleared and the beer was free. We could get as wild as they could, often wilder.

At home, though, the Pyramid was our steady date.

by Tim Lee   57

The Pyramid featured cheap drinks (it didn't get much cheaper than J.R. beer for 50 cents on Thursday nights), loud music, a table-top Space Invaders game, and a place for the oddball musicians to hang out. The interior of the oddly-shaped building was square with a rectangular bar situated in the center of the room. If I wasn't playing a gig elsewhere, I was there. It's just what I did.

Short-lived as it ended up being, it was a scene of sorts, and that weird hotel bar played a big part in my world at that point in time.

Ultimately, though, it would mean even more for my future. The Pyramid is where Bobby Sutliff and I started hanging out more regularly. But most importantly, it is where I first spent any significant time around my future wife, Susan Bauer.

9. THAT GIRL: SHE'S SOMETHING ELSE

June 28, 2015

The band laid into a thick swampy vibe. The drummer put down a groove so hard, you could "drive nails with it," the singer said. The young guitar player closed his eyes and cradled his aging Telecaster, wringing out stinging notes between the front man's vocal lines.

Susan leaned against a post, swayed to the beat, and sang along.

It was Ray Wylie Hubbard's second and final encore for the rowdy east Tennessee crowd, and the ageless Texas outlaw-country-artist-turned-senior-country-blues-shaman was singing about a "Chick Singer, Bad Ass Rockin'." I looked over at Susan and thought, "Yep."

Less than 24 hours earlier, I'd watched her from across the stage at the Basement in Nashville, admiring the way she swayed to the beat with her beloved '72 Precision Bass strapped around her neck while laying down a groove of her own that was deeper than deep. I love to see her plant her feet and dig into the low end, occasionally dipping her left shoulder in time with the music. I love watching her sing, the way she cocks her head to the left and looks over at me from the corner of her eye. I really dig her voice, especially when she lets a little growl creep in at certain moments.

All of that's reason enough for me to put up with the bullshit that goes with playing music.

There's not much of a story of me without Susan, so as I recall …

The small room was throbbing. People danced on the floor, on tables, chairs, and on the mantle over the old fireplace. It was all bodies, booze, and the beat as my band, The Occasions, played for the wild frat party at the infamous Pike House on the Millsaps College campus.

We blasted out our versions of Beatles, Four Tops, Grass Roots, and Ramones songs, one after another, as fast and loud as we could. I was in the moment, pounding out eighth notes and leaping about like a junior league Pete Townshend. Still, I couldn't help but notice the girl with the plastic frame glasses and straight, shag haircut. She wore bright clothes and danced with abandon.

Love at first sight, you might say. I certainly do, because it's true.

When we took a break, I tracked her down and introduced myself. We spoke for a moment, just small talk. She was there to help out her younger brother, Scott, who was rush chairman (damned glad to meet you). I tried to keep her engaged in conversation, but she seemed distracted, busy, and not too impressed with the likes of me.

I was crushed.

Over the the next few weeks, I saw that girl at some of our regular gigs at the Pyramid. She knew Bert, so I just figured she was coming around to hang out with him.

Bert and I would be sitting at a table, just shooting the shit, and she'd come sit down with us. I'd have to get up and leave. Being that close to her was just too much to bear.

I'd asked about her; found out her name was Susan, that she worked at WZZQ.

I'd call the station and ask for her on the pretense of finding out when a spot for one of our local shows might run. You know, so I could listen for it and make sure they got the information correct.

Yeah, right. I was obsessed.

I just wanted to hear her voice, even if a little piece of me died every time I heard it.

This went on for a few months, before Bert eventually sussed out what was happening and hipped me to the fact that ... "that girl Susan likes you."

I couldn't believe it. What? Really? All this time, I thought she had no interest in me whatsoever.

Emboldened by this particularly exciting knowledge drop, I asked her out in December of 1980. After one date, we were inseparable. Within a year, we were married.

It was a church wedding (our families wouldn't have it any other way), and my father conducted the service. Susan and I stood at the altar and giggled conspiratorially, until the moment that Clay got a bit emotional and his voice cracked as he addressed the attendees. We straightened up real quick and made it to the end of the ceremony without incident and got hitched without a hitch.

Forty years later, we're still married and still laugh at inappropriate moments.

Underaged drinking … er, Nuthin' Fancy … on the patio at Everybody's, circa '77 (left to right): Tom Gober, Robert the bass player, me, Keith Treadwell, Benny Douglas.

by Tim Lee

Snowblind, circa 1978 (left to right): "Spooky" George Reid, me, Benny Douglas. I suspect the boys were indeed back in town at this moment.

What's up with the skinny tie, dude? Snowblind, circa '78 (left to right): Me, Eric Arhelger's North drums, Lisa Goodman Palmer.

I Saw A Dozen Faces...

More skinny ties. The Occasions, circa '79 (left to right): Eric Arhelger, me, Mike Walters, Bert Wallace (who apparently didn't get the skinny tie memo).

New wave, new wave, new wave! Tuesday night at the Lamar! The Occasions, circa '80: Me (testing the surly bonds of gravity) and Mike Walters.

Susan and me on our wedding day, November 7, 1981.

I Saw A Dozen Faces...

PART 3: IN ORBIT

I Saw A Dozen Faces...

10. A NOISE OF OUR OWN: ANY MONKEY WITH A TYPEWRITER

"I read in *New York Rocker* that Mitch Easter guy has a studio in North Carolina. Wouldn't it be cool to go record there?"

One night early in 1982, Bobby and I were sitting on the living room floor of mine and Susan's apartment, listening to music and talking about our desire to make another record, some kind of follow-up to *Meet the Windbreakers*. A name we'd seen in the credits of many of the singles and EPs we were digging was Mitch Easter. He'd been in the North Carolina combos Sneakers and the H-Bombs. He played on Peter Holsapple's "Big Black Truck" single and had a couple of his own songs on a compilation record called *Shake to Date*.

Obviously, this guy had something going on.

One thing led to another and soon, thanks in no small measure to liquid courage courtesy of the Anheuser-Busch Brewing Company, I was on the phone, dialing directory assistance in Winston-Salem. Moments later, I was talking to Mitch, who seemed quite surprised to hear from these yokels a few states away.

He was encouraging, though, and offered affordable rates at the Drive-In Studio, which was located in his parent's converted garage. Eventually, we booked a date and that June, Susan, Bobby, Eric, and I (Jeff had since left to form his own band, Radio London) piled into Eric's station wagon and hit the road for North Carolina, pulling a U-Haul trailer, like the Clampetts heading for Beverly Hills.

When we reached Winston-Salem, we drove straight to Mitch's house, where we met him and Faye Hunter, his then

by Tim Lee   67

girlfriend and bandmate. They immediately whisked us off to the Piedmont Triad International Airport for a dinner of "3-D burgers," as they dubbed the on-site diner's excellent triple-decker hamburgers.

This was my first inkling that I'd just met two of the coolest people who would ever enter my orbit.

We'd booked a single day at the Drive-In with the intention of recording and mixing two songs, which we accomplished by staying up nearly all night to finish, fueled by Hostess snacks, pork rinds, and Budweiser. And we were delighted with the results. Mitch was knowledgeable and helpful, willing to break out all the tricks we'd heard about and wanted to try.

Backwards guitar solo? No problem. Tape loops? Hell yeah. Entertaining stories? That too.

This was a whole world away from our *Meet the Windbreakers* recording experience. If nothing else came from the day at Mitch's, I learned to love the process of making records.

During our brief visit, Mitch played some recordings of Let's Active, the band he had with Faye and Sara Romweber. Hearing rough mixes of songs like "Every Word Means No" and "Room with a View" was revelatory and further convinced us we were in the right place with the right guy.

When we hit the highway the next day, en route to a gig we'd somehow managed to finagle in Atlanta, we popped our fresh cassette into the boom box and listened to those two songs over and over, barely able to believe we'd been involved in something that sounded so cool.

Bobby and I returned to the Drive-in later that year (sans Eric, who was beginning to drift farther out of our world), and recorded four more songs with Mitch on drums. Coincidentally, Richard Barone and Jim Mastro of the Bongos were in Winston-Salem, tracking songs for what would become their album *Nuts & Bolts*.

Those guys took a couple days off for our reserved recording dates, but Richard hung out while Jim blasted off to visit a girlfriend further south. Richard is a great guy, and fun to have around, cheerful and outgoing. We asked him to add an e-Bow guitar solo to my song, "You Never Give Up," which he gladly obliged.

As with our previous experience, we had a blast working with Mitch. The Drive-In had such a happening vibe. Despite its relatively small size, it was a comfortable work space. Mitch was a gracious recording host, equally at home engineering as he was playing a myriad of instruments or just kicking ideas around.

He remains one of my favorite studio collaborators, simply because he has a sixth sense of sorts about what each situation needs. If all a band needs is someone to get their thing on tape, he's happy to man the board and capture the sounds. If they need cool production ideas, he has plenty of those and is generous with his skills and knowledge. Looking for some unique instrumentation? He's probably got what you need *and* knows how to play it.

In our case, we welcomed his input. We had plenty of ideas of our own, but Mitch knew how to implement them. His involvement allowed us to expand on our limited knowledge and make the kind of recordings we heard in our heads.

That type of experience is priceless for young artists and musicians trying to find their footing in the recording studio, which is a completely different setting than a live stage or a practice space.

Again, we left Winston-Salem thrilled with the results.

With six total tunes in the can, we set out to release the Windbreakers' sophomore EP, *Any Monkey With A Typewriter*, our smart-ass take on the old notion that a thousand monkeys with a thousand typewriters could eventually write the works of Shakespeare.

We figured if that was true, then any old simian could write fifty Windbreakers songs in one sitting. We had self-deprecation in spades.

Being from the deep South, I don't think we ever really expected anybody to take us seriously. We may have had a Mississippi-sized chip on our shoulders, but that didn't stop us from trying. We wanted to make records, dammit!

Following the release of the first Windbreakers EP, Susan and I learned all we could about the fledgling independent music scene that was developing around the country. We read every fanzine we could get our hands on. If we found an address for a college radio station, we sent them two or three copies of *Meet the Windbreakers* (you know, just in case they lost the first one).

by Tim Lee   69

When other local bands released their own singles, we got copies from them to send out with ours in an effort to make it look like there was something going on in Jackson.

"New York Rocker reviewed our record!"

I was breathless as I all but ran from the mailbox to our tiny apartment. Susan and I were dedicated readers of the venerable Manhattan-based rock and roll 'zine, so it was exciting to land a review of **Meet the Windbreakers** *among the pages where we read about our favorite bands.*

Overall, the write-up was positive, although it did compare "That Girl" to a Rick Springfield song. In a good way, mind you, but still ... Rick Springfield?

That review signaled a small step forward in the grand scheme of things.

But it was a giant leap for our little band from The Magnolia State.

Susan and I were zealots, not just for the Windbreakers, but for the independent music scene in general. We bought every self-released or small-label record we could get our hands on. When we visited larger cities with rock clubs and cool record stores, we asked about local releases and took home as many as we could afford.

That scene, which was just starting to grow legs in the early 1980s, represented something more realistic, more achievable, than the big-time show-biz world of Boston and Kansas (the bands, not the geographic locations). It required a lot of work, but folks like us could run a small label out of our living room and actually have a chance at fanzine press and college radio play, which hopefully would lead to gigs in clubs that welcomed original music.

The existence of that scene allowed one to believe that they could make music and that music might actually find an audience, no matter how small. There was something in the air, and we wanted to be part of it.

Scraping together what money we could, Big Monkey release number 007-11 (a nod to the Ventures tune) was a six-song, 12-inch EP with a flimsy two-color paper sleeve, as we couldn't afford traditional cardboard jackets. *Any Monkey With a Typewriter* featured three of Bobby's songs and three of mine. In many ways, it remains my favorite Windbreakers release. I dig the energy, the quirkiness, and the sense of adventure of which I'm reminded with every listen. To my ears, we sound like a backwoods version of XTC or something like that on the record, and how can that be bad?

A humble release, we sent it out into the world, where it actually got a fair amount of attention despite its low-rent packaging. Against all odds, *Any Monkey With a Typewriter* got great reviews from fanzines and significant college radio play. A handful of discerning distributors wanted copies to sell to stores. We were picking up steam.

Of course, timing helps. That it was 1983, still quite early in the realm of the indie rock scene, probably worked for us. There were fewer releases coming out to compete with for that attention. Also, the fact that Mitch's name was getting out in the world as his early work with R.E.M. became more well-known surely helped shine some light on more modest releases such as ours. Sometimes, you just get lucky, and being lucky is often better than being good.

At the end of the day, what separates your band from every other act that puts out a record is what you do with that record. Do you find a way to get copies out into the world, or do you just let them gather dust in your closet?

I suppose one could place the early 1980s American independent music scene in some sort of historical context, pointing to post-Vietnam-War disillusionment, the rise of corporate rock music, and the transition into the Reagan era as catalysts for youthful expression. They would be largely correct, too. But on a personal level, we were really just rock-and-roll-crazed kids who wanted to make some noise of our own.

Somewhere along the way, though, I became one of those kids who wanted a little more than just a stack of record boxes in the back of his closet. I had ambition to do more, to get some music out there in the world. I wanted to be heard.

Unfortunately, there is no roadmap for that trip; it's a lot like feeling around for a light switch in a dark room.

But, I was ready to give it a try. As with starting my first band, I knew that every step I took would be up to me, regardless of who I collaborated or worked with. Having someone like Susan by your side, working through all this with you, was a bonus.

I'm always fascinated by the people who make a few inroads into the biz and immediately feel it's their duty to inform younger artists on the necessary steps to "making it." They act like anybody who follows their exact steps will achieve the same things that they have. Like there's a set of rules or something. C'mon, there are no rules in rock and roll (okay, except maybe the one about shorts and sandals on stage). That's what attracted most of us to this racket in the first place.

You don't have to look too far to see how arbitrary the whole show biz thing is. All I can figure is you just have to do the work and put yourself out there in the world. Everything else is completely up to the fates.

Bottom line: you've got to do the work. That's the only advice I've got.

That, and keep your publishing. Don't sell it away. Those dozens of dollars will come in handy some day.

Oh, and one more thing: Take your work seriously, but not yourself.

Beyond that, I'll just share this little tidbit of advice handed down from Arkansas singer-songwriter Jim Mize one night while he, Susan, Laurie Stirratt, and I were closing down a crappy chain restaurant bar: "Sometimes you just gotta get out and get some inspiration: piss on an electric fence or stick a knife in an electrical socket!"

Preach on, brother Mize!

The whole point of art, in my not-so-humble estimation, is the doing it. You've got to ignore the biz, get off your ass, and make something happen. That's how every cool thing starts.

With our second release, despite making inroads into the bigger world, the Windbreakers were still just a local band who could play three sets of cover songs and just happened to have a pretty cool record that was getting some attention beyond its humble birth.

To my mind, we were just spinning our wheels, going nowhere and getting there in a hurry. It just wasn't fun anymore.

I'd lost the rest of what little interest I had in performing multiple sets of other people's songs; I wanted to play short, tight sets of original music. I'd mention this to musicians and get the response, "How are you going to make money like that?"

I never picked up a guitar because I thought I'd make a dollar from it. I only ever did it because it was cool. I wanted to be part of the bigger thing that was going on outside our little town, and I was getting impatient. It was high time to stop following convention and start cutting my own trail.

So I quit the band.

II. BEAT TEMPTATION: CONCERNED ABOUT ROCK MUSIC?

"It's OK to Like Nick Lowe"

The message emblazoned on the badge stood out every bit as much as the raven-haired young woman's black leather motorcycle jacket to which it was pinned. She browsed the strings and picks at the counter in the strip mall music store where I was working.

"Nice pin," I said, letting her know I was hip to the Basher. She lit up at my acknowledgement.

Thus, I met Sherry Cothren, at the time still a high school student in a small town in south Mississippi. She was in Jackson to visit her sister when she stepped into my world. Over time, she would make quite an impact there.

Dark-eyed and quiet-spoken, even as a teen, Sherry exuded Joan Jett levels of cool.

This was probably 1979, and she was the first person I met who was totally committed to the "new music," punk and new wave.

And she played guitar.

Within a year or so, Sherry moved up to Jackson and we hung out a bit. Eventually she fell in with some folks, and along with Carla Westcott, Joe Partridge, David Minchew, and John Wagner, started a band called the Germans who excelled in covers of songs by the Pretenders, Ramones, the Clash, and others. They also released one of my favorite local singles before they broke up.

Following my exit from the Windbreakers in 1983, I approached Sherry and my percussionista pal Bruce Golden about starting a band. Though she played guitar in the Germans, Sherry had recently taken up bass. Additionally, she is a prolific lyricist, a damned good one at that, which is a skill that comes in handy when you're building a new band from the ground up, songs and all.

Bruce and Sherry were the players in town I most related to, so why shouldn't the three of us be in a band together?

I'd first seen Bruce performing with the free-improv group Ars Supernova in the late-'70s. As a teen, I wasn't really sure what to make of them, but the combination of Bruce, keyboardist Evan Gallagher, sax player George Cartwright, and bass man Jeb Stuart created a marvelous sonic world.

My introduction to Ars came in the House of Representatives chamber of the Old Capital Museum downtown. I was 17, and had read in the newspaper about this odd music event, which I attended out of curiosity. Even if I wasn't musically astute enough to understand purely improvised works, I admired anybody who did things out of the ordinary, especially with music.

Of course, I had no idea the part some of these individuals would play in my life over time.

One afternoon a couple of years after that Old Capital show, while thumbing through the import bins upstairs at the BeBop Record Shop on State Street, I recognized Bruce and Evan, who were perusing another box of albums. I nodded to them as an unspoken greeting.

They chatted excitedly as they rifled through the racks, eventually pulling out a record, about which one of them exclaimed, "I heard this was just two guys who sat down with guitars in front of a tape recorder and just made a bunch of noise!"

Butting into their conversation, I displayed my wealth of 19-year-old wisdom concerning the world of recorded music, sniffing, "Yeah, I guess they'll just let anybody make a record these days."

Bruce and Evan grinned and looked at each other. Then they blurted out simultaneously, "Yeah, that's cool, isn't it!"

Cue the re-education of little Timmy, courtesy of the fine folks at Ars Supernova. In time, Evan and Bruce invited me to join them in various musical adventures (the rest of the original Ars had moved away), mostly providing backing or intermission sounds for the Kinetic Dance Collective. Trust me, every smart-ass know-it-all rock kid ought to get a crash course in oddball and improvised music from masters of the form. I had a lot to learn and a couple of excellent teachers from whom to learn.

In addition to improvised pieces, Evan would provide charts for others scribbled on poster board with instructions such as, "Hit fuzz bass with mallet, then play duck call." Pure genius.

Bruce and I became particularly close after he filled in on a couple Occasions shows and we played a weird one-off church gig together. His outlook on life and art is a beautiful thing, and he has been a consistent inspiration to me over the years.

The same could be said of Sherry.

Sherry, Bruce, and I called our new thing Beat Temptation. Everybody had screwy schedules, so for a while we could only practice on Saturday mornings at 10 a.m., but we wanted to play music together badly enough to tolerate that very non-rock hour. As a band, we made a joyful noise, and rehearsals had the feel of teenage kids in the basement, making racket for the very first time.

It was magic.

Pulling lyrics from Sherry's notebooks filled with poems, prose, and various writings, we immediately got to work cranking out songs of our own. Musically, there were no proprietary ideas: everything got thrown in the mix. We were on fire with creativity and stayed that way for the life of the band, burning through concepts and songs at a rapid rate. We probably forgot as many cool ideas as we actually implemented. It was exciting to be part of such a creative combination of personalities.

Our $50-a-month cooperative practice space on State Street, which we dubbed Noise Central, was located above a beauty salon owned by our landlord, a former NFL player who drove a Mercedes with what looked like bullet holes in the trunk. One corner of the brick-walled space held a refrigerator box that functioned as a beer can receptacle for us and our space-mates Used Goods, a band recently formed by our friends Robert Crook and Joe Bennett. It didn't take long for that massive cardboard container to overflow with scrap aluminum.

It was a great place to practice, although the load-in up the stairs was a bitch. But it was in the middle of downtown, which was pretty much dead after 5 p.m. and on weekends in those days, so we didn't disturb anyone with our manic doings. And nobody disturbed us on the occasions we used the crude equipment on hand to make recordings.

Sadly, Noise Central is now a parking lot.

Around that time, Robert discovered a hole-in-the-wall beer joint called Sidetracks and talked the owner into hosting Used Goods for a show. There wasn't much to the place, just a square wooden building sitting behind a convenience store on West Street, alongside the railroad line that inspired the name. A few beer neons and two pool tables constituted the décor.

But it was suitable for rock and roll. I'm pretty sure I either played bass or ran sound for the Goods when they played that first show there. Either way, it turned out to be ground zero for a new scene. A few of the local faithful showed up, and we ultimately staked a claim in that unlikely location.

The timing of Robert's discovery couldn't have been better, as our previous hangouts, the Pyramid and Skidmarks, had both run their courses, leaving our little group of musical misfits without a home stage. In classic D.I.Y. form, we took advantage of the situation and put together our own shows.

Not long after the Used Goods debut there, Sidetracks was sold and the name was changed to W.C. Dons (short for We Couldn't Decide On a Name), but the old guy who bought it still allowed us to occasionally bring in our bands. He'd sell beer and we'd charge two or three dollars at the door for live music. And everybody went home happy.

Bruce and Evan knew guitarist Eugene Chadbourne, who wanted to bring his avant-psychedelic band Shockabilly, which also featured Mark Kramer and David Licht, to town. So we booked them into W.C. Don's, where Bruce, Evan, and I played an opening set under the name D.O.N. (Dance-Oriented Noise), performing Evan's original compositions "I Love the Big Pig" and "I Wanna Fuck Stockhausen's Daughter." That understated affair helped set the stage for much of what happened in that old double-wide building in the subsequent years.

Beat Temptation eventually debuted at Don's sometime in 1983, and for the next year we played there at least once a month. The three of us were capable of making a pretty big sound. I remember after our first gig, somebody asked me who was playing organ on the Velvet Underground cover we played. We never had a keyboardist.

At Don's, we never performed the same set twice and went to great lengths to challenge the audience, which built pretty quickly, due primarily to the fact that you never knew what we were going to do. It's a fine line between challenging and annoying listeners, and like children playing with their food, smearing that line brought us great pleasure.

We generally saw a couple dozen faces and we rocked them all … whether they liked it or not.

Eventually, Bobby's brother, Robin Sutliff, joined Beat Temptation on saxophone and the unit was complete. Bringing his Bobby Keys/Ornette Coleman-hybrid skronk to the table, Robin was the perfect fourth for our trio. A veteran of the Oral Sox and local blues rockers the Roman Hands, he could rock and roll with the best of them but was also quite knowledgeable of a wide range of musics, from jazz to punk. It didn't hurt that his subversive attitude fit hand in glove with ours.

As long as Bobby and I have worked together and hung out, Robin and I have easily as much in common, just on different levels. He's a great dude to know and have in your corner.

Beat Temptation was loud and obnoxious at times, quite musical at others, often simultaneously. We were proud to be among the first all-original combos on our little scene, and we were happy to play with people's expectations. We would kick off the set with a recognizable riff from a popular tune, and as soon as folks were up and dancing to the familiar, we'd take a left turn and segue straight into our own songs.

We were wild cards who would do anything to get a rise out of an audience.

One of my favorite bits we did was Request Time, which, like most of our schticks, was only performed once or twice. For Request Time, we'd take anybody's request and play it to the tune of the Muddy Waters' "I'm a Man" riff. Ba-duh-duh-dunt.

"Play U2!" someone would yell.

"If you walk away, walk away." Ba-duh-duh-dunt. "Then I will follow." Ba-duh-duh-dunt.

"Play Free Bird!"

"If I leave here tomorrow." Ba-duh-duh-dunt. "Would you remember me?" Ba-duh-duh-dunt.

Works for most anything.

One night, we opened with a medley of "Iron Man," "I'm a Man," "Free Bird," "Folsom Prison Blues," and "Should

I Stay or Should I Go?" that lasted all of five minutes. We laughed at the confused looks on people's faces as we ping-ponged from one song to the next before laying into a dozen or so of our own compositions.

The thing is, for all of our conceptual performance tendencies and general wackiness, we were a really good band. We played together with a chemistry that allowed us to fray the edges of a song pretty hard before returning to the center. There was a confidence that built among the four of us that allowed us to venture into improvised bits or perform tight arrangements with equal ease.

On the other hand, our irreverence didn't particularly endear us to a lot of folks. It was no secret that many local musicians didn't care for us. It was fashionable among some to refer to us as Beet Plantation. I thought it was hilarious.

Don's was our home. The only two times we played elsewhere, the plug was pulled on us before we could finish the first song. That's not technically true, but it's our story and we're sticking to it. I do remember playing a Rock Against Racism show, and Sherry recently showed me a bunch of old flyers that would prove me wrong in a court of law, but that's not the way I remember it. Oh well, the mind is a terrible thing …

Once, we were invited to play at a small punk rock festival on the Gulf Coast that took place at a local park. We almost made it through a song before the power was cut off, as we were deemed a disturbance to the families who were cooking out and playing nearby. The whole thing wound up being a bust.

Another time, a local crafts guild asked us to play during their annual holiday sales event. In retrospect, what were they thinking? We even tried to start out quiet, but an irate vendor unplugged the power box just minutes into our set. A couple of failed attempts at compromise eventually led to us giving up and packing up our gear.

Not long after our first gig, Beat Temptation hit the studio with the help of a friend who wanted to help us get something on tape. We recorded two songs in a proper facility, albeit one in which the decrepit multi-track recorder regularly had to be started by hand before tape would roll. Taking our approach into the studio was a blast. We added touches such as bowed cymbals and employed lots of Bruce's "found" percussion toys. Soxman J.T. dropped by and was pressed into service for a cornet solo at the end of "On Your Mark," although he was not given a chance to hear the song beforehand. We just hit the record button and gave him one shot to wail alongside Bruce, who was blowing equally manic saxophone. The results are pretty cool.

We tracked two more songs on Evan's eight-track machine at Noise Central. We mixed those particularly lo-fi numbers at local musician Sergio Fernandez's jingles studio, much to his bemusement.

We pulled those four songs together to make up the self-titled *Beat Temptation* EP, which became the fourth Big Monkey release.

As part of our scene-building schemes, several of us planned a full-fledged compilation album of Jackson bands. Having done the math, we knew how much money each artist would have to chip in to pull it together. Everyone agreed, but it was a logistical nightmare to pull all those disparate recordings together, especially considering the various personalities involved.

Most of the Jackson bands were buddies, but we were all in our 20s, young and full of ourselves, so there was no shortage of jealousy and backbiting. I guess it's the same with any kind of scene.

Naturally, we called the record *Familiarity Breeds Contempt*.

Bands included the immediate Big Monkey Records family (Windbreakers, Beat Temptation, Used Goods) and anybody else who wanted to participate.

Sixteen songs altogether, *Familiarity* ran the rock and roll gamut from the more pop-influenced fare of Bert Wallace and Joe Bennett to the raw punk of "Lovesick" by the Germans. In between was a Whitman's sampler of garage rock, new wave, power pop, bar band rock, and rockabilly, even a bit of improvised music in the form of Ars Supernova's "Shoats."

Because it took so long to pull together, *Familiarity Breeds Contempt* finally came out in 1985 to little, if any, fanfare. But the lessons learned from that experience have served me well for future compilation endeavors. If nothing else, I learned the importance of hard deadlines.

I was having fun with Beat Temptation — immeasurable amounts of fun — but independent record labels were now contacting me to see if the Windbreakers were interested in making a full-length album. Bobby and I talked it over and decided to give it a shot. What did we have to lose?

Susan and I were planning to move to Atlanta in fall of 1984, so Beat Temptation was soon to be put on hold regardless of what Bobby and I did with the Windbreakers. Because our little rental house was being taken over by imminent domain, Susan moved late that summer, a month or so before I did, and stayed with her grandmother in Atlanta until I arrived. I hung around Jackson, waiting for our displacement check, and closed out that Jackson chapter by squeezing in a few more Beat Temptation gigs.

Although we never went on the road or promoted Beat Temptation much to the outside world, that era proved to be important in my development as a musical artist. Being one of the components of such a wildly creative group was a crash course in collaboration that has influenced every thing I've done since. You can't be involved with people like Bruce, Sherry, and Robin and not grow on some level. If you don't, you're just not trying.

The three of them are still among my favorite humans and best friends. Some combination of us usually gets together whenever I visit Jackson. We're all older now, but whenever we gather, it doesn't take long for that mischievous gleam to return to our collective eye. Some chemistry never dies.

Beat Temptation never broke up, Bruce says, just broke down. After Sherry, Bruce, and I played a hastily-assembled three-song set for a 2017 Bob Dylan tribute in Jackson, the three of us reconvened for a couple of reunion shows with Robin the following year and had a ball. I have no doubt there will be more.

You can't keep a good band down.

12. SECOND HELPINGS: TERMINALLY SPEAKING

"What are you doing?"

"Nothing much," Bobby replied.

"Why don't I swing by? We can go get a beer at CS's and shoot pool or something."

In my mind's eye, Bobby and I never didn't hang out together. Memory can be a funny thing, and maybe mine's a bit screwy after all these years, but I can't think of many times we didn't go out for beers together or sit around and play guitars. It didn't matter whether we were in a band together, or even getting along. As long as we lived in the same town, we just did.

Even if the previous statement is merely a figment of my imagination, we definitely spent time together after interest in a follow-up to *Any Monkey with a Typewriter* developed. We had drifted apart for a while after I left the Windbreakers, but in time, things between us got back to normal.

Sam Berger, who had launched the new Homestead label as part of the Dutch East India Trading distribution company, expressed interest in releasing a Windbreakers full-length album in 1984. I don't recall how we showed up on his radar (although it was likely because Dutch East was one of the distributors who owed us money for *Any Monkey*), but we didn't need much convincing. We liked the idea of making another record and couldn't believe someone was actually willing to pay to have it pressed.

Moving forward, Bobby and I knew that a new Windbreakers chapter would be our project, just the two of us. Eric had moved away for college, and nobody else we knew seemed particularly interested in joining us. So we kicked some songs around, patched together some crude demos, and worked on a plan to make that full-length album.

Eric's departure from our world was a bummer to me, as he and I had been through several bands together. We'd been pals and spent a lot of time hanging out over the years. Being a dumb kid, I said some crappy things about him in a couple local interviews. I wasn't capable of handling it any better. That's one of my few regrets. Eric didn't deserve that, was always a good friend.

It was a happening time for me. Beat Temptation was still playing, but Bobby and I did a few Windbreakers shows as well with various rhythm sections. Susan and I had stepped up our scene-building efforts, booking touring bands from the coasts into W.C. Don's. We fed them and put them up in our little rental house situated next to the big Baptist church on the I-55 frontage road. Bands such as Rain Parade and Green on Red from Los Angeles and the Neats and the Lyres from Boston came to stay and play. Most became life-long friends.

At the very least, it felt like a time of great promise.

I don't have a lot of distinct memories of mine and Bobby's preparations for recording, except of the time we were working on a double-cassette-deck demo for "Running Out of Time," a rare Sutliff/Lee co-write. Bobby started it at his house and then brought the tape over to mine.

The version he presented already featured his guitars and the rhythm machine of a cheap Casio keyboard keeping the beat. We decided we were going to overdub a marching snare drum of Bruce's that was lying around, so we set it up in the spare room and plugged in a borrowed Shure SM57 microphone. Naturally, we didn't have a mic stand handy so we draped the cable over the ceiling light fixture in the center of the room, positioned the mic a few feet above the drum, and proceeded to hit it on the two and four beats.

That's just an example of the janky-ass extremes to which we would go in the pursuit of demo-making during the time just prior to the availability of the ubiquitous 4-track cassette machines of which we'd both become quite enamored.

"From a Distance" was another co-write. Much like "Running Out of Time," it started with Bobby. I just helped finish it. I recall him coming by the house one day, when I was home sick from work, to get my input. The details elude me, but I'm pretty sure I just helped sort out the last verse or the bridge or something.

That sort of collaboration was rare among the two of us. We both tended to write separately and bring completed songs to the table, and our approaches to the process are different. I'd say Bobby probably starts with the music in most cases, and I tend to begin with the lyrics. Our outlooks on recording are quite different as well. Bobby tends to have pretty solid idea of what parts he wants to hear from the various instruments, while I'm looser about it and generally prefer to just see what the individual players can come up with on the spot. He makes elaborate demos of his songs with all the parts included, which I also did for a while in the latter part of the 1980s before jettisoning that practice for a more spontaneous approach to arrangement.

Ultimately, the Windbreakers' reputation became that of a band with two distinctly different singer/songwriters. Bobby was considered the more melodic, polished pop-oriented guy, while I was portrayed as a little rawer and rougher around the edges.

As a selling point, I doubt that approach gets mentioned much in Marketing 101, but there's certainly a degree of accuracy to it. If the shoe fits, huh?

In preparing for our first full-length album sessions, Bobby put together a great batch of songs. Since I'd been writing collaboratively with the members of Beat Temptation during the previous year or so, most of my contributions were written specifically for what became the *Terminal* project. The opening riff to "All That Stuff" came about after I'd bought a Silvertone bass at a yard sale. It just seemed to play itself. "Changeless" was an attempt at making something that was a bit darker and grittier, a little less power pop, and "A Girl & Her Bible" was deliberately psychedelic as hell. "Again" was the only Beat Temptation song I brought to the Windbreakers table.

I was already straying from the formula we'd established with the first two EPs. I'd been drawn into this music thing by the lure of power pop, but once I got into it, I had no interest in being a one-trick pony. There were too many paths to follow, and I wanted to see where some of the other ones led. Barely into what would turn into a lengthy recording life, I was already chafing at the notion of pigeonholing. Any kind of expectations, even self-inflicted, felt a bit too much like all those times I had to put on a suit and tie and go to church, where I was expected to sit still and behave.

I've never had much interest in sitting still or behaving.

We booked a session with Mitch at his newly expanded Drive-In and made another trek to Winston-Salem in June of 1984. As always, working with Mitch was an education and a pleasure.

Among the numerous joys of working at the Drive-In was that you never knew who might be hanging around and could happily be pressed into service. As with Richard Barone's guest turn on *Any Monkey With a Typewriter*, we took good advantage of the arrangement. Faye Hunter played bass on "Changeless." We met Don Dixon, who had worked extensively with Mitch on the early R.E.M. records and other notable releases, and just happened to be in town. Dixon's vibe was low-key, yet energetic, always encouraging, so his was a good attitude to have on hand. He wound up laying down the low end on four of the six songs we completed. Mitch again played drums.

In addition to "Changeless," we also completed and mixed "Off & On," "A Girl & Her Bible," "Can't Go On This Way," "From a Distance," and "Running Out of Time."

The spirit of the session was pure fun, and you can hear some of that wackiness in the spaces between songs (dig the spontaneous "blues jams" at the beginning and the end of "Running Out of Time"). Our ideas blended well with Mitch and Don's sensibilities, and the work rolled along easily.

Besides his many musical and technical strengths, Mitch is also an astute and often dryly hilarious commentator. In time, I found that quality to be fairly common among his North Carolina contemporaries. During the sessions, he pointed out his appreciation for our decidedly unpretentious appearance. "Y'all just show up, looking like pig farmers or something, but you make this cool music," was one of his comments.

"I like that y'all bend guitar strings in your solos," Mitch said another time, "It's like most new wave bands are scared to do that."

We wrapped up after three or four days, and Susan, Bobby, and I took a little northward road trip before heading back to Mississippi. We drove up to Hoboken, New Jersey, to hang out with Howard Wuelfing, who was working for JEM Records after moving up from the D.C. area, where he'd been a member of the Nurses and Half-Japanese.

We went with Howard to the famed rock club Maxwell's for beers and dinner before trekking out to a tiny bar somewhere in the boondocks of Jersey to see the Trypes, a Feelies offshoot.

It was fun to meet some new folks in a new place, to get out in the world a bit. More than anything, though, that trip also gave me a better idea of where I thought we needed to be.

This southern boy also learned about being "buzzed up" to someone's apartment. We spent the night with some folks in Hoboken, and the next morning I got up to move the car or something. When I returned to their place, I rang the bell and kept hearing this buzzer in return but had no idea what to do. Eventually, one of our hosts came downstairs to open the door for me.

What a yokel.

Back home, we listened to the results of the Drive-In session, which felt like another step forward for us. Bobby and I were excited about the tracks, but it wasn't enough material to fill a complete album.

Around the same time, the French label Closer contacted us and offered to release an album-length version of *Any Monkey With a Typewriter* with some new tracks, ultimately dubbed *Disciples of Agriculture*. The title was a nod to our southern heritage and a play on Little Steven Van Zandt's Disciples of Soul.

On the other hand, *Terminal* got its name from a Sneakers song, "Be My Ambulance," the first line of which ends with the word "terminal." We were always taken by the way Chris Stamey sang "terminal," both accenting it and slightly elongating it, so we chose that word as our first album's title.

Before we could actually use those titles, though, we had to get a few more songs committed to magnetic tape.

Our pal Randy Everett, who I knew from my guitar shop days, told us he'd been doing some studio engineering in a guy's living room in the suburbs with some good gear. He introduced us to Rick Garner, who owned the aforementioned house and equipment and we went into negotiations. We were cash-poor but idea-rich, you might say, so ultimately Bobby traded Rick a Fender Jazzmaster guitar for the studio time to track four more songs.

Rick called his home studio Master Tracks; we just referred to it as "Rick's Palatial Estate."

Figuring we could kill two birds with one stone, and working with limited finances, our plan was to use those four songs to complete both *Disciples...* and *Terminal.*

The only catch to recording at Master Tracks? The house was located smack dab in the center of a subdivision with other dwellings in close proximity on all sides, which meant this was no place to record drums. Our only real choice was to to rely on Rick's Oberheim drum machine (which was almost state of the art at the time) to lay down the beat for "All That Stuff," "Stupid Idea," "Again," and "New Red Shoes."

The decision to use a drum machine was not one to which we gave much thought. It was the hand we were dealt, so we just rolled with it.

These days, I find it pretty funny that at least three of the most listened-to Windbreakers songs feature a drum machine rather than a real person behind an actual kit. Kinda forward thinking for a couple of techno-peasants, however accidental.

Despite the lack of real drums, we layered our usual instrumentation on top of the mechanical beat, and wound up with enough material for an album, plus a version of Television's "Glory" on which we collaborated with the Rain Parade (but that's a story for later).

Concurrent to development of the *Terminal* project, Susan and I set our sights on a bigger pond and ultimately moved to Atlanta that September. With help from Bruce Golden and bassist Fritz Martin, Bobby and Randy finished up the four songs in my absence.

By the time the leaves started turning colors with the first hint of fall, the first Windbreakers full-length LP was done.

We pulled the 11 tracks together, came up with a sequence, had a friend produce the artwork, and turned it into Homestead for *Terminal.* At the same time, we sent tapes overseas to Closer, with the addition of Bobby's home demo of an instrumental titled "Lonely Beach," for *Disciples of Agriculture.*

*There are a couple funny typos on the back jacket of **Disciples**, which I chalk up to poor translation and human error. Mitch is credited with the various instruments he contributed, as well as "baking vocals." The **Any Monkey** tracks are listed as "Mixed by Mitch, Booby and Tim."*

To this day, I refer to Bobby as Booby Stuliff. Hell, he calls himself that half the time.

*Ironically, **Terminal** has its own errors. The track listing on the record label is completely wrong. I can't remember how that happened, but somewhere along the line, someone hadn't checked the order against the back album art.*

Hey, it's not a Windbreakers project if everything goes right!

Between the time I left Jackson in September of 1984 and *Terminal* came out the following year, a lot went down. I barely got settled in Atlanta before Mitch called and asked if I'd go on the road with Let's Active for their U.S. tour supporting the *Cypress* album.

Of course, I signed on immediately. This was everything I'd worked toward, and I couldn't believe my luck. Nor could I wait to report to Winston-Salem for rehearsals in November.

There had been some changes in Let's Active land. Original drummer Sara Romweber had exited the band after their recent English tour. Mitch and Faye were splitting up as well, but had chosen to continue working together.

Former Crackers drummer Jay Peck and I were pegged to fill out the combo for the upcoming dates. My job was to provide whatever guitar and keyboard parts from the recordings that the basic trio didn't cover. The rehearsals went smoothly and we jelled quickly. It was a pretty rocking band by the time we played the first dates in the Northeast late in 1984.

By this point, Let's Active was pretty popular and, for the most part, the band was headlining medium-sized clubs. As you can imagine, I was in heaven traveling around the country, playing great songs with cool people and meeting loads more folks along the way. We did two complete U.S. tours, hitting most of the major cities, almost none of which I'd ever visited before. Every day was a new experience, which was exciting for the kid who'd rarely ventured too far out of the deep South.

I Saw A Dozen Faces...

As I'd suspected, Mitch and Faye were great folks to be with on tour with, as was Jay. They always knew of some oddball place you needed to visit when time allowed. Days off, or even just a few stray hours, involved trips to the Jay Ward Museum in Los Angeles or the Strategic Air Command Museum in Nebraska. There were few dull moments during those days.

One of my first shows with Let's Active was at the infamous former disco, Studio 54, in New York. We played a short set during the *College Music Journal*'s annual awards ceremony where Mitch collected the Best Producer trophy for his work with R.E.M. Afterwards, we attended a reception upstairs with free drinks and food. I met former New York Dolls singer David Johansen, who was then in his Buster Poindexter phase. He was super cool and friendly to the kid who told him how much the Dolls records (as well as Johansen's first two solo albums) meant to him.

A few minutes after that, I turned around and ended up face to face with another hero, Lou Reed.

"Hi, Lou. I'm a big f…"

"You're in my way."

"…fan?"

Boy, talk about playing to type.

Toward the end of the first tour, we played a club in Phoenix. We'd gotten to town in the middle of the night, so I used the next day's free time to do some record shopping. I found a cool store where I got into a conversation with the guy behind the counter. He told me about the local scene, so I asked if he knew the guys in the Meat Puppets, told him I was big fan of theirs. He said, yeah, he knows bassist Cris Kirkwood, would probably see him later that day. So I told him to let Cris know he'd be on the guest list if he wanted to come to the show.

Cris did show up, so it was cool to meet him and hang out a bit. He was a sweet guy, and told me that he and his friends usually had to sit outside and try to listen to shows, because they rarely could afford tickets. I was surprised, as the Meat Puppets were pretty much universally loved among the musicians I knew. Those guys should've been on every guest list.

Prior to the second tour, a television crew showed up to film a segment for an upcoming episode of the Cutting Edge, an IRS Records-sponsored MTV program that Susan and I watched every Sunday night in hopes of hearing some new

by Tim Lee   89

act or catching a glimpse of one of our favorite bands, perhaps even a friend. It was pretty happening to be part of a show we dug so much.

The Let's Active footage appears in a North Carolina-centric episode that opens with the band set up in the field behind Mitch's parents' house, playing the MC5's "Shakin' Street" with Don Dixon and Cutting Edge host Peter Zaremba (front man from the Fleshtones) adding backing vocals.

I was still a kid and a big fan of many of the artists of whom I was now a de facto contemporary, so my excitement level generally stayed somewhere off the charts, as we played shows with folks like Tommy Keene, the dB's, Chris Stamey, Don Dixon, the Hoodoo Gurus, and others.

One of the early shows of the second tour was a benefit held in the auditorium of Winston-Salem's Reynolds High School Auditorium featuring Let's Active, the dB's, and Chris Stamey. The event was a homecoming of sorts, as Mitch, Faye, Chris, Peter Holsapple, Gene Holder, Will Rigby, and Stamey drummer Ted Lyons had all attended Reynolds as teenagers. It was a very cool kickoff and quite an evening to be a part of.

Billed as the "Who's on First?" tour, the Let's Active/dB's/Chris Stamey lineup stayed intact through the South and across to Texas before the dB's set off in a different direction in Oklahoma.

At Center Stage Theater in Atlanta, I walked onstage for the Let's Active set only to find that the members of the dB's had covered my side of the stage with cards from a deck featuring hardcore nude photos of men. The front of my amp, between the guitar strings, the keyboards ... nothing was spared their pornographic prank. And sitting atop one of my Fender Twin amps was a clay sculpture of an old cowboy with a ten-inch cactus growing up out of the front of his pants.

Susan and I kept that cactus around for years. The cards? Naturally, I threw them one by one into the audience.

Stamey stayed on to open most of the shows on that tour, but midway through the trek, half of his band flew home for various reasons. Mitch, Jay, and I stepped in to join remaining keyboardist Mary Mac where we could and fill out his band. I

I Saw A Dozen Faces...

played guitar on a few songs and even provided sparse drums on Chris' song "Oh Yeah."

As the tour progressed, I ended up rooming with Chris a lot and we spent some time sitting around and playing guitar. Like Mitch, he has a deep knowledge of six-string technique. I learned a lot from him on the afternoons we had time to kill before soundcheck. Between Mitch, Chris, Bobby, and eventually Matt Piucci, I was hanging out with some pretty good guitar mentors.

Chris had originally founded the dB's but left the band for a solo career after their first two albums. He'd also been responsible for releasing some of the early singles and EPs that had inspired Bobby and I to make our own records. Between Mitch, Chris, and the dB's guys, I found myself traveling around the country with a good chunk of the folks who'd cleared the path for the road I was on.

Following a show in Chicago in late 1984 that members of the band Shoes attended, a group of us went out for pizza. Over deep dish deliciousness, brothers John and Jeff Murphy invited Mitch and I to visit their band studio the following day.

We took them up on their offer and drove down to Zion, Illinois, where we had a great time, hanging out and comparing notes on recording. The Murphy brothers and Gary Klebe played some of the songs they were working on for us and regaled us with tales of major label excess from their early stint on Elektra Records.

It was a fun day, meeting and hanging out with yet another one of the bands that initially inspired me to go down the road I was following.

In the midst of such heady times, I don't doubt that my youthful enthusiasm got the best of me on occasion. I was the youngest person in the band, and I may have shown my ass a couple times, metaphorically speaking, but I like to think I acquitted myself well as a hired hand in a groovy touring combo.

The first of the two tours concluded with a Monday night gig in Los Angeles, followed by a day of press interviews the next day, and a final show on that Friday in Atlanta. I was anxious to get home to see Susan, so I caught a ride with a couple of crew members rather than wait on the band. We left L.A. Tuesday night around 11, and drove nearly non-stop (minus a five-hour stop in Jackson for a nap) across the country and arrived at the 688 Club, where I'd arranged to meet Susan, 48 hours later.

There was an Alex Chilton/Get Smart! show that night and, as I recall, I got there just as Chilton's set was starting and made my way through the crowd to find Susan. I've since heard an audience recording of that show in which you can hear her scream when we were reunited after being apart for a couple months.

I owe Mitch a lot, both for all the things I've learned from him and his willingness to give me a chance with his band at a time when I really needed a boost in figuring out where to take my own work. The experience was invaluable, and he's still a good friend.

Coming away from the Let's Active experience, I definitely felt better prepared to tackle my own path that lay ahead.

13. IN THE TRENCHES:
THE X FACTOR

Between wrapping up a pair of albums and touring with Let's Active, the previous twelve months had been a bit of whirlwind, and a damned enjoyable one at that, but by the spring of 1985, it was time to get serious about the Windbreakers again.

Not long after the Let's Active tours wrapped up, *Terminal* came out as Homestead Record's fifth release, following on the heels of cool bands such as Salem 66, the Dogmatics, and Great Plains.

Homestead did a good job of getting the record out into the world, and it received shining reviews from a lot of fanzines, even landing a mention in my beloved *Creem*.

Around that time, the venerable *Rolling Stone* declared the Windbreakers one of the nine best-unsigned bands in the country. Within a year, of course, the other eight bands on that list were all signed to major labels. Us? Not so much.

> *While I was growing up, my father never expressed much of an opinion concerning my musical pursuits. But after he heard about the Rolling Stone mention, I think he looked at me a little differently. He must have figured that, if what I was doing got my name in a real magazine that he'd seen in the grocery store, maybe I was doing all right.*
>
> *Years later, we were browsing in a book store together and I picked up a copy of the* Trouser Press Guide to Records *and showed him that it contained an entire page about the Windbreakers and my other projects. He got a big kick out of that.*
>
> *Hey, we get our validation where we can.*

With the feeling that we were starting to build some kind of momentum, plans were made for a follow-up to *Terminal*.

Bobby, Mitch, Randy Everett, and I congregated in Jackson that summer to record the second Windbreakers album, *Run*. We tracked the songs at Rick Garner's new Terminal Studio (no relation to the album of the same name, Rick's joint got its name due to its proximity to the airport).

Run features some of my favorite songs of Bobby's such as "Visa Cards & Antique Mirrors" and "Ghost Town." Overall, it's a solid follow-up to *Terminal*, but it does sound at times like he and I were maybe trying too hard. We had a lot of big ideas, so we just kind of threw the kitchen sink at it.

Yeah, I can be pretty critical of my own work, but I will always take full responsibility for any artistic or commercial missteps (of which I've had many).

As kitchen sink productions go, though, it does rock. *Run* is a sonic departure from *Terminal* for the most part, more guitar heavy (as Bobby's former roommate Jimmy Dukes would say, "Son. That's some damn git-tar playin'!"). We definitely got a bit adventurous with the production touches as well. It could be said that *Run* is short-hand for "we decided to *Run* everything we could through a Leslie rotating speaker cabinet." Nothing was spared the Leslie treatment, not even vocals or bass guitar.

Our over-zealous use of studio trickery was just a natural result of our love of the recording process. Self-editing is never the artist's first lesson. But, hey, we were having fun.

Following the attention *Terminal* got upon its release, we received offers from a few independent labels to put out the next record. Ultimately, we decided to go with Danny Beard's Atlanta-based DB Records. Danny and I had become friends, and I was a big fan of many of the acts whose records he'd released like Pylon, Love Tractor, Oh OK, Kevin Dunn, Method Actors, Swimming Pool Qs and others.

At the time, I remember being surprised that Danny was interested in the Windbreakers. Although we were pals, I didn't figure my band was cool enough to join a roster that included so many happening and primarily left-of-center acts. Blame that Mississippi-sized boulder that sat squarely on my shoulder.

I originally mentioned to Danny that we were looking at offers from a couple of labels and asked if he had any advice to offer. His unexpected reply was: "Why not put it out on my label?"

That was the beginning of a long relationship, both professionally (as much as either of us has been) and personally (he's still a great friend).

The DB connection was our first experience with a "real" record contract. Our previous arrangements with Homestead and Closer had been P&D (production and distribution) deals that involved us providing the completed master tapes at our expense (which required plenty of rubbing pennies together as we were basically young working stiffs with no other visible means of support). The label's responsibility was to pay for manufacturing and get the physical product out in the world. With Danny, we actually had a recording budget (a typical one for the time, but it seemed huge to us). Our job was just to show up and make the record.

DB had just released Guadalcanal Diary's debut wax, which was getting a great push from Landslide Records, the label that was overseeing the promotion and marketing for Danny's releases. Naturally, we wanted that sort of support as well.

Danny introduced me to artist Flournoy Holmes, who was best known for designing the cover of the Allman Brothers Band's iconic *Eat A Peach* album. He and I visited Flournoy at his home one night to check out a new series of paintings he'd done and picked one out for the *Run* jacket.

The Windbreakers were not the only thing that kept me busy in 1985. The Let's Active experience had built my confidence a bit while catapulting me into a community of music people I only dreamed of joining previously. So I went in search of projects to pursue. One of those was the week I spent in Rochester, New York, producing Absolute Grey's final release, *What Remains*.

I'd met the members of that band when Let's Active came through Rochester on tour and stayed in touch with drummer Pat Thomas, who sent me their early recordings, which I dug a lot. When the opportunity arose to work with them, I accepted and took the Amtrak from Atlanta to upstate New York.

Traveling econo was cool, but my train arrived in New York City a bit late, giving me little time to travel from one station to the other to catch the second train that would carry me north along the Hudson River and deliver me to Rochester. I remember hailing a cab and, playing the part of the big shot, promising the driver that there was a hefty tip in it for him if he got me to the station on time.

In my mind's eye, I carry an image of that big yellow taxi hauling ass through traffic, dodging cars, and all but taking to the sidewalks in order to drop me off at the proper depot. I doubt it was that dramatic, but that's how it felt.

The rube in me was also pretty proud to have negotiated such a big city moment with some degree of competency.

Absolute Grey was a very young band (bassist Mitchell Razor and guitarist Matt Kitchen had just graduated from high school), but they had a cool sound, jangly and moody, thanks in large part to singer Beth Brown's vocal chops. She has a great voice, large and full, like Grace Slick but all her own.

I don't recall if I knew they were on the verge of breaking up before the sessions (Mitchell and Matt were going off to college) or if I learned about it once there, but that certain knowledge hung over the sessions like a dark cloud. Not to say that the recording wasn't fun — it was. Beth, Pat, Mitchell, and Matt were all easy to work with, and cool folks to be around. I recall much local pizza and pitchers of Genessee Cream Ale during my stay. But the subject matter of songs such as "What Remains" and particularly "Grey Farewell" seemed to dig deep into conflicted feelings among the four band members. Those songs truly embody the feeling of watching the cool thing you built with your friends come apart.

When recording Beth's vocal on "Grey Farewell," the last song on the band's final recording, you could cut the tension with a knife as she sang lines that faced those conflicted feelings head on.

On one level, these were the yearnings of teenagers, too young to have experienced true heartbreak. But, if you've ever seen your band dissolve, you know it's a raw experience, one that can cut as deep as any knife.

Beth got emotional during her performance. Fighting back tears — and giving into them at times — she delivered an impassioned and powerful vocal performance, wrapping up the band's recorded history with a solid, pronounced finish.

I Saw A Dozen Faces...

On the other end of the spectrum, during the summer of that year, Sherry, Bruce, Robin, and I reconvened for a particularly raucous studio weekend to make a full-length Beat Temptation record with Randy Everett at the Terminal.

Gerard Cosloy, who good-naturedly inherited the Windbreakers when he took the reins at Homestead Records in 1985, dug the seven-inch Beat Temptation EP and offered to release an album for the label.

We were bonkers during that recording session, happy to be reunited and ready to make some racket. Let's just say there was a lot of beer involved and probably a moment or two that made it on to tape that I'm not particularly proud of (fortunately, most of those wound up on the proverbial cutting room floor). But, as always, the four of us had a damn good time.

This was during the era of Tipper Gore and the Parents Music Resource Center, who were trying to get albums rated like movies, you know, to "protect the children." Somewhere in there, I caught a news program that referenced another parents' group called CARM, or Concerned About Rock Music. That name cracked me up, so we turned it into a rhetorical question for the Beat Temptation album, *Concerned About Rock Music?*

As if 1985 wasn't busy enough, I also collaborated on a record with Howard Wuelfing of the Nurses, of whom I was a fan. I can't really remember how he and I first became acquainted, but he was a solid supporter of the Windbreakers early on.

Howard and I had talked a lot on the phone, and eventually kicked around the idea of making some kind of recording together. We traded some demos back and forth and narrowed it down to a few songs. Howard convinced the New York indie label Midnight Records to pony up a $300 budget (the biggest part of which went to malt liquor purchases).

I was living in Atlanta, so we decided he'd take the train down from New Jersey and we recorded in a local 8-track studio located in a guy's house. I'd already laid down some rhythm tracks with some local players, so we used those drum tracks for my songs and recorded new ones for Howard's songs and a cover of the Alex Chilton/Tommy Hoehn song, "She Might Look My Way."

I got really sick with food poisoning during the session and played most of my parts laying on my back in the middle of the floor. Despite my illness, we got it completed and released *Howard & Tim's Paid Vacation: I Never Met a Girl I Didn't Like* on Midnight in 1986.

It was good fun, sickness be damned. Howard's a kickass music publicist these days, and the Windbreakers played his songs for several years. We recorded his "Things We Never Say" for the B-side of the *I'll Be Back* 12-inch single.

By autumn, with *Run* in the can and my other projects completed, my main concern became getting some version of the Windbreakers on the road. Since I was living in Atlanta, and Bobby was in Jackson, the decision was made for me to take a Georgia-based band on tour in fall of 1985.

The first order was to find a combo for the task at hand. Through an ad in the community entertainment rag, I hooked up with some local guys: brothers Scott and Chris Mowry on keyboards and bass, drummer Stewart Bird, and guitarist Jon Byrd. They were already a band, so it was pretty easy just to plug me and these songs into their existing formula. We rehearsed a set and the plan was made to hit the road in early October.

Prior to this, our friends from the Rain Parade had hipped Los Angeles booking agent Marc Gieger to the Windbreakers. He became a fan and was kind enough to put us on a handful of dates opening for the band X in the Midwest. Following our first Atlanta gig with Game Theory at the 688 Club, we were playing to full houses in grand old theaters in Michigan and Ohio.

We showed up for the first show in Cleveland, where X's road manager immediately cornered me and let me know, in no uncertain terms, that she wasn't there to do anything for us. We were on our own, had our own contracts, and we were not her problem.

Okay, I wasn't expecting much else. Hey, welcome to the world of being your own road manager!

Soon enough, she turned out to be a sweetheart who quickly went to bat for us a couple days later when the promoter in Columbus added a local band to the bill. After the locals drank all the beer in our dressing room during our set, X's road manager found out and went on the hunt for the culprits. All of the sudden, we were "X's special guests," dammit. The promoter ended up delivering another case of beer to us in person.

I Saw A Dozen Faces...

After that first Cleveland show, a few folks came backstage to meet us. It was strange to have our own dressing room in which to receive guests, as I was used to just hanging out at the bar afterwards. It was just like you see in those documentaries about famous bands. One very earnest young couple asked if we had a place to stay. Since we didn't, they invited us to follow them down to Akron to crash with them at their pad (this is where any comparison to famous bands ends).

Happy to have a landing spot, we took them up on their offer, getting in at a very late hour. I laid out my sleeping bag on the den floor while the other guys found their own spaces.

The following morning, I was awakened by a small child who used my sleeping body as a means of support in order to lean back and watch cartoons. We didn't even know the nice couple had offspring.

Welcome to show biz, kid!

X was on their **Ain't Love Grand** tour, and while it would be their last outing with the original line-up for many years, they were amazing to watch every night on stage, furiously rocking like a well-oiled machine.

John Doe and Exene were super cool, dropping in to hang out in our dressing room regularly, while Billy Zoom talked to me about his self-designed amps and pedalboard every chance he got (even mid-song if he saw me standing on the side of the stage). John and Exene watched our set every night from the wings.

One night, I gouged a hole in the meat of my right hand when it got caught on the bridge pieces of my Telecaster. The wound bled profusely over the front of my guitar. When we arrived at the next day's venue, Exene tracked me down to check on my injury.

A week's worth of shows opening for a band of X's stature was not a bad way to kick off one's first lengthy tour. It was a bonus that the stars of the show were cool to the nobody band who was just lucky to be there.

Once that portion of the X tour ran its course, it was back to the rock club trenches. Fortunately, we were aligned with a good booking agency, Frank Riley's Venture Booking, with whom I'd become acquainted through Susan's and mine booking efforts in Jackson, and agent Joe Brown kept us busy. We played some really fun shows with bands like Dumptruck, the Lyres, and Game Theory as we worked our way across the rest of the Midwest and back to the East Coast and home after five weeks. We even played a show in D.C. with a very young Fishbone on their first tour. They were mostly still teens, so their road manager asked us if we minded getting our band beers from the bar. He said he couldn't trust them if there was beer on hand in the 9:30 Club's shared basement green room.

> D.C. power pop hero Tommy Keene, who I'd met during the Let's Active tours, came to the 9:30 show. He was wearing a pair of tan suede boots, the type we called "desert boots" or "chukka boots" in junior high school. In 1985, that footwear was a pretty obvious fashion anachronism. I hadn't seen a pair in years. I complimented Tommy and made a big deal out of them. Once it was ascertained that we wore the same size shoe, I talked Tommy into letting me borrow his boots for our set, handing off my sneakers for him to wear.
>
> I always liked to say that Tommy was such a nice guy, he'd give you the shoes off his feet.

At the Rat in Boston, we shared a bill with Dumptruck. Following our set, I succumbed to exhaustion and laid down for a few minutes in the green room. Apparently, I fell asleep as I eventually woke to the sound of guitarist Kirk Swan's voice from the stage, asking me to come up and join them for the last song of their set.

That's easily the quickest I've ever risen from slumber and strapped on a guitar.

Howard Wuelfing joined us onstage in Hoboken, where he played percussion with a drumstick on a Budweiser bottle and sang his song, "That Won't Make You Love Me," from the yet-to-be-released **Howard and Tim's Paid Vacation** record.

At one gig with Game Theory in the basement of a dorm in Milwaukee, we ended our set with GT leader Scott Miller joining us for our version of Led Zeppelin's "Tangerine," one of their more pastoral psychedelic songs. It's a simple song, but it goes to a more complex chord structure for the solo, which needs to be played like Jimmy Page's original in order for all the pieces to mesh. Our band worked pretty hard to get that section together in rehearsals, but that night, Scott just waltzed in and nailed the solo like he'd been playing it all his life.

I gained some valuable experience as a touring band leader during the Windbreakers' maiden voyage. Every day was an adventure as we navigated our way through five weeks of new places and faces, sleeping on floors and playing well-known rock clubs like the Rat, the 9:30 Club, Danceteria in NYC, Maxwell's in Hoboken, the West End in Chicago, and others.

As a group, we decided our favorite fast-food lunch was Long John Silver's chicken planks, which became a staple of our daily diets. It's a miracle none of us died in the van of a cholesterol overdose. We often joked that we should sport a Long John Silver's logo on the side of the van with the motto, "You can't spank our planks!"

The night we were in Columbus, Ohio, with X at the Newport Theater, was the night I met Mark Wyatt, the keyboard player in Great Plains, who were label-mates of ours at Homestead. Gerard Cosloy suggested I get in touch with Mark, as he was generally cool about putting bands up.

I called Mark out of the blue and introduced myself, adding rather enthusiastically that I owned a copy of Great Plains' **Mark, Don, and Mel** EP, their self-released debut. I'm not sure Mark believed me at first (it was true), but he invited us to crash at his place that night, and we've been pals since.

I've spent many a night on couches or in guest rooms at his various places of residence over the years. Great Plains stayed with Susan and I the one time they came to Jackson, and Mark ended up playing on the last couple Windbreakers albums and went on the road with us for the **At Home with Bobby and Tim** tour. We have occasionally worked together since and still hang out when the opportunity arises. Even if it's been a matter of years, he and I seem to pick right back up whenever we get together.

Like a lot of folks, Mark has been a recurring part of this whole crazy musical journey I've been on my entire adult life. It takes a village to raise a post-middle-aged rocker, you know.

We eventually returned to Atlanta without much to our names but some great memories, new friends, and stories to tell.

It felt good to know I'd been able to pull off a tour with my own band and looked forward to more. If nothing else, I felt like less of a yokel for having herded cats through several major cities without losing anyone along the way.

Jon Byrd is still a pal. He lives in Nashville now, and is a great traditional country music singer and songwriter. It's always good to see him these days, although I've lost touch with Scott, Chris, and Stewart. It was a pleasure, as well, to meet Game Theory members Scott and Gil Ray, who became long-term friends.

Soon after getting home, I got a letter from a guy in Hoboken who'd seen our Maxwell's show. He spoke highly of our set, then added that the evening inspired him to make a bank withdrawal the next day and buy a guitar.

All these years later, I'm still blown away by that one.

With **Run** in line to be released after the new year, Susan and I opted to move back to Jackson. She'd decided to return to school at Millsaps College, and I figured Bobby and I would pick up our partnership where we'd left off and the Windbreakers would be our band again.

But things have a funny way of working out sometimes.

14. (TURN AND FACE THE) STRANGE CHANGES

"I can't go on tour."

Bobby has this way of saying things when he's being adamant. It's almost monotone, but a little aggressive, as if to discourage active questioning. Kind of a "these are not the 'droids you're looking for" vibe.

I'm just enough of an asshole to be immune to his Jedi mind tricks. "What do you mean, you can't go on tour?," I said.

"I can't do it," was the extent of his explanation.

I didn't know what to make of this. Bobby and I were partners. We'd just made the second full-length Windbreakers album together. Touring was what bands who released records did. That was the truth that I'd accepted.

It wasn't Bobby's truth necessarily, just mine.

The ensuing conversation was tense. To my memory, Bobby agreed that you can't be a member of a band and not do the road work associated with it (unless you're Brian Wilson, which neither of us is). According to Bobby, I fired him from the band.

It's an argument we've had a few times over the years, and I'm too old to care one way or the other about it now. It's just the way things turned out.

I'm a pretty pragmatic guy, so I just accepted that it was my sole responsibility to take the Windbreakers on tour again.

It was a bummer that things didn't work out the way I'd hoped but during my ventures in the world of music, things rarely did.

After the shock and disappointment wore off a bit, I approached Sherry Cothren and her former bandmates in the Germans, guitarist David Minchew and drummer Joe Partridge, about joining me for the tour to support *Run*, which had been

by Tim Lee   103

released to good initial reviews. They were up for the adventure so we went to work on a bunch of songs in early 1986.

We played a few shows not long after getting together, and at the beginning of April 1986, we set out for a couple months of gigs, bringing along our friend Thom Eason, who'd offered to run sound and help with the driving. We started with an outdoor show at Mississippi State University in Starkville with Jason & the Scorchers and the Producers. From there, we hit Memphis for a night at the Antenna Club (and the time-honored band tradition of visiting Elvis' Graceland) before kicking off a string of club dates with ex-Television guitarist Richard Lloyd in Nashville and working through the Midwest.

After a few days off, we headed to Texas for shows opening for Australian band the Church (another assist from Marc Geiger). When we arrived at the first gig in Austin, Church guitarist Marty Wilson-Piper and drummer Richard Ploog came out to the van to greet us.

"The Rain Parade told us all about you guys," Marty enthused. "We're looking forward to seeing you!"

Those Rain Parade boys were doing a pretty good job spreading the word about our little band. We should have put them on salary.

We played shows throughout the Lone Star State and across Tennessee to Georgia with the Church (including the night we played an early opening set at the Uptown Lounge in Athens, then packed up and hauled ass over to Atlanta where we quickly set up and hit the 688 Club stage for our own gig just after midnight). From there, we headed back to the Northeast, where we shared stages with the Reducers, the Lyres, the Neighborhoods, Translator, and more of our favorite contemporaries.

We played at CBGB for the first time, and I was pleased to stalk the same stage as so many of my heroes from the first wave of New York arty punk rock. It was a big deal for me.

I suppose some folks would get a tattoo as a memento of such an important personal benchmark. I didn't have to; I have a scar to commemorate the event.

As we were loading out through the club during the Lyres set, I was carrying a speaker cabinet and watching front man Jeff "Monoman" Connelly cast his garage rock spell on the audience. I wasn't paying good attention to where I was going. Turning

I Saw A Dozen Faces...

sideways to slip through the crowd, my left leg got caught on a rough-edged piece of the old plywood that comprised the stage surface, ripping my jeans open and cutting a big gash in my upper thigh.

The cut bled profusely, and I had to clean it regularly over the following days to stave off infection. If you see me around sometime and I'm wearing shorts (nearly a statistical impossibility), ask to see my CBGB scar. It's still visible.

I've got several stories about Monoman and the Lyres, having met them early on when Susan and I booked them in Jackson. The Windbreakers played many shows with them over the years, and Jeff would often stay with us when he was in town.

One night, our bands shared a bill in Columbia, South Carolina. Somehow Jeff and I missed each other at load in and sound check, but when I returned to the club after dinner, I saw him in a corner behind the stage, wearing sunglasses in the dark and hugging himself in his oversized leather jacket.

"You okay?" I asked him.

"Tim, she left me," Jeff replied, obviously still upset. "My girlfriend moved out. I came home and there was nothing. Just three keys in the mailbox."

I offered my sympathies and went up to play my set.

When we were done, I grabbed a beer and found a good spot from which to watch the Lyres, who hit the stage hard, with Jeff leading the band through the slow version of "She Pays the Rent." He threw himself into the song like a possessed Percy Sledge plowing through "When a Man Loves a Woman." It was completely unexpected, but absolutely amazing and gut-wrenching, one of those great moments that makes you look forward to getting in the van.

One of our odder gigs on the tour was opening for a latter-day version of British stalwarts Wishbone Ash at the Lone Star Cafe in New York City on a Monday night. It was rather surreal to wind up on the bill with one of my teenage favorites, even if the only remaining original members were guitarist Andy Powell and drummer Martin Upton. I was still pretty excited to meet those guys.

Both bands arrived at the club only to be informed that there was supposed to be two shows: an early one and a late one. Immediately, Upton pulled me aside and intoned gravely, "We're too old to play two shows, Tim … much too old."

Maybe it was just his staid British accent, but it came across as one of the most "Spinal Tap" moments ever.

They were nice guys, although their bassist, a noted journeyman musician, kept asking Sherry to join him in their dressing room. "I've never met a female bass player," was his opening line. She respectfully declined.

We eventually agreed to play two Windbreakers sets, one before them and one afterwards. As you might imagine, on a Monday night, pretty much no one hung around after Wishbone Ash's show. Performing the second set to a quickly emptying room, we just sat on the front edge of the stage, dangling our legs, and played "Free Bird" for the departing patrons with one eye on the clock until our contracted time was up.

> Joe recently reminded me that, after our sound check at the Lone Star, we met a young Asian guy with a brand new leather jacket who "spoke no English and clearly had never seen a rock band."
>
> Young dude ran up to us and insisted that we sign his new jacket with a sharpie. "I remember us trying to convince him that was not a good idea, to no avail," Joe said. "We were the coolest shit he had ever seen. We looked at each other warily and defaced his property.
>
> "I have to wonder if, in later years, he had regrets over that."

Touring with Sherry, Joe, and David was fun. They're all easy-going, cool folks with sharp wits. Despite the usual fatigue associated with living in a van for weeks at a time, I don't recall many tensions, just good times and loud music. Thom fit in and was an energetic presence who loved to drive all night after gigs. One recurring mental image I carry from that tour is Thom, with his left hand on the steering wheel, lit cigarette between his fingers, right arm draped over the back of his seat, Coca-Cola can in that hand, looking backwards over his shoulder, talking to whoever sat behind him.

I Saw A Dozen Faces...

The rest of us kept at least one eye open and one foot on our imaginary brake pedals.

Thom also stepped into the role of guitarist for a couple of Texas shows after David was called home for a death in the family.

Back during the MySpace days, I got a personal message from a guy who told me he'd come to a Richard Lloyd/Windbreakers show in Iowa City during that 1986 tour. He recalled that he and a friend sat at a table next to ours before the show. We looked like we were having such a good time, just hanging out, eating, drinking, waiting to take the stage, that he decided he wanted to be part of something like that. So he took up the drums and ultimately became a professional musician. He just wanted to offer thanks for the example we displayed that night.

I have a photo of us on stage that night that hangs over my writing desk, and graces the cover of this book. We do look like we were having a ball.

It was hard not to notice that, as the tour went on, there was little or no promotion for us from the label. I called the DB office and Danny said I should check with Landslide, the partner label in charge of promotion. One of the reasons I was happy to sign on with DB Recs was that their alliance with Landslide had been working well for both labels and the associated artists.

I got someone from Landslide on the phone, and when I mentioned that there seemed to be a lack of promotion, they acted like they didn't know what I was talking about. What they apparently didn't tell me, or Danny for that matter, was that Landslide had decided to end their relationship with DB immediately.

That would've been a handy piece of information to have before hitting the road for several weeks.

After wrapping up the **Run** tour, we kept that version of the Windbreakers together for a few months, working on material, planning a new album, and playing shows around the region with the Primitons, 10,000 Maniacs, the Swimming Pool Qs, and others. Eventually, it all sputtered to a halt when Sherry and Joe decided the touring lifestyle wasn't commiserate with their worlds at the time.

The death of that combo was hard. It's always tough to see a band go off the tracks when everyone seemed to be working well together and having fun, especially when you really like the people involved. But they do. Sherry and Joe are still great friends of mine, and I've been fortunate to play music with them at various times since.

David stuck around for a while, and he and I found another rhythm section in Chris Hall and Mike Yarbrough. We played a short East Coast tour before that line-up fell apart when David split, looking to be his own band leader.

*For that two-week East Coast trek in early 1987, we brought along a young band, Drivin'-n'-Cryin', to open the shows. They had recently released their **Scarred but Smarter** debut album on 688 Records, which was run by my pal Cathy Hendrix, who helped arrange what was their first road foray of any length. Kevn Kinney, Tim Neilson, and Paul Lenz were cool guys that I knew from my Atlanta days and a lot of fun to be around.*

The last show of the run took place at the Brewery in Raleigh, North Carolina. Because his band was playing the following night, Jimmy Zero of the legendary punk band The Dead Boys was on hand, hanging out backstage and regaling us with cool stories. Afterwards, both bands stayed at a nearby Econolodge. As we were pulling out to head south the next morning, we looked up to see D-n-C bassist Tim leaning over the rail outside their second-floor room in nothing but his boxer shorts, pumping his fist and singing/shouting "You've gotta fight for your right to party!" to us.

David lives in Atlanta now and plays in several bands, including one with some other friends of ours called the Skylarks. It's a small world, especially the music world. David and I cross paths from time to time and, despite our initially awkward split up, it's always a pleasure.

But, at the time, I had no band and no real plan. The future, as Tom Petty once sang, was wide open.

I Saw A Dozen Faces...

15. FISHING FOR A GOOD TIME (STARTS WITH THROWING IN YOUR LINE)

"Hey Tim, do y'all wanna play a couple shows with us in February?"

Will Rigby's distinctive North Carolina drawl oozed out of the telephone receiver and into my ear.

His band, the dB's, were one of my favorites and an early inspiration for the Windbreakers. I'd met and hung out with them during my tours with Let's Active, so they were now my pals. Will and I had hit it off right away.

The *Run* touring version of the Windbreakers had just come together, so we quickly made plans for a couple of shows with Will and company. In early 1986, we met the dB's in Athens, Georgia, to open for them at the famed 40 Watt Club on a Thursday. As always, it was great fun to see, hear, and hang out with those guys.

The show was a good one. The dB's were popular in Athens, and we were at least a somewhat known quantity, so there was a good turnout. Some of the R.E.M. guys, who the dB's had toured with previously, were on hand, a couple of them joining in on an encore of Elvis' "Suspicious Minds."

The day after the 40 Watt show, the dB's went one direction and we drove to Atlanta, where we were part of a DB Records (no relation to the band) showcase at Center Stage Theater with headliners Swimming Pool Qs and openers the Coolies. We served as the meat in that new wave sandwich, and it was a great evening celebrating Danny Beard's influential label alongside a couple of our favorite bands.

The show kicked off with the Coolies entering stage left, dressed in … you guessed it, coolie uniforms, carrying singer Clay Harper on their shoulders in a P.O.W.-style tiger cage before breaking into songs from their rock opera *Dug*.

Hell, we saw more than a dozen faces that night … and you know what we did with them.

On Saturday night, the dB's and the Windbreakers reconvened in Tuscaloosa, Alabama, at the Chukker, a classic old rock dive near the university campus, for what ended up as one of the coolest gigs of all time in my estimation.

Not only were we sharing the bill with one of my favorite bands, but another pal, Matt Piucci of the Rain Parade, had flown into Atlanta earlier in the day and caught a ride to Tuscaloosa with his brother Andy. Matt and I were planning to make a record together in the next few weeks, but tonight we were all just hanging out for the rock and roll show. It turned into a big party.

We kicked the evening off with a spirited Windbreakers set. Matt joined in for a few songs before Will and Peter Holsapple took the stage with us for a set-ending "White Light, White Heat."

Next up, the dB's were on fire, kicking out a barnburner set in the packed, sweaty little club. I plugged my guitar back in and joined them for their encore. We played one song, and I figured I was done, but they kept me up through four or five total songs including their "Spy in the House of Love" and the Beatles' "Why Don't We Do It in the Road?"

It was a great night, consisting of everything I love about live music, but I was also hyped to get back home and into the studio with Matt.

Upon our arrival back in Jackson, Matt and I dove straight into the Terminal with Randy to begin work on what became the *Gone Fishin'* album.

For the next month, we tried out every idea either of us had. A chord progression and a vocal phrase might end up as a chorus, which could be combined with another piece that became a verse. Sometimes we'd have a complete instrumental track done before any words were written. Although we recorded three or four songs that existed prior to the sessions, our on-the-fly approach to songwriting was a new thing for me. But it was fun, even exhilarating at times.

Matt had convinced the California label Enigma to finance the project for their Restless imprint. I have no memory of the initial budget, but I know we went well over it. I mean, three dudes working a mere three hours from New Orleans in February needed to go to Mardi Gras for research, didn't they?

During that Louisiana trip, we wound up at the Dream Palace, a rock club where Will's calamitous side project Wipe Me, Mommy was playing. Naturally, I wound up on stage playing guitar for their set.

It reminded me of being at the same club a year earlier to play a Let's Active/dB's/Chris Stamey Mardi Gras triple-bill. Over happy hour crawfish and Dixie beer, the dB's hatched a plan for me and Janet Wygal to join them onstage for a version of "Devil Woman" at the end of their set.

When we got back to the club, Will insisted that he and I have a shot of Jagermeister. I went along for one and then curtailed that activity, as Let's Active was playing last. On the other hand, Will had a few, which resulted in his being barely able to function by the end of the dB's set and spoiling the "Devil Woman" plan.

I got serious side-eye from Will's bandmates as their drummer turned green and the set eventually ground to a halt. I just shrugged my shoulders with my palms upward. Sometimes blowing off a little steam just gets carried away.

At one point during the sessions, Matt called the label to ask for more money. He claimed that we had already spent all of the money on the project, and that the studio was holding the tapes hostage until they got more dough. Randy and I stood behind him, stifling our giggles, as he pulled off an Oscar-worthy performance for the beleaguered label rep. In front of Matt was a yellow legal pad with a detailed list of our expenses, including one line item that was simply a crude drawing of a marijuana leaf and the figure $300. To my knowledge, no expense report was ever shared with the label.

As hard as we worked in the studio, we played equally hard away from it. In addition to our New Orleans foray, we were regular after-session visitors to CS's, a local bar located around the corner from mine and Susan's house. There, we ate Inez burgers and red beans and rice, played pool, and imbibed cold Budweisers while plotting our next moves.

We found out the Primitons were scheduled to play at W.C. Don's on a Wednesday night, so we insisted that we'd be the opening band. Thus, Matt, Bobby, Bruce Golden (who drummed on the *Gone Fishin'* project) and I performed an impromptu set under the guise of Crosby, Stills, Nash, and Piucci.

We played a couple songs from the current sessions plus covers of Television, Neil Young, and Love songs. The Used Goods' Joe Bennett joined us to sing a set-closing version of Donovan's "Atlantis."

There was no real rehearsal; we just dove in and played with excessive volume and joyful glee.

In the studio, friends dropped in and contributed, including both of the Sutliff brothers and singer Kris Wilkinson. For the song "Something Better" (a hangover from Beat Temptation), we used a basic track Randy and I had previously recorded with George Cartwright on sax so we could keep George's parts. Matt's brother Andy even contributed some low end piano notes and handclaps before heading back home to Atlanta.

Toward the end of Matt's stay, we hunkered down and put the finishing pieces on everything. I have a memory of sitting on my front stoop in the early morning with a notepad and a cup of coffee, feverishly writing the final lyrics in order to wrap things up.

The finished product, **Gone Fishin': You Can't Get Lost if You're Going Nowhere** was released into the world in late 1986, one of the total of five releases I was involved with that year.

If nothing else, that prodigious output gave reviewers an angle to use in write-ups. More than one referred to me as "the hardest working man in rock and roll."

I took their praise and put it together with 50 cents. I was still short a cup of coffee.

16. POST-PARTY DEPRESSION: PICK UP THE PIECES

In the first half of 1986, I was busy with the *Gone Fishin'* sessions and the *Run* tour. With the dissolution of my band, though, I found myself in need of something to do to fill the second half of the calendar.

A call from Marti Jones' management provided that something: the opportunity to hit the road again, this time playing guitar and keyboards as part of the former Color Me Gone singer's band on a fall tour to support her sophomore A&M Records release *Match Game*.

I had seen Marti on her first solo tour in Athens, and her band included Don Dixon and Chris Stamey. I remembered her show being cool and pretty straightforward, so I signed on and soon headed to Raleigh, North Carolina, to prepare for the work ahead. Upon my arrival, I met Marti when she gave me a ride to my motel. Like her set I'd seen the previous year, she was cool and pretty straightforward, so I liked her. That evening I met the rest of the band, a trio who played around the region in a great rock and roll combo called the Woods: drummer Terry Anderson (who wrote the song "Battleship Chains," a hit for the Georgia Satellites), bassist Jack Cornell, and guitarist David Enloe. They were good dudes, but we didn't spend a lot of time together before the tour, as they all worked their day jobs right up until we hit the highway.

Through Marti's manager, Harry Simmons, we had access to a music club in Chapel Hill called Rhythm Alley where, for the next couple weeks, we met every evening for practice sessions. During the day, I hung out in my nondescript Days Inn room with little to do but practice the songs or walk down the road to the nearest lunch spots. Marti dropped in from time to time to work out parts, and one day Faye Hunter came by to visit when she was in town to take her aging dog Buford to the vet.

Other than that, though, I was just killing time most days.

Some nights after practice, I entertained myself by hanging out at the Brewery, a club where Harry booked shows, checking out friends and contemporaries like Mojo Nixon & Skid Roper, the Dream Syndicate, and the True Believers, who I saw perform a particularly monumental rock and roll show, filling out their seemingly never-ending set with raucous versions of Mott the Hoople, New York Dolls, and Stooges songs.

> *One distraction involved the couple of days spent shooting a music video for Marti's cover of a Dwight Twilley song, "Chance of a Lifetime," for which the label hired famed film-maker D.A. Pennebaker. At least I got to follow him around and pester him with questions about "Don't Look Back" and "Monterey Pop." He was generous with his time, as I recall.*

After a couple weeks of rehearsals, Marti's band hit the road. With the support of A&M, we played some pretty cool gigs like the Bottom Line in New York (where the members of the dB's sat at a side bar and heckled me in a good-natured fashion) and an MTV special called the *Spin* New Music College Tour that was filmed at the University of Maryland. The MTV taping was emceed by Larry "Bud" Melman and featured several other bands such as Beat Rodeo, the Screaming Blue Messiahs, and the Call. It was a fun gig, but later that night at the motel, someone broke into the equipment truck and stole Marti's guitar and keyboard. Dixon showed up the following day with replacement gear so the show could go on.

This tour was more relaxed than the ones I'd been used to. Rather than playing six or seven shows a week, we were doing more like four or five, so there was plenty of free time to do more tourist-y stuff than I'd done in the past. That was all fine, but ultimately it just amounted to too much time on my hands. I loved playing music, and I enjoyed touring, but when we weren't busy, I was bored. I learned that you can only visit so many museums before they all start running together. Next stop, hotel bar.

I Saw A Dozen Faces...

Dixon, who was Marti's producer (now husband), joined us on parts of the tour, so they were together as much as possible. The Woods were all long-time friends, so they naturally hung out as a group. I mostly passed the time by myself or with the crew: road manager/sound man Cliff Atchison, who'd performed the same duties (and taught me a good bit about the trade) with Let's Active; Gilbert Nestor, who I knew through the dB's and his role as lead guitarist in Wipe Me, Mommy; and Jeff Wygal, the brother of my friends Doug and Janet Wygal of the Individuals.

That tour did have a few hectic periods, including one particularly crazy Boston-to-Nashville haul. Following a Monday night show in Beantown, our next gig was at a Cat's Record Store Convention showcase in Music City on Wednesday afternoon. Sending the equipment truck off after the Boston show, the band van hit the highway on Tuesday morning and we drove all through the night. I took the first shift and got into one of those unreasonable zones where you just don't want to turn the driving duties over to anyone else. At about the 12-hour mark, they finally pried my hands off the wheel and put me in the backseat with a pillow and a drink. We got to Nashville early on Wednesday morning, with just enough time for a quick nap before the mid-day soundcheck.

The gigs were fun enough, but it was tough to enjoy myself with so much free time. Everybody involved was cool, but my brain just wasn't wired for that kind of schedule.

After a couple months, we all returned home for a couple of weeks before flying out to reconvene in Los Angeles for a string of West Coast shows opening for the British band Everything But The Girl.

There were plans for a European tour after that, but the calendar got shuffled around a few times, so I opted out. Being a hired hand on a major label dime was nice enough, and it kept me employed for a while at a time when I needed it. And I liked Marti a lot. Once it was done, though, I was ready to get back to my own grindstone and try to figure out the next step of my so-called career.

Going into 1987, Randy and I were still at work on the songs that started out as the beginnings of an album for the Tim-Sherry-Joe-and-David version of the Windbreakers, and morphed into a Tim-and-David project, before ultimately becoming a de facto solo album as band members dropped off.

Despite the ever-evolving nature of the process, Randy and I had fun working together on the material, and we figured out a lot of recording technique along the way. He's been a great friend and collaborator over the years. His curiosity, humor, and enthusiasm made what otherwise was a pretty trying time all the more enjoyable while we were in the studio.

As low-key as they come, Randy exudes quiet energy. Wiry and tall, with a nest of blonde hair and a wry grin that stops just shy of a smirk, he's all heart. A smart engineer with a solid musical background and a hell of a jazzy guitarist as well, he's yet another one of those great folks to have in your corner.

Because we kept backing up and starting over during the process, it could be argued that we overworked the recordings, but if that's the case, it was my fault. I was obsessed with getting something done and moving forward, despite the near-constant stream of circumstances that conspired against our doing so. I found myself getting wrapped up in the idea of production, perhaps to the detriment of the finished product. But it was a blast, you know, so that's what we did.

> People wonder why records from that era have so many of what are now considered novel sounds on them. That's an easy one: it was brand-new technology, and it was fun to play with that gear and make new noises that hadn't existed before (and mostly not in nature).
>
> As much as all of us appreciated the recording techniques of the past, we were living in the present, and this now offered a whole new array of colors to choose from. Why would you use that measly 8-pack of dollar store crayons when you have access to a massive 64-count Crayola box? Of course, now I can think of several reasons (some good, some not so much), but it was a different time in the 1980s.

Eventually, Randy and I wrapped up the batch of tunes we were working on. I picked out some songs and played them for Danny Beard, and we talked about a plan for the new record, which would come out under the Windbreakers name at DB's suggestion.

A Different Sort lived up to its name. Although the 11 songs involved many of my Jackson friends (even my high school bandmate Lisa Goodman Palmer, who sang on a couple numbers), it was essentially a solo album wrapped in Windbreakers clothing.

In the meantime, Bobby recorded his first solo album, *Only Ghosts Remain*, for the JEM label, where Howard Wuelfing was still employed. It was slated to come out roughly at the same time as *A Different Sort* in 1987.

So, with two separate solo projects, what did Bobby and I do? Planned to take on a tour together, of course! Having quit his job and moved temporarily to Austin, Bobby was back and now apparently free to hit the road.

The idea originated with JEM, and when I was approached with it, I figured we should just do a wide-ranging Windbreakers set that included songs from both of our new releases. That made sense to me, but Bobby's label folks didn't like that idea, preferring that he play an opening set under his own name.

Thus, plans were laid for a Windbreakers/Bobby Sutliff tour, one of the craziest endeavors in our shared history. I'd lined up drummer Ric Menck and bassist Paul Chastain from Illinois for the *A Different Sort* tour, and the three of us also formed Bobby's backing band for his set. Thom Eason had already signed on to play guitar and keyboards, so he played on the Windbreakers set with the plan for Bobby to join us for a couple songs.

Following a few days of rehearsal, we headed out for a month of rock and roll adventures around the eastern half of the country.

The concept worked well enough. Both Bobby's and the Windbreakers' sets were well received and different enough from each other to justify the double billing. Ric and Paul, who later started their own band Velvet Crush and backed Matthew Sweet, were great and had no trouble covering both sets each night.

Early on in the tour, Bobby lost one of his cowboy boots, leaving him with just one of a really nice pair. It was unfortunate, but after he also lost a single contact lens, I spent a lot of time reminding him that he was just half the man he'd been at the onset.

A week or two into it, our Rent-A-Wreck (seriously) van blew a head gasket in the middle of the night in Orangeburg,

by Tim Lee

South Carolina. After piling all five of us and our gear into a room at the local motor court, we limped the van down the road to a shade-tree mechanic's front yard next to a trailer park.

The old guy diagnosed the van, and somehow knowing the exact amount of cash in my front pocket, proclaimed the repair would cost $900.

Our options were limited, so we decided just to go with the flow (thank goodness for credit cards). After calling ahead to cancel our upcoming show in Raleigh, North Carolina, we made ourselves at home at the motor court when we weren't hanging out and drinking beer (our purchase) with the old guys in the shade-tree mechanic's yard.

We asked for input on local restaurants, but our new friends' recommendations were pretty unsavory, so we stuck with the Wendy's Super Bar, a cheap staple of mid-1980s tour cuisine.

Not long after that, I got a message to call Lisa Roach (now Maddox) at the DB Recs office. Lisa was a friend of mine who had been working promotions for the label. She'd done a great job of getting the *A Different Sort* tour promo started, but was calling to apologize because she'd been offered a real job, one that she really needed to take.

Sense another pattern developing here?

That was a tough one, though. Of course, I couldn't argue with my friend's personal decision to improve her life, but there was no one on deck to take up the task of tour support.

As per usual, it felt like one step forward, two steps back.

17. GLORY DAYS

"Where's Tim?"

A familiar face whipped around the corner and through the doorway to the — shall we say, spartan — dressing room at CBGB.

"Hey Richard," I said, standing from my slumped position to shake his hand.

"Hey man, how're you doing?"

Enter Richard Lloyd.

The renowned guitarist from first-generation CBGB band Television dropped by to say hello.

You could've pushed me over with a guitar pick.

I'd met Richard the previous year when he and the Windbreakers played a string of dates together. At that time, he was fresh out of rehab and releasing a new solo album called *Field of Fire*, so our mutual booking agent thought it was a good idea to put the returning hero together on a double bill with his acolytes.

One of the things the Windbreakers were known for was our version of the Television song "Glory" for which we'd teamed up with our pals the Rain Parade on the *Terminal* album.

Remember when I said the Windbreakers/Rain Parade collaboration was a story for later? There are a couple funny things about that recording and its origin. Susan and I booked the Rain Parade in Jackson when they were first touring as a four-piece after David Roback's departure. They stayed at our house, and we hit it off famously and had a great time hanging out together.

The night they played at W.C. Don's, the Windbreakers opened the show. Matt Piucci asked me to come up and play a song with them. "Sure," I said, "What do you want to do?"

"'Glory,'" he replied.

Misunderstanding him, I said, "'Gloria?' Like E, D, A, right?"

Matt misunderstood me as well and answered, "Yeah!"

Okay, I thought as drummer Eddie Kalwa counted us in.

It didn't take me long to realize that we were not playing the Van Morrison and Them song. I quickly corrected course and, watching Matt's hands closely, I caught right up and was playing Television's "Glory," not Them's "Gloria," in no time.

Out of fear of embarrassing myself, I don't think I ever told them that story.

> *Sitting in with bands and misunderstanding them is a recurring theme for me. In 1988, on a tour for my first solo album, my band played in Toronto with a cool local combo called the Whammee, who took us in, cooked for us, showed us around, and such. Great dudes.*
>
> *During their set, they invited me up to sit in on a song. We, of course, had spent our post-set time imbibing local brews, so I probably wasn't at my best.*
>
> *When the guitar player said, "'Folsom Prison Blues' in the key of G, eh?" all I could come back with was, "Okay, which one, G or A?"*

A few days later, the Rain Parade was coming back through town so we booked studio time at the first place we could find. After meeting at my house, we headed out to the studio, which was in Clinton, west of town.

En route, we stopped at a sandwich shop for fortification. Over po-boys, we sketched out ideas for the arrangement of the tune on the back of a brown paper bag. The song didn't really call for keyboards, so I suggested Will Glenn play a violin solo toward the end.

"My violin only has three strings on it," Will said. "I broke one."

"You can work around that, can't you?"

Will's part on "Glory" was recorded with three of the standard four strings on his instrument. His solo ultimately gave our version a slight country-ish feel, despite Steven Roback's slithering bass and Matt's, Bobby's, and my cranked up guitars.

So here I was at the Bowery dive, hanging out with Richard Lloyd. Not only was there a bit of Windbreakers fan-boy connection to Television, but reading about the CBGB scene in *Creem* and *Rock Scene* had been one of the main things that made me want to get out in the world and play music in the first place.

As an early teen, I was completely enamored of Patti Smith, Television, Richard Hell, the Ramones, Blondie, and all the others that comprised their world. The influence of that time and place on me is immeasurable. Just being at CBGB to play a show was a really big deal to me, even on the second or third time, so for an actual founding member of that scene to come around to say hello was mind-boggling.

> *On another occasion at CBGB, my cousin Dana Ong brought "Handsome" Dick Manitoba of the Dictators to see us. Dana was living in the city and had become friends with him. She knew that I was giant Dictators fan dating back to their first album. I got Manitoba to sign the* **Dictators Go Girl Crazy** *sticker on the back of my battered Telecaster. He was a cool guy.*

You've got to remember where I come from. The odds were very much against this kid from Mississippi, who spent afternoons sprawled on the floor at the Rexall drug store, poring over the photos of Television, the Dictators, and the Ramones in *Rock Scene*, ever getting to visit the Big Apple, let alone play one the legendary rock clubs of that era.

I remember something Richard told me that night. He asked me about our new record, the usual kind of touring small talk. I told him it was going pretty well, but recited a not-so-great review to him verbatim.

"Yep, you always remember every word of the bad ones, don't you?" Richard replied.

He was right. You do.

The previous year's tour with Richard had been a load of fun. At the least, getting to watch him play the guitar tour de force "Field of Fire" every night was nothing short of amazing, like going to school. A really cool school.

The first show we did together was in Nashville on a Sunday night. I was introduced to Richard backstage at the Exit/In. He seemed a little out of it, like he was jet-lagged or something.

He said he'd heard that we also covered a song from his *Alchemy* album called "Blue and Grey." When I replied in the affirmative, he asked how many times we'd played it and made a lame joke about us owing him 72 cents.

It was an awkward kickoff to the tour.

The following day, however, somewhere on the interstate between Nashville and Louisville, Kentucky, Richard's band's van caught up to pass us in the left lane. We looked over to see Richard hanging out of the passenger seat window, wearing a child's felt cowboy hat and shooting rubber darts at us from a toy gun at 65 miles per hour.

We laughed our asses off at the thought of one of our guitar heroes hamming it up for our amusement.

A couple days later in Iowa City, we were hanging around while the audio guy tweaked the P.A. system. I have long said that, "Where there be sound men, there be Steely Dan albums," and sure enough a cassette of one of that band's low-key recordings blared from the speakers.

Richard walked over and sat down next to me. "You'd think they'd play some disco or something like that instead of this," he said. "I mean, something with some low end."

It made sense, so I nodded in agreement.

"You know what song I really like on your new record?" he asked.

What? One of my guitar inspirations actually listened to something I'd done?

We ended up getting along well. It was also cool to befriend Jon Klages, the former Individuals guitarist who was playing second guitar to Richard for the tour.

Again, experiences like that are why you do this stuff in the first place.

It was a packed bill at CBGB that night I reconnected with Richard. In addition to the Windbreakers and Bobby Sutliff sets, there was True West guitarist Russ Tolman (who joined us that night for "Glory" and later worked with the WBs on our *Electric Landlady* album) and our Alabama neighbors Carnival Season.

Oh yeah, there was also some young new wave band from Boston, who opened the show, making their New York City debut, called the Pixies.

18. ROCK AND ROLL HOTEL: TALK TO STRANGERS

"I don't wanna be weird or anything, but my name's Tim and you guys look like you need a place to stay."

The young band members exchanged glances before the leader answered.

"Yeah?" she replied timidly.

Finding a cheap, preferably free, place to stay is an important part of life for touring bands who fly beneath the radar of fancy motor-coaches and fine hotels. A veteran of that world, which I was in my late-twenties, could spot the lost ones a mile away, might even know they needed a place before they did.

In a perfect world, every band would be able to afford decent motels and bunk no more than two to a room, but the world — particularly in the sphere of rock and roll — is rarely perfect. Money is usually in short supply for any young touring outfit, and one of the quickest ways to save a bit is to stay in peoples' homes. Besides, having a sofa to yourself is sometimes better than sharing an Econolodge room with three or four more people.

Sometimes. It depends on the situation.

When the Windbreakers toured, we never hesitated to announce from the stage when we needed a place to crash. Of course, you're always taking a chance. Like the night in South Carolina when the kid who ran sound at the club offered us his living room floor when no audience member came forward with better accommodations. After we got to his house and got settled, he and his buddy got knee-knocking drunk and sang the 1970s Frito Bandito jingle at the top of their lungs in the kitchen, non-stop, until we gathered up our sleeping bags and slunk out the side door to find a Motel 6 in the middle of the night. Ai yi yi, indeed.

by Tim Lee

The occasional bad stay aside, most people were quite gracious in sharing their homes. The vast majority of experiences were positive ones.

I recall one night at the Continental Club in Austin when, after we made our plea for lodging from the stage, we received multiple offers, all of which seemed good. None of them were from people we knew, so we had an impromptu meeting to compare the relative merits of our various would-be hosts.

None of the candidates stood out from the pack, so we opted for a quick round of questioning with a single query: do you have This is Spinal Tap *on VHS? Following a quick quiz, we found a winner based on that sole criteria.*

After Susan and I settled back in Jackson in the mid-1980s, she'd returned to both school and her old job at the radio station. Between work, college classes, studying, and running the student darkroom on the Millsaps campus, her life was non-stop.

I returned to my old job, screen-printing t-shirts for Paul Canzoneri, and spent the rest of my time writing songs, planning tours, and recording. Sensing that our kitchen was on the verge of becoming a wasteland, I learned how to cook for the two of us.

Still, I had plenty of time on my hands, so I spent many an evening at W.C. Don's, hanging out at the bar and checking out the touring bands that passed through. It gave me something to do and kept me out of Susan's hair while she was studying.

She was cool with the fact that I might bring home stray bands from time to time. It was certainly nothing new for us. Hosting musicians had been part of our world for quite some time.

During the couple years Susan and I spent in Atlanta, W.C. Don's had taken on a life of its own. After word spread about the shows we had booked there, bands began calling around after we'd left. A couple intrepid souls took up the mantle and promoted some shows (including a Flipper gig booked by Robin Sutliff), but eventually the little bar on Jackson's northwest side was sold to a guy named Terry Butler.

Phone calls continued from touring bands looking for another gig in the deep South, and Terry obliged, booking acts any night of the week that was requested.

For the second half of the 1980s and through the '90s, Don's served as a home base for the regional bands that began to flourish as "alternative" music became a prominent thing, opening a floodgate for young Southern creatives looking to make their own mark on the larger world. Thanks to Terry's little bar, young local bands who wanted to play their own songs had a stage to inhabit.

Regular visitors to Terry's joint included the Hilltops from Oxford, Mississippi, which featured future Wilco bassist John Stirratt and his twin sister Laurie, who eventually formed Blue Mountain with fellow Hilltop Cary Hudson. I remember a teen-aged Pat Sansone (Wilco/Autumn Defense) sneaking into the club under aged, offering to play his demos for anyone who would listen (and they were good). Will and the Bushmen came up from Mobile, Alabama, on a regular basis before moving to Nashville and setting the stage for leader Will Kimbrough's wide-ranging career as an award-winning instrumentalist, singer, and songwriter in the Music City. Starkville, Mississippi's Cafe Des Moines featured a young Jimbo Mathus, years before he left the Magnolia State for the Carolinas and the Squirrel Nut Zippers. North Alabama band Adam's House Cat was populated by several eventual Drive-By Truckers.

The most exciting of the young Jackson bands to pop up at Don's was a trio of Black teenagers playing hardcore punk and metal who called themselves The Men With No IQs.

In the grand scheme of things, W.C. Don's was just another piece of the puzzle that comprised the deep South's bourgeoning indie rock world, one that would ultimately make a few marks in the wider world. Like the Nick in Birmingham, the Antenna in Memphis, the Tip Top Cafe in Huntsville, the Chukker in Tuscaloosa, or the Kingfish in Baton Rouge, Don's was a landing spot for young bands working to build a following as well as a helpful tour stop for national (and international) acts such as the dB's, Scruffy the Cat, Game Theory, Alex Chilton, Raw Power, and the Swimming Pool Qs.

Unlike most of those other venues, though, Don's had a particularly weird reputation as a place where anything could happen, and often did. Stories were plentiful of bands who collected their pay in weed or cases of beer, as there never seemed to be much money on hand at the end of the night. Double bookings were common, although a complete and functioning P.A. system was not.

by Tim Lee

Somehow, though, the place managed to plug along for a couple decades, longer than most rock clubs.

Terry was a friendly, outgoing fellow (still is) who meant well, but no one was going to accuse him of being a great music promoter. He could be pretty creative, though.

On one New Year's Eve, a couple of our local bands played at Don's. Being a traditional party holiday, the room was packed.

Just before midnight, Terry got the bright idea to hand out sparklers to everyone in the audience with the notion that they'd light them all simultaneously at the stroke of twelve in a spectacular display.

Sure enough, as the minute hand and seconds hand met at the top of the clock, dozens of sparklers were lit.

What no one considered was how quickly the oxygen would evaporate in the cramped end of the small building, leaving dozens gasping for breath and stampeding to get outside to the fresh cold air.

Under pressure from the crush of people, the wall at stage right gave way, opening up one side of the room and allowing revelers to escape sure suffocation. The entire side of the structure fell over in one piece.

To most folks, a missing wall might present a problem. For Terry, it just gave the building some flexibility. The side of the building would stay in place during the colder months but with its newly removable status, when the weather got nice, that wall was opened up to expose live music to the outdoor patio area and a hastily constructed volleyball court.

On this particular night at Don's, I'd seen an intriguing combo from Virginia called the Future Neighbors. I was among the dozen faces they set out to rock that night. I liked their music, but it was obvious they were probably on their first lengthy tour.

I knew the scene well. It might have been Wednesday night in Jackson, but as far as I could tell it was Tuesday night in Pittsburgh. With a lesser-known act in a smaller town on a weeknight, it was hard to tell one weeknight from the other.

So I offered to let them follow me home, where they'd have a relatively comfortable place to crash.

"You just have to be quiet and not wake up my wife," I said, both as an explanation of the situation and to telegraph to the two young women and two young men that I wasn't inviting them to an all-night rave.

They conversed amongst themselves before tracking me down at the bar to let me know they'd take me up on my offer.

The following morning, while I made coffee for our impromptu guests, the band leader called home. During her conversation, she explained the band's situation to the person on the other line.

"What did you say your name is?" she asked me with her hand over the receiver.

"Tim," I replied. "Tim Lee."

She relayed that information to the person on the other end of the line and soon seemed to relax for the first time since we'd met the night before.

"He knows who you are," she explained after hanging up. "He said you were okay."

The rock and roll hotel is an important aspect of the up-and-coming band's cosmos. Someone in the band that takes up space on your floor tonight is likely to be your host the next time you visit their town.

During that time, Susan and I welcomed a lot of bands into our home, many who we knew and several that I happen to meet randomly on a slow night at W.C. Don's. Glass Eye and the Wild Seeds from Austin. Get Smart! from Chicago. Amy Rigby's first touring band, the Last Roundup, from New York. Fetchin' Bones from North Carolina. Ohio's Great Plains and Scrawl. The F.U.s from Boston. Mojo Nixon and Game Theory from the West Coast. The mighty Plan 9 from Rhode Island stayed with us on two Thanksgivings in a row, their converted school bus parked on the street guarded by their pet Doberman.

Putting folks up is just what we did. In turn, several of them offered dependable stops for me and my bands when we were on the road.

Couch space was valuable currency in a world where cash was always in short supply. To this day, Susan and I still stay with friends or family on most of our road forays. Hanging out and visiting with good folks adds a wider dimension to the touring experience.

However, we don't follow strangers home any more. Not very often, anyway.

by Tim Lee   127

19. GOING SO LOW IN A NEW YEAR

"Happy New Year!"

The clock struck midnight and the impromptu accordion-and-mandolin duo of Jim Mastro and Ted Lyons strolled through the crowd at Maxwell's playing "Auld Lang Syne" as we revelers sang along.

As the calendar page turned over to 1988, Susan and I were in Hoboken, New Jersey, ringing in a new year with some of our beloved music pals in one of my all-time favorite rock clubs.

We were there because, feeling like I'd made good progress as a songwriter and with several years under my belt as a bandleader, it seemed like the time was ripe to make my first real solo album. I had a batch of songs I was happy with and a slightly different sound in my head.

Songwriting was a task that I approached much like every other endeavor I undertook. As putting words and music together didn't come naturally to me any more than anything else, I simply had to practice, practice, practice. Nearly every morning, before heading out to work at the t-shirt shop, I spent whatever time I could spare in front of my four-track cassette machine, working on songs.

In time, the shadows and light didn't come from the same direction as much any more, and the verbiage became a bit less clunky. But trust me, I threw away plenty of songs and pieces of songs.

Recently, I heard back-to-back songs by Guy Clark and John Prine on the radio. Listening closely, I was struck by the grace displayed in their words, a quality that sets such artists apart from the rest. I suppose you could call it a literary sense.

I Saw A Dozen Faces...

I hear that same grace in the work of Townes Van Zandt,
Leonard Cohen, and my pals RB Morris and the late David
Olney. It's a rare and beautiful thing.

On the other hand, I can write a pretty good rock and roll
tune, which is a different animal altogether: more direct, less
poetic (unless you happen to be Chuck Berry). I've been doing
it a long time, so I should be relatively capable. If there's an
idea, I can usually run with it; some things eventually become
natural. I love literature, but I don't think there's anything
particularly graceful about the songs I make up. Still, I feel
like I'm pretty good at the thing that I do.

To move forward, I faced a tough decision: should I keep
to the path I was on, working with the same people, or should
I branch out and try a different approach? Although I hated to
break from my friends Randy and Danny, my gut told me to
strike out in a new direction. To try something different.

So I did.

Steve Fallon was the owner of Maxwell's and had turned his
family's restaurant into one of the hippest rock and roll joints
in the country. Everybody loved playing there, from the rookies
to the veterans. It was just a small rock club located behind a
neighborhood pub and restaurant, but it was like home to many
a wayfaring rock and roll combo.

The crowd at Maxwell's generally consisted of the most
hardcore of music fans. It was not unusual to get requests for
songs of yours that you'd never recorded, but that someone in
the audience knew from trading demo tapes with like-minded
types. They were serious about this stuff and often tried to
out-obscure each other with their shouted requests. I saw
Richard Thompson, the ultimate cult artist, there one night when
he humorously chided the crowd for being a "bit too chatty"
with their constant pleas for lesser-known songs.

It was always a fun and unique experience to play there.

In addition to Maxwell's and his other Hoboken business interests, Steve had started the Coyote Records label and
released recordings by the Feelies (and their various offshoots),
Chris Stamey, Gigolo Aunts, the Neats, and others.

I figured Steve might be my ticket to a different way of
doing things. He'd always been supportive and was never

anything less than a joy to be around when I'd played his club. I approached him with the idea, and he agreed to release my first solo album, **What Time Will Tell**, on Coyote.

Recording officially commenced on January 1, 1988, at Water Music in Hoboken.

Gene Holder of the dB's signed on to play and co-produce the project with me. I was a fan of the records he'd worked on before, but figured we'd ease into the producer/artist relationship by sharing the producer's role. After we'd been in the studio roughly a half hour, though, I knew he needed to take charge. "You're the producer!" I blurted out. Gene had the right temperament and skill set for the job and was no stranger to the particular studio we'd chosen, as well as the engineer and the players we'd lined up.

Gene and I had gotten to know each other during the Let's Active/dB's tour of 1985 and we had a great rapport. There was plenty of good-natured ribbing that passed between us, but the work progressed smoothly. On the surface, he's a pretty quiet guy, almost stoic. But he has a sharp wit and a wicked sense of humor. Oh yeah, and he knows a lot about getting records made. Plays a mean guitar too.

Gene was just the kind of Swiss-army knife partner I needed to make **What Time Will Tell**.

Both Ted Lyons, from Stamey's band, and Doug Wygal, of the Individuals and the Wygals, agreed to play drums. My former Let's Active bandmate Faye Hunter joined in, providing duet vocals on the title track and my cover of her song "Back in September." Doug's sister Janet Wygal, also from the Individuals and the Wygals, sang on several songs and the aforementioned Mr. Mastro of the Bongos added accordion and e-Bow guitar.

It was a great lineup of New York/Hoboken area friends who were supportive of my new endeavor.

While in Hoboken, Susan and I stayed in Steve's apartment above Maxwell's and she ventured into the city on most days to visit friends and museums. As Gene and I were in the studio at Water from 10am to 10pm everyday, on most nights, she and I had a late dinner then headed to Steve's place to decompress and watch TV before crashing.

With Gene on bass (and snarky dialogue), we tracked the 11 songs, recorded overdubs, and mixed everything in six days. We'd budgeted for seven, so we finished a day early.

Steve decided we should use the extra dough to take everyone involved to Sunday brunch. Along with a few stragglers such as Stamey and Peter Blegvad, who tagged along for the celebratory meal, we piled into a couple of cars and drove into Manhattan on a cold sunny January morning.

I remember listening to a few of the just-finished tracks in Steve's car on our way into the city. He remarked that some of my vocals reminded him of Bob Pfeifer of the band Human Switchboard. It's always interesting to see what comparisons people come up with. I, of course, have no real idea of what I sound like, so I can't really agree or disagree.

It was a festive gathering with plenty of laughs and loud conversation over beverages and a sizable spread at an old Irish pub. In the midst of it, a few of us decided we wanted to perform that night at Maxwell's. Singer-songwriter Joe Henry was scheduled to play a record release show for his A&M Records debut *A Murder of Crows*, so Gene, Jim, Doug, and I figured we should be the opening act and convinced an initially skeptical Steve that it was a good idea.

That evening, after we'd all recovered from the heavy brunch, we showed up at the club and made our way though an impromptu set that consisted of a few songs from **What Time Will Tell** and culminated with a spirited take on Buddy Holly's "Not Fade Away." Faye and Janet took turns on backing vocals, so we arranged a couple of chairs on the side of the stage for them to occupy when not singing, just like Elvis Presley's harmony singers.

The whole thing was a bit ragged, but a bunch of fun.

> *I was happy to see Joe, as we'd shared an acoustic bill at CBGB's Record Canteen during the College Music Journal convention the previous year. Peter Holsapple was also on that bill. Neither Peter nor I had heard of Joe, who opened the show, but he was pretty great.*
>
> *I'm glad to see he's made something of himself in the biz these days. You may have heard of him.*

What Time Will Tell felt like a big step forward to me. I'd ventured outside my previous comfort zone and worked with new people in an unfamiliar setting on a batch of songs I believed were moving me in a different direction, whether it was obvious to anyone else or not.

Upon its release, the reviews were good, really good in some cases. Jon Young, writing in *Music/Sound Output* called it "a stunning album, the kind of unexpected triumph that restores your faith in the power of art."

Now, if there are any rules to this stuff, number one is don't believe your own press. Still, if a review like that doesn't give you the big head, nothing will. I'm also kind of partial to the one where the reviewer referred to me as "part Lynyrd Skynyrd and part preacher."

There were even reviews that complimented my voice, which was certainly a new twist.

I was particularly excited to have sung with Faye and Janet on *What Time Will Tell*. I'd long been a fan of the male/female vocal dynamic, so I was thrilled to include that approach on my first solo record.

Back home in Jackson, while looking to put together a band to tour behind *What Time Will Tell*, I became friends with a local singer/songwriter named Jill Giddens. We hung out a bit and cobbled together a combo we dubbed Love Shack (named after the Knitters/X song, being that we predated the B-52s hit of the same name by a few years). After trying a couple variations, the line-up settled in with Charlie O'Connor on lead guitar and the returning Joe Partridge on drums. Jill played acoustic guitar, I played bass, and the two of us traded vocals.

In addition to a few of Jill's songs, some new ones of mine, and a big chunk of *What Time Will Tell*, the band learned a handful of Gram Parsons songs to use as a template of sorts. It was a happening little combo.

I have fond memories of Jackson during the late 1980s. Susan and I both stayed busy: she with school and work, me with work and music.

Susan had found a place on the local art scene, garnering attention for her black and white photography. It was fun to attend gallery openings with her, a pleasure to see her get the spotlight after the years she'd put her support behind my musical efforts.

I, in turn, enjoyed my role as the artist's spouse.

When not on tour, I continued to work at the t-shirt shop. Also, I landed a few gigs producing records, working with bands such as Mobile's Will & the Bushmen, Even Greenland from Tuscaloosa, and the Skeeters, a DB Recs act featuring a couple ex-members of Fetchin' Bones, who came over from Charlotte, North Carolina, to record with Randy and me at the Terminal.

In fall of 1986, R.E.M. came through town on their *Life's Rich Pageant* tour to play at the Civic Auditorium. The opening act was the aforementioned Fetchin' Bones, my DB Recs label mates, who planned to stay with Susan and me. The afternoon of the show, R.E.M. guitarist Pete Buck (who I knew through the Mitch Easter connection and who'd sat in with the Windbreakers on a couple of occasions in Athens) called me at the t-shirt shop to let me know that we were on the guest list, and when we got to the venue, he asked me to sit in and play their encore with them. We decided on a song, I was given the proper instructions on where to be when, and Susan and I found our seats to take in the show.

At my appointed time, I reported to the guitar tech back-stage, who asked, "What kind of guitar do you want to play?" I looked around at the couple dozen guitars on stands, each some color and model variation of Rickenbacker, and answered, "A red one?"

Armed with red Rickenbacker, I joined the four members of the band on the big stage for a version of "Goo Goo Muck," an old song first recorded by Ronnie Cook and the Gaylads, but better known from the Cramps' version.

After the show, Pete jumped in the car with Susan and I as we headed home (after a stop for beer) to meet the members of Fetchin' Bones.

A few drinks later, we decided to trek down the street to W.C. Don's, where local punk band Workin' Muthas was playing. The R.E.M. bus somehow found us and eventually we took over the stage. Me, Pete, Mike Mills, Hope and Aaron from Fetchin' Bones, Will Kimbrough (who happened to be in town), and no telling who else, borrowed the Muthas' instruments and bashed out any and all three-chord rock and roll songs we could remember until last call.

Again, one of those magical evenings.

Upon the release of *What Time Will Tell* in June of 1988, Love Shack hit the road for a quick jaunt up and down the East Coast.

It was a little weird supporting my solo record with an actual band that played Jill's songs as well as mine, but it worked musically and we had a good time.

One of my favorite memories from that tour didn't even involve playing. We showed up at a club in Columbia, South Carolina, only to find a note on the door that it'd been closed down by the tax commission the night before. The door was open, and some guy who didn't seem to give a damn was sweeping the floor. He explained that the club wouldn't be opening that night.

So we grabbed a couple cases of beer from behind the bar (fair compensation, right?) and high-tailed it to Dillon, South Carolina, where we spent the night at one of the world's tackiest tourist traps, South of the Border. SOB was a regular stop for touring bands, and their neon-colored stickers adorn many a guitar case to this day.

We didn't just roll in for kitschy souvenirs this time. We stayed over in one of the three or four crappy motels on the premises, enjoying an unexpected day off and a few cold brews outdoors on a warm summer evening.

As I adapted to this particular lineup, I found myself digging the change of pace. We were a bit more laid back and rootsy than most of my previous bands, although we could rock pretty righteously when needed. I even enjoyed playing bass and was content to share the front spot with Jill. Joe and I had some history together, so it was cool to have him around and our friendship grew during the tour. Charlie was a unique individual, a fun hang, and quite the bluesy shredder.

Among my favorite stops from that tour was a night in Boston when we played a particularly raucous show opening for my old friends Dumptruck at T.T. the Bear's. The evening ended with me on stage with my local pals for a cover of Humble Pie's "30 Days in the Hole." Another fun one was a bill with Fetchin' Bones at the 9:30 Club in D.C., at the old F Street location that backed up a shared alley with the infamous Ford Theater.

Joe recalled what he called our "ultimate Spinal Tap moment" from the tour on a Saturday night at CBGB. Jill and I were singing the quiet introduction to "Love Hurts," an Everly Brothers-through-Gram Parsons cover we played most nights. "I'm keeping time on the high-hat," Joe said, "and the bass rig

I Saw A Dozen Faces...

starts making horrible intermittent noises at an unbelievable
volume before the sound man bounds up on the stage to make
repairs. We never missed a beat."

For once, the promo machine, courtesy of Coyote's alliance
with Twin/Tone Records in Minneapolis, didn't grind to a halt
mid-tour, and we actually had some decent press to go along
with the shows.

We were moving along, rocking faces a dozen or so at a time.

Following that trek, we settled back into daily life. On the
horizon was a West Coast tour, which would be the first I'd ever
pulled off with my own band.

My booking agent, Bob Lawton, totally outdid himself,
arranging a well-routed series of dates that would wind through
the Southwest and the West, then back across the Midwest
for a few shows, before heading back home to Mississippi.
Pretty much all of the gigs were opening slots for Camper Van
Beethoven or the Mekons, two of the most happening indie
bands at the time, and there was even a Chicago show at Cabaret
Metro opening for Iggy Pop for a change of pace.

For the first time in a while, things seemed to be going my way.

I was excited and ready to get this show on the road. But,
ultimately, it was not to be. The rest of the band quit a couple
weeks before the tour was slated to begin.

Sense yet another pattern?

Thus was the conundrum of my so-called career. There were
labels who would release my records, agents who would book
the tours, good press, radio play, all of that stuff. And I could get
people on board to go out and tour, but almost none continued
after the initial experience: they were one and done, as they say
in sports.

I'm sure it was hard for any of these folks to feel a vested
interest in a gig in which they'd leave their daily lives behind
to go away for a few weeks and make what amounted to part-
time wages. And for what? Having fun is great, but you can't
pay your bills with cool stories. Obviously, I was trying to build
a career of sorts, but that couldn't have really meant much to
anybody else, could it?

That was why I continually strived to give everyone some
creative space so that these oddball combos might actually

by Tim Lee   135

grow into real bands, in hopes that everyone else would feel they might ultimately benefit from this activity. There's strength in numbers, you know. But this way of life just doesn't work for most folks, regardless of how much they love playing music and traveling. I was up front with everyone about the lack of glamour in this endeavor, but it requires a lot of sacrifice and it's an unrooted way of living, so it was pretty bold of me to assume other players would want to pursue this passion of mine with me.

So my so-called career continued as a solitary quest.

I recently re-read Tommy Womack's excellent **Cheese Chronicles** *about his time in the Bowling Green, Kentucky, band Government Cheese. It's a highly entertaining tale of four (sometimes five) young guys who meet in college and go on a wild rock and roll adventure that lasts for the next seven years.*

In a lot of ways, Tommy's story is pretty typical of most folks' in the indie music world. Some friends get together, make a band, get some gigs, and gain some momentum. If they stay together, they'll likely venture out from their hometown into neighboring areas. They might make a record or two. Somewhere in there, they'll eke together the money to buy a van, then widen their area of playing shows, maybe go on tour.

But, by God, they'll be in it together, for better or worse, toughing it out until they reach the end of their 20s or the onset of their 30s, at which point some will likely settle down, get a real job, have kids … you know, grown-up stuff. Some will stick it out, pursuing new bands or lineups or even solo careers, but that number dwindles with age. Not everybody is a lifer.

Of course, there are the occasional combos who manage to figure out a way in the music biz, perhaps gain some popularity and develop a plan for making a living at this stuff. But most people who go down this trail will reach that proverbial fork in the road and face a big decision: chuck it in for the straight life or take another running leap face first into that brick wall called "progress."

On my path, there was just me most of the time. There were no bandmates with whom to invest in a Ford Econoline. And I had no hope of affording something like that on my own.

I Saw A Dozen Faces…

Hell, Susan and I had one car between for most of those years,
so touring generally involved renting a van which cut deep
into any money that was made. There were no other direct
participants with whom to share frustrations and triumphs,
just a revolving cast of players with lives of their own to deal
with. I had a hell of a good time with many of those folks, and
most are still good friends, but my journey was not theirs, and
vice-versa.

Of course, Susan was a supportive partner, but she was
not playing music yet so all she could do is stand by and
watch me run headfirst into that brick wall time and time
again.

It broke my heart and crushed my soul to have to call Bob
and tell him all of his hard work was for naught. We had to
cancel the whole thing.

For a year that had started with such promise, the last part
of it was looking pretty grim. My solo career was becoming a so
low career.

I still managed to grind out one more Midwest/East Coast
fall tour for that record with a patched-together (yet quite good)
combo that included Primitons drummer Leif Bondarenko and
the late Matt Kimbrell, founding member of Birmingham's Jim
Bob and the Leisure Suits and the Ho Ho Men, on bass. On
guitar for my second official solo tour? Bobby Sutliff, of course.

Leave it to my pal Robert to step in and help out when I
needed him. As one reviewer noted, we had "a hard time staying
out of each other's bands."

Somehow this rag-tag collection quickly gelled into a pretty
rocking band, and we had a damned good time during our
five weeks together. We got into the habit of learning a random
cover song every day at sound check to play that night. From
"Rumble" to "Hard Day's Night" to "This Diamond Ring" to
"Let it Rock," if we could figure it out in ten minutes, we'd break
it out in that evening's set.

That kept us on our toes and provided a daily break from the
more mundane aspects of touring.

The tour was fun, but in retrospect it should have been
obvious that the nails in the coffin of my so-called career were
getting plentiful.

20. THE LATTER DAY WINDBREAKERS

"We should think about making another Windbreakers record. Want another beer?"

Although I could feel the indie scene's best days fading, along with those of my own so-called career, I continued to work at the music thing pretty hard, and in spring of 1989, I was still plugging away at my quietly flat-lining solo endeavor. At the same time, Bobby and I decided, over another round of beers, to team up to make a new Windbreakers album.

The two of us had been hanging out a lot following our adventures on my tour the previous year, so the idea of making a record together eventually made its way into the conversation. In some ways, it came out of nowhere. We hadn't discussed the concept at all, until the day we did. From there, it grew legs pretty quickly.

I was straight off recording my second solo album, *The New Thrill Parade*, and was working towards its release, but recording with Bobby sounded like fun, so we made a plan and got Danny Beard on board.

The sessions, which were helmed by Randy Everett at the Terminal, were among the most relaxed and fun Windbreakers sessions since our earliest collaborations with Mitch Easter. Joe Partridge signed on to drum, and he was playing better than ever. Mark Wyatt came down from Ohio to play keyboards, and Bruce Golden brought in a van load of percussion toys to add to the proceedings. Local bassist Raphael Semmes was brought in as a ringer, someone none of us had played with but who I felt would bring a different flavor to the mix.

Although he was the unknown in the equation, Raphael brought a lot to the table. As we'd hoped, his playing added a great feel. His years of club experience provided him with the proper combination of loose and tight, an excellent quality for any rock and roll rhythm section. I'm kinda dancing about architecture here, trying to describe it, so we'll just say it worked well. Also, his sense of humor and enthusiasm for the project made him an easy fit with the rest of us.

Prior to recording, Bobby and I both went through our existing stock of songs and pulled together the eleven that ultimately comprise *At Home with Bobby and Tim*.

Bobby brought in some of his most rocking tunes to date, including "Cold, Cold Rain" and "I Thought You Knew" along with two of his coolest ballads, "On the Wire" and "Our Little War." He also worked up a version of "Portrait of Blue," a song written by our pal Russ Tolman from True West.

Having recently pillaged my stockpile for *The New Thrill Parade*, I pulled together a hodgepodge of tunes, including "Just Fine," which I'd originally done with Love Shack. "Ill at Ease" had been around for several years (and recorded more than once), and "Closer to Home" was a newer experiment in a folkier direction.

With any ongoing collaboration like ours, there's a balance that constantly changes. Sometimes, Bobby was on a prolific streak and had more songs to contribute. Other times, it was me who brought more material to the table. With our latter day records, it pretty much depended on our work outside of the Windbreakers. With *At Home with Bobby and Tim*, he definitely had the upper hand, song-wise.

In all, the sessions had a more collaborative feel than most previous Windbreakers' recordings. Having come back together without an agenda or expectations, Bobby and I were free to relax and enjoy ourselves more than usual. We traded vocals on "Our Little War" and guitar solos on a few tracks, crediting the individual solos on the jacket, in homage to the liner notes on Television's *Marquee Moon*.

Bobby's particularly crazed first guitar solo on "Cold, Cold Rain" wasn't even recorded during the album sessions. He'd previously made a demo of the song at my apartment when Susan and I were out of town once. At that time, I had a cool eight-track setup, so we just left him a key while we were gone. He produced that amazing piece of playing, but didn't feel he

> *could recreate it in the studio. So we just dumped the tracks*
> *from the demo recording onto the studio's tape machine and*
> *played along with it in our headphones to get the basic track.*
> *Then we erased everything from the original but the solo. And*
> *it worked.*

After all we'd been through, together and separately, *At Home...* was a fun and easy album to make, and thus remains one of my favorites among the Windbreakers' catalog. We'd shed a lot of baggage and just dived into the process, much like we had done at the beginning of this whole sojourn.

At Home with Bobby and Tim came out on DB Records in the fall of 1989 and we celebrated its release with an East Coast swing, oddly enough, the first official Windbreakers tour with Bobby and I both on board. We called on bassist Brad Quinn and drummer Mark Reynolds from Carnival Season to make the trek, and Mark Wyatt, who was reeling from the recent breakup of Great Plains, signed on as well. He later told me that he'd pushed the issue with his employer for a leave of absence in order to do the tour, which eventually worked against him in his annual review. "No raise for Mark that year," he said with a laugh.

Susan and I had moved back to Atlanta by then, so the band gathered there for a few days of rehearsal before hitting the road for a couple of weeks.

Once out on tour, we could see that the indie landscape was changing quickly. Traveling around the country once or twice a year to play club shows gives you a certain perspective on what's coming up (or on the way out). For instance, when touring for *What Time Will Tell* in the late 1980s, we shared bills with bands like the Blood Oranges and the Jayhawks, who were laying the groundwork for the alt-country movement of the coming decade. One of the final shows for the Windbreakers tour was in Atlanta with Too Much Joy, a fun band that was definitely a harbinger of the punk-pop scene that was on the horizon.

More than anything, we didn't seem to play as many shows with our friends and contemporaries. By the time of that December 1989 Windbreakers tour, many of our friend bands had broken up or moved on to some other level. When we hit CBGB in New York, instead of a bill featuring friends like the ones we'd been on in the past with the Lyres, Hetch Hetchy

(Linda Stipe's post-Oh OK band), Russ Tolman, or Carnival Season, we were thrown in the middle of five local acts, none of which we were familiar with.

There were a few instances on the tour where we shared stages with more familiar fare, such as the Maxwell's show we opened for Alex Chilton and the night at the Georgia Theater in Athens where I pulled double-duty, playing bass with Homemade Sister, an Atlanta band I was in at the time, on the set that preceded the Windbreaker's headlining slot. Athens band Time Toy was also on the bill at my request.

Recently, Mark reminded me that the mid-December tour put us in several college towns after school was out for the holidays. That Athens show was a particularly acute example of being booked into a larger venue than merited, especially since the University of Georgia was closed up tight for the year.

> *Speaking of which, hey Tim, what was the most extreme example of being overbooked you experienced? Well, kids, that would've been Bogarts in Cincinnati toward the end of the* **Run** *tour in 1986. A year earlier, the Windbreakers had opened for X in front of a full house at that thousand-seat hall, and for some reason, someone thought it was a good idea to bring us back as the sole act on a Friday night.*
>
> *Once the doors opened, I peeked out from backstage to see a whopping total of four ticket-buyers in their seats. Of course, I bought them all a drink and we rocked our set as if the room was full. Still, it was pretty hard to keep a straight face when your audience filled exactly one of every 250 seats in the place.*

It was a quick run up the Eastern Seaboard and back. With all the good people involved, naturally we had a good time. But overall, it was a pretty quiet ending to the Windbreakers touring era.

One year after recording *At Home with Bobby and Tim*, almost to the day, Bobby and I reconvened with Randy at the Terminal to track the songs that became *Electric Landlady*, the final release of the original Windbreakers run.

As I was living in Atlanta and playing bass with the Swimming Pool Qs, we timed the sessions to coincide with a Qs set at Jubilee Jam, Jackson's annual spring music festival. That got me to town, but also allowed us to avail ourselves of the talents of Qs drummer Billy Burton and guitarist Bob Elsey, with whom we recorded four tracks on the Saturday night following the Qs' afternoon Jam show.

The rest of the Qs returned to Atlanta without me, and Bobby and I continued work for the following week with Russ Tolman, whom we'd invited to fly in from the West Coast to produce the record. Joe returned to man the kit for the remainder of the songs, and Mark once again came down to play keyboards. Rounding out the band for basic tracks was bassist Michael Thorn, a friend and veteran of many local bands. Michael had been assisting Randy at the Terminal, plus he and Joe had been playing together live and in the studio with several projects. The two of them were airtight as a rhythm section, so it was a natural choice.

Russ was great to have around, but I think it took him a couple of days to get used to the Bobby-and-Tim dynamic. At one point, he proclaimed that he wasn't producing so much as "refereeing Tim and Bobby's fights." I don't think either one of us thought we were at war, we just have that weird push-pull dynamic that long-time friends who work together are prone to develop over time.

To that point, I think it's safe to say that Bobby and I generally communicated better in the studio when we were living in the same town and hanging out regularly in the time leading up to our recording projects. That's just natural. It's easier to understand where the other guy's coming from if you've been sitting around talking for weeks leading up to recording rather than just getting a feel from a handful of phone conversations and handwritten notes stuffed in demo cassette cases.

Still, the sessions were fun and we did a lot of work in a short period of time. This time around, I was the one who had the most songs to choose from, although Bobby certainly had his highlights, including "Big Ideas" (one of my faves) and "Girl from Washington," a longtime favorite among Windbreakers fans.

Recording songs written by friends was a habit of ours by then, dating back to my inclusion of Faye Hunter's "Back in September" on *What Time Will Tell*, the version of Howard Wuelfing's "Things We Never Say" that Bobby and I recorded for the b-side of the "I'll Be Back" 12-inch single, and our take on Russ' "Portrait of Blue" on *At Home with Bobby and Tim*. For the *Electric Landlady* sessions, we took on John Thomas' "Elayne Lies Looking at the Sky," a psychedelic homage that was written by the former Oral Sox front man partially as a spoof of mine and Bobby's previous dabbling in the genre. We, of course, thought it was hilarious to include the song on our record. It's really quite good, too.

We also recorded a song called "Waltzing Matilda" that was written by Lee Barber and Elaine Barber, whose cool combo The Barbers also included Joe and Bruce. "Waltzing Matilda" was one of my favorite Barbers songs, and we recorded it pretty close to the original, although for some reason we edited it down a bit lyrically. Elaine played harp and Bruce manned the vibraphone with Joe on brushes for the basic track with Bobby on acoustic guitar, and it turned out quite beautiful and very different for a Windbreakers song. Michael added a fretless bass solo that carried it even further out from our usual sonic spaces.

As I recall it, "Devil & the Sea" was a song that Russ had given, unfinished, to Bobby who added some lyrics and passed it on to me. I came up with the last verse, and somehow through the democratic process ending up singing it as well.

Ultimately, *Electric Landlady* (the title was Danny Beard's idea, and of course none of us knew that Kirsty MacColl would release an album with the same title around the same time) is a bit of an odd duck among the Windbreakers' collected works due to the use of some different players and (for us) an unusual selection of songs. We definitely went guitar heavy for the sessions, borrowing cool gear from friends and using it to great effect. Between the two of us, Bobby and I have a lot of combined experience playing a lot of styles, so it was fun to turn the guitars up a notch and cut loose a bit. Throw Bob Elsey into the mix and you've got some serious riffing. For better or worse, only a few songs on the record have the "jangly" (or the "J word" as Michael Hall of the Wild Seeds humorously called it) sound associated with our earlier records.

In keeping with the prevailing media trends of the era, *At Home with Bobby and Tim* and *Electric Landlady* were the first Windbreakers records to be released on the new compact disc format. Still novel to the marketplace, CDs initially featured retail prices in the neighborhood of twenty bucks, more than twice what a vinyl album was going for at the time.

Bobby and I decided since those prices were so high, we'd make them more of a deal by adding previously-unre-leased-on-CD records at the end of the discs. Thus, if you come across a copy of *At Home with Bobby and Tim* in your local used CD bin, you also get *Terminal* in its entirety. *Electric Landlady* discs include the whole of *Any Monkey with a Typewriter*. Bargain shopping with Bobby and Tim!

Electric Landlady was unleashed on a largely disinterested world in 1990, bringing the previous decade and the initial Windbreakers' run to a close. Going into a new decade, Bobby and I set off on divergent paths, and while we stayed in touch, it would be several years before we worked together again.

The Windbreakers *Run* tour, circa 1986 (left to right): David Minchew, me, Sherry Cothren, Joe Partridge's drums. Opening for Richard Lloyd at Amelia's in Iowa City. (Photo by by David Conklin)

I Saw A Dozen Faces...

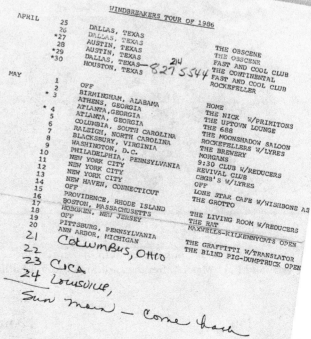

THE WINDBREAKERS

CONFIRMED ITINERARY

DATE		CITY	VENUE
APRIL 11	FRI	STARKVILLE, MS	MISSISSIPPI STATE UNIVERSITY
12	SAT	MEMPHIS, TN	ANTENNA CLUB
13	SUN	NASHVILLE, TN	§ EXIT IN
14	MON	LOUISVILLE, KY	TEWLIGAN'S
15	TUES	COLUMBIA, MO	§ THE BLUE NOTE
16	WED	IOWA CITY, IA	§ AMELIA'S
17	THURS	MINNEAPOLIS, MN	§ SEVENTH STREET ENTRY
18	FRI	MILWAUKEE, WI	THE SPRUCE GOOSE
19	SAT	CHICAGO, IL	§ THE WEST END
30	WED	HOUSTON, TX	# ROCKEFELLER'S
MAY 3	SAT	ATHENS, GA	# UPTOWN LOUNGE (EARLY)
3	SAT	ATLANTA, GA	688 CLUB (LATE)

§ Show is with Richard Lloyd
# Show is with The Church

Itinerary for the Windbreakers *Run* tour, 1986. Shows with * on second page were with the Church. (From Sherry Cothren's archive)

WINDBREAKERS TOUR OF 1986

APRIL	25	DALLAS, TEXAS	THE OBSCENE
	26	DALLAS, TEXAS	THE OBSCENE
	*27	AUSTIN, TEXAS	FAST AND COOL CLUB
	28	AUSTIN, TEXAS	THE CONTINENTAL
	*29	DALLAS, TEXAS	FAST AND COOL CLUB
	*30	HOUSTON, TEXAS—827 5544 214	ROCKEFELLER
MAY	1	OFF	
	2	BIRMINGHAM, ALABAMA	HOME
	* 3	ATHENS, GEORGIA	THE NICK W/PRIMITONS
	* 4	ATLANTA,GEORGIA	THE UPTOWN LOUNGE
	5	ATLANTA, GEORGIA	THE 688
	6	COLUMBIA, SOUTH CAROLINA	THE MOONSHADOW SALOON
	7	RALEIGH, NORTH CAROLINA	ROCKEFELLERS W/LYRES
	8	BLACKSBURY, VIRGINIA	THE BREWERY
	9	WASHINGTON, D.C.	MORGANS
	10	PHILADELPHIA, PENNSYLVANIA	9:30 CLUB W/REDUCERS
	11	NEW YORK CITY	REVIVAL CLUB
	12	NEW YORK CITY	CBGB'S W/LYRES
	13	NEW YORK CITY	OFF
	14	NEW HAVEN, CONNECTICUT	LONE STAR CAFE W/WISHBONE AS
	15	OFF	THE GROTTO
	16	PROVIDENCE, RHODE ISLAND	
	17	BOSTON, MASSACHUSETTS	THE LIVING ROOM W/REDUCERS
	18	HOBOKEN, NEW JERSEY	THE RAT
	19	OFF	MAXWELLS-KILKENNYCATS OPEN
	20	PITTSBURG, PENNSYLVANIA	THE GRAFFITTI W/TRANSLATOR
	21	ANN ARBOR, MICHIGAN	THE BLIND PIG-DUMPTRUCK OPEN
	22	COLUMBUS, OHIO	
	23	CICA	
	24	LOUISVILLE,	

Sun main — come back

One of the first Beat Temptation shows at W.C. Don's, 1983 (left to right): Me, Bruce Golden, Sherry Cothren.

Beat Temptation, outside the Terminal during the recording of *Concerned About Rock Music?* after the addition of Robin Sutliff (bottom right), 1985.

I Saw A Dozen Faces...

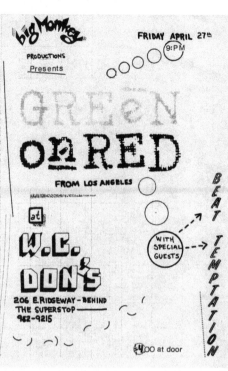

A variety of flyers from mine
and Susan's early promotional
attempts at W.C. Don's. (From
Sherry Cothren's archive)

by Tim Lee

The Windbreakers at the Drive-In, 1982 (left to right): Bobby Sutliff, Mitch Easter, me (not sure what's up with the evil grin). Photo by Susan Bauer Lee

Flannel as far as the eye can see. The Windbreakers at W.C. Don's sometime in the mid-'80s (left to right): Me, Bobby Sutliff, Barry Brown.

I Saw A Dozen Faces...

This is what I look like when I'm concentrating (or playing keyboard).
Onstage with Let's Active, somewhere in Baltimore, 1985.

Howard and Tim's Paid Vacation: Howard Wuelfing and me (with Howard's
son Severin with the photobomb) in Atlanta, 1985. Photo by Susan Bauer Lee

by Tim Lee

The Windbreakers *Run* session, Jackson, Mississippi, 1985. Me and the brains of the operation, Randy Everett and Mitch Easter. Photo by Susan Bauer Lee

Wacky hijinks with the dB's at the Chukker in Tuscaloosa, Alabama, 1986 (left to right): Sherry Cothren, Will Rigby, me, David Minchew, Joe Partridge on drums, Peter Holsapple.

I Saw A Dozen Faces...

Matt Piucci and I practice our angelic harmonies before hitting the stage at W.C. Don's for the first (and only) live performance of Crosby, Stills, Nash, and Piucci, 1986 (below, left to right): Bobby Sutliff, Bruce Golden's drum kit, Matt Piucci, me. Photos by Susan Bauer Lee

by Tim Lee   151

Susan and I with our basset hound Beatrice on the back steps of our apartment in Atlanta, 1985. Photo by Howard Wuelfing (from author's collection)

Pregaming for the Windbreakers *Run* release party in the living room at mine and Susan's house on Duncan Avenue in Jackson, 1986 (left to right): Randy Everett, Matt Piucci (with back to the camera), Danny Beard, me.

I Saw A Dozen Faces...

The Windbreakers *Run* tour in Minneapolis, 1986 (left to right): Sherry Cothren, Joe Partridge, me, David Minchew. Photo by Thom Eason (from Sherry Cothren's collection)

Me onstage with Marti Jones on her *Match Game* tour, 1986. Photo by Susan Bauer Lee

The Windbreakers warm up show for the *A Different Sort* tour, W.C. Don's, circa 1987 (left to right): Thom Eason, me, Ric Menck's drums, Paul Chastain. This would've been the damn good hair era.

Hanging out at the rock show, the Chukker, Tuscaloosa, Alabama, circa 1986 (left to right): dB's roadie/Wipe Me Mommy guitarist Gilbert Nestor, Danny Beard (with back to camera), Gene Holder, me.

I Saw A Dozen Faces...

Me joining R.E.M. to play "Goo Goo Muck" for their encore, City Auditorium, Jackson, 1986 (left to right): Mike Mills, Michael Stipe, me, Bill Berry on drums, Peter Buck.

We get by with a little help from our friends, Niagara Falls, 1988 (left to right): Matt Kimbrell, Bobby Sutliff, and Leif Bondarenko sight-seeing before we crossed over into Canada on the *What Time Will Tell* tour.
Polaroid by Tim Lee

by Tim Lee

I Saw A Dozen Faces...

PART 4:
CRASH LANDING

I Saw A Dozen Faces...

21. HIGH TIMES AND LOW WAGES

Laying in the darkness, my sleeping bag stretched out on some stranger's living room floor, I mentally counted and recounted the money wadded up in the left front pocket of my jeans. The equation never changed: the total of what we'd made the previous few nights, minus what was spent on gas and meals, equaled just enough to keep going with hopes of having a few bucks left over to split at the end of four or five weeks on the road.

I was in my mid-20s. The people with whom I'd gone to high school were mostly fresh out of college and beginning careers in the real world. I worked screen printing and restaurant jobs that allowed me to disappear for a month at a time to chase this elusive thing. Many of my friends around the country were progressing with their musical careers, garnering larger support and opportunities, so there appeared to be some sort of potential path forward.

Susan and I had been married a few years, and she was still in my corner, offering support and belief in the crazy endeavor I pursued. She understood what it meant, and was a willing participant in the "artist's lifestyle." Having returned to college, she'd discovered a passion of her own in photography.

My relationship with Susan was the launching pad that made it possible for me to even imagine that I could do any of this. I would have never had the confidence on my own. Without her support, there's no way I could have done a fraction of what I did. That much can't be over-emphasized.

Eventually, I rose from my hardwood nesting spot, gave up on shut-eye, and wandered out the front door to check out another neighborhood I'd never seen in daylight. If I was lucky, there was a convenience store down the street with a coffee

by Tim Lee   159

maker. Or maybe our host or hostess was up, getting ready for work, with a pot of joe on the burner.

It didn't matter where the coffee came from. There just had to be coffee. And these were the days before a Starbucks (or even better, a local mud spot) populated every other corner, definitely pre-dating smart phones, laptops, GPS, and all the other amenities that make being organized on tour a lot easier these days. Hell, phone company calling cards were a brand new convenience at the time.

> *Communications were usually a tough proposition on the road. Pay phones were still pretty plentiful then, but even if you had a calling card, it wasn't easy to advance gigs from a booth outside a gas station, let alone foster relationships. I saw one band member try to salvage a marriage from a pay phone outside a White Castle in the snow in Ohio at 3 a.m. It was not pretty.*
>
> *One year, I was on tour in the fall when Susan's birthday rolled around on October 25. I made it a point to get up early to call her. We were in Boston, staying with my cousin Dana, who played in the band Slaughter Shack. She had one of those phones with the long coiled cord, so I pulled it out the front door and sat on the steps outside her top-floor walk-up apartment and called Susan at work while everyone else slept in.*
>
> *She and I spoke for several minutes, running up our phone bill in the process. It was always nice to hear her voice and to catch up with our parallel lives when I was gone. We eventually hung up, and it never crossed my mind that I'd forgotten to actually say the words "happy birthday" to her. I was so proud of myself for making the effort, but I didn't remember the two words I'd called to utter. Like Eric Burdon, my intentions were good, but it took a while to live that one down.*

Inevitably, my thoughts turned to the day ahead. How far was the drive? Where were we going? Had we been there before? What day is it?

For a borderline bottom-feeder band like mine, that "what day" question was important.

Our early records resonated with critics, fanzines, and college radio. We'd even gotten the odd mention in larger publications. So when we were booked in one of the bigger cities on a weekend, we generally played to a decent audience. Not large by any stretch of the imagination, but reasonable. Weeknights, however, particularly in smaller markets (yes, actually typing such a show biz term makes me a bit queasy), tended to be another story. It was rare that we drew more than a handful of folks to a midweek club gig.

We were lucky to have a good booking agent, though, who could get us an okay guarantee for most dates despite our lack of clout. I always imagined the conversations like this: "Yeah, I'll get you the Replacements for that Saturday, but I'm gonna need you to book the Windbreakers on a Wednesday for $200. Deal?"

Those weeknight shows were necessary to fill the void between the weekend shows in New York, Boston, Washington, or Chicago. But, man, sometimes it took a toll on you to climb out of a van after a long drive, pep up your band members, and play your best for a handful of people.

But, you see a dozen faces and you rock them all. Every time. It's what you do.

I refused to give anything less than my best on those nights, and got bent out of shape with anyone in our entourage who did. My philosophy is that if there are only ten people on hand for a show, it's not their fault that 90 other people stayed home. That group of folks made the effort to be there and deserved the same thing you'd deliver for a bigger audience.

Their five dollars goes in your gas tank the same as anyone's.

The memory of one particular Tuesday in Pittsburgh always stuck with me. We showed up to the club, and there were exactly four paying customers. So, I went out and introduced myself and chatted with all four of them, even offering to buy them each a drink.

I needed them in my corner. Just moments earlier, one band member complained to me, "This sucks; there's nobody here," implying that somehow such a small turnout was beneath their dignity. That kind of thinking is alien to me. We'd shown up to do a job, to play some rock and roll for anybody who was there, not to be some kind of preening wannabe stars with fragile egos.

We played our set that night, and everybody had a great time ... well, except for that one band member.

by Tim Lee   161

Regardless, we saw a quartet of faces and we rocked them all.

To this day, I still refer to midweek shows as "Tuesday night in Pittsburgh" as a reminder of that particular evening.

It could be tough, though, to watch as some of your friends' bands broke through that weeknight glass ceiling, wondering if it might ever happen for you. Every morning, you'd wake up in somebody else's living room and wonder if today might be the turning point. Perhaps there was some kind of local press that might drum up a respectable Monday night crowd, or maybe a couple local fans would talk a bunch of their friends into coming out on a Wednesday.

Anything could happen. (Hint: it never did.)

A Baltimore City Paper "Best of" issue from September 1989 awarded a couple of intrepid local fans, Terry Harris and Rich Spiegel, the mantle of "Best Rock Scene Cheerleaders" for being the music fans who "logged more cool-school club-going hours than any dozen other alleged scene-makers combined." The story's opening example? A "particularly foreboding" night on which most of the city's rock fans "traipsed off to the Towson Center to see the overwrought Midnight Oil" while the true believers such as Harris and Spiegel were among the "nine people" at a club called Max's on Broadway "to see the infinitely superior Tim Lee and Bobby Sutliff."

Apparently, even the club owner skipped out to see the Aussie MTV stars.

If you can't be successful, I guess you can at least be known for being unknown.

But you continued your daily routine: drive all day, load in, sound check, eat pizza and drink beer, play the show, eventually look for a place to stay so you can start over again the next day.

Put a few bucks in your pocket, put a few bucks in the gas tank, hand out a few bucks for a fast-food lunch, and keep the cycle alive.

Paying your dues, they say.

But what was the goal? Rock stardom was out of the question. That was for a different sort of person, a certain type of ego. There seems to be a general assumption that a person who does this music thing is doing so in hopes of achieving some sort of fame. Those people do exist, for sure, but I was just a guy who wanted to play music, make records, and go out and meet people.

I knew my goals were generally modest, but I hoped to be able to eke out an "artist's lifestyle" and at least pay my bills.

Wish in one hand and shit in the other, and see which one fills up first. That's what my t-shirt boss Paul Canzoneri always said. I'm hard-headed, though. Like everything else, these lessons had to be learned first-hand.

Did I think of playing music in terms of mass acceptance when I was a teenager? Was the dream of being a star an early motivation for learning the guitar? Honestly, I don't think so. Sure, initially I wanted to be like those folks on "Midnight Special," but from the time I mastered a few chords and riffs, the goals all became more immediate. First, I wanted to learn more chords and riffs, because having a recognizable sound come out of a guitar I was playing made me feel good. From that small accomplishment, I learned about the feeling one experiences when playing with other people, so that was the next goal. After that, I wanted to be in a band. Once I was in a band, I wanted to play gigs. Then more gigs. From there, I wanted to shed the cover band thing and come up with my own material. Then, I wanted to make a record, wanted to go on tour … you get the idea.

If the notion of rock stardom had crossed my youthful mind when I first picked up guitar, the actual coolness of making racket with other folks quickly kicked it to the side of the road.

On my own terms, I was pretty successful at nearly every step of the way. Anything else — the good press, the hanging out and collaborating with cool people — was lagniappe.

Actually, my so-called career was going to plan. Until it wasn't anymore. Then the progress stopped. There was no next step that I was able to achieve. I plateaued.

Any forward movement at that point would've required some kind of show business acumen, which I didn't possess, or maybe a manager who could navigate that world. Again, nothing.

During my occasional close brushes with the biz, I was often told things like, "Your problem, Tim, is that you make too many records" or the particularly damning line I got from one artist manager, "Your problem, Tim, is that you don't want to be a star."

Okay, why would I want that? I just want sushi tonight instead of pizza. I didn't get it.

A record executive from a mid-sized label once suggested that the aforementioned manager have one of their artists get together with me so I could provide assistance with that singer-songwriter's tunes. The manager's response was, "Oh no, Tim would be a bad influence."

The record exec and I had a big laugh over that one.

In 2019, a guy named Jason Lee Usry put together a podcast about the beginnings of the music scene in Jackson called "Play Dead: The Jackson, MS, Music Scene of the '80s and '90s." He interviewed me, Sherry Cothren, David Minchew, Joe Partridge, and several other folks about the early 1980s in our hometown. When I listened to that particular episode, I noticed that my personal ambition was a recurring topic in the various interviews. Without being critical, most of my hometown contemporaries did mention it.

Not long after its release, Robin Sutliff and I were having dinner and we talked about that podcast. I quipped, "Yeah, I only came across as semi-ruthless."

Robin replied quickly, "But you were," half-joking but entirely serious, in that way that only one of your oldest friends can pull off.

The biz folks didn't think I was ambitious enough and my friends thought I was sort of ruthless. As with most things, I imagine the truth lay somewhere in the middle.

The independent music scene of the early 1980s was originally all about taking the artistry back from the biz, albeit as much out of necessity as any grand notion of integrity. Still, we were just building on the foundation laid by adventurous souls such as Terry Ork of Ork Records, Chris Stamey, who had Car Records, Greg Shaw of Bomp!, and others who'd put out exciting recordings by the likes of Alex Chilton, Television, Chris Bell, and Shoes and figured out ways to get them out to the handful of freaks who wanted to hear them. That was the business model, as much as it was one, to which we initially aspired.

At some point, that indie thing took on a life of its own, with enough labels, fanzines, and rock clubs to make it feasible for a scene of sorts to emerge. There had to be some precedent in place for some hick kid from Mississippi to be able to do all the things

I was able to do. I've never taken for granted that I just showed up at the right time and place. If not ground zero, then at least close enough for collateral damage.

When Alex Chilton died in 2010, I was fascinated by the way the news resonated in my little corner of the rock and roll world. I always had a somewhat difficult relationship with the man. I love his music and was around him a few times in the 1980s, but never knew him or claimed to. He was always a bit standoffish, and I generally took that to mean he appreciated his personal space, so I was happy to give it to him.

Chilton's passing, though, reminded me that I was once part of a scene of sorts. Really just a loose conglomeration of misfits who played music but weren't aspiring to any brass ring. We made records, hit the road, populated the College Music Journal charts, and slept on a lot of couches. Other than that, we were all very different in our personalities and approaches. But one of the main things we all had in common was Big Star's recorded output.

Sure, we all loved the Beatles, the Byrds, Brian Wilson, the Ramones, the Who and the Kinks, but in the late 1970s/ early'80s, owning a well-worn copy of **Radio City**, **#1 Record**, or **Sister Lovers**, or a 45 of Chris Bell's "I Am the Cosmos" on Car Records, was the equivalent of the key to a secret society.

Like the Velvet Underground before them, Big Star is credited with launching more bands than they ever sold records. And many of those bands were part of a short-but-thriving era of independent rock and roll in the early- to mid-1980s.

We were the in-betweeners, coming along at a time when our forebears — Big Star, the Velvets, Flamin' Groovies, Television, etc. — were either gone or on their last legs, but before "indie rock" became an actual genre, one big enough to be co-opted by the major labels. And we were just kids at the time, mostly well under 30, so everything had a heightened sense of importance.

by Tim Lee

A day or two before I heard about Chilton's passing, I also learned of the death of David Lee, one-time Neats bassist. Like Chilton, I didn't really know Lee (obviously no relation), but had met him. His band stayed at our house once, and true to their name, they washed the dishes in the sink before leaving. Good folks.

Of course, David's passing didn't have the same seismic impact in my community that Chilton's did, but it's always sad to see a contemporary go. These individuals are all part of this continuous ribbon that runs from the days of wire recordings through the birth of country and the blues and jazz and rock and roll and the British Invasion and the original punk rock and hip hop up to today and into the future.

You hate to know that a link in that chain gets broken, although it's comforting to know that there's likely some kid out there listening to Big Star or the Neats and composing his or her own teenage symphonies that will lay the groundwork for another generation and forging that chain whole again.

Dedicated to the cause, I believed whole-heartedly in that scene; wanted that world to flourish and grow, so my attitude was deeply invested in a certain distrust, bordering on wholesale rebellion, toward the real "music biz."

Sure, I'd go along for a while, but as always, my ultimate goal was just to see cool stuff happen, not to play games or jump through hoops. I was too busy making music.

The music was everything. Under the best circumstances, you were traveling with like-minded friends on a shared adventure— folks who were up for stopping at bizarre roadside attractions for a grin, who didn't bitch about "Pizza again?", who were in the moment, enjoying it for what it was.

It was fun while it lasted. Very fun.

22. THE GUTTERS OF FAME: MAJOR LABEL NEUROSIS

So what happened to the fun?

I'm sure everyone has their own opinion, but here's my personal crackpot theory: the music biz happened to the fun.

Early on in the great 1980s indie scare, R.E.M. signed a contract with IRS Records, a subsidiary of A&M, making them one of the first acts of the American independent music scene to make the leap to the next level.

It was a cool move. It put their records out in the world, and got them on television and commercial radio, all of which eventually landed them on the Warner Brothers Records roster. Plus, IRS was a happening label that featured a new waver's dream line-up. During my brief tenure as a touring member of Let's Active, my experiences with IRS were all positive. They seemed like good people who really were into the music they manufactured and distributed.

In time, R.E.M. got big. Really big. It was inevitable. They had strong chemistry, an exciting front man, bucketloads of charisma, great songs, and a herculean work ethic. Love 'em or not, they towered over most everybody else from our world on nearly every level.

And they were rewarded handsomely for those attributes.

On the heels of their success, other indie darlings saw a new possibility: maybe *we* can make something real of this music stuff.

Goals and aspirations shifted. The pursuit of fun and cool art became the dream of gaining a foothold in the music biz, which eventually gave way to full-blown major label neuroses. With few exceptions, everybody worried about getting a record deal. The big companies were snooping around, trying to find their own R.E.M.: you know, a hip, respected band that could move some units with those college radio kids.

Naturally, as those college radio kids graduated and moved into the music biz, many of them landed jobs with the major conglomerates. Once there, they championed the acts they'd played on their free-form university airwaves, in some cases viewing it as a kind of holy crusade to expose their favorite music to the masses.

Hooray! The revolution was here!

On paper, it looked good. Money was flowing down from the world of Van Halen and Styx to the gutters of fame, where we were all hanging out, hoping for some of that sweet, big time trickle-down goodness.

Many independent labels landed distribution deals with majors, cementing their status as farm league feeder systems. Bands got signed directly and indirectly. Checks were cashed, new vans were purchased for touring, shiny guitars were ordered, and thrift store fashion shopping reached historic highs.

Oh yeah, and a thousand or so new bands were launched. Prior to this explosion, there weren't more than a few dozen acts exploring the American indie landscape in any type of serious fashion. At this point, though, every kid with a credit card now owned a Fender guitar and a pair of Beatle boots.

Like the majority of my contemporaries, I bought into it for a while, cranking out demos for one major label that expressed interest.

"We see you playing to 15,000 people a night," said the college radio programmer-turned-artist relations rep, who called almost daily. "Like John Cougar Mellencamp or someone like that."

Okay? I mean, I couldn't really picture it, but sure, you wanna hear more songs? Cool.

At the height of that interest, after months of regular phone conversations and mailings of demo tapes, my band came through New York on tour and played at CBGB, where some of the label folks came out to see us. There was a new song in our set called something like, "Calling Me Back Home." It was a song that never got recorded, just another one that came and went in the set list, but which apparently made a bit of an impact.

Maybe not the kind you'd want, though.

Later that night, one of the biz people I'd been dealing with said something to the effect of, "You were up there, but you were singing about wanting to be home. We didn't know what to think." The message was simple: big companies aren't willing to invest in a potential asset that might not be totally committed to being a full-time asset to said multi-national corporation.

The phone calls stopped the next day.

When that interest dried up, I pushed the indie labels I was working with to convince their major distributors to include me among their hybrid rosters. None were ever able to make it happen.

Again, was I trying to get famous? No, like any artist, I wanted my work to get out in the world where people could experience it and judge it for themselves.

Like R.S. Field says, I had some intellectual property I wanted to zone commercial.

At one point, a person I knew at one of the major labels hired me to produce demos for my Birmingham pals Carnival Season at the Terminal. My friend flew into Jackson to hear the final product and I picked them up at the airport. On the way to the studio, we talked about the session and about the whole music biz thing.

At one point, the rep said, "You know, Tim, you should be signed to a major label."

The irony was not lost on me that this pronouncement came from one of the few people I knew who could actually make it happen. The whole thing was getting pretty absurd.

My work fell into a funny place in the music world. I loved making records, actually enjoyed touring, and wanted to be able to keep it up, make a little progress with my so-called career. My releases got good reviews, and I was willing to put in the hard time.

As mentioned previously, "Your problem is …" was a sentence opener I heard from plenty of biz folks who felt it was their solemn duty to fill me in on the shortcomings of my attempts. You know, like "… you don't want to be a star."

I guess my true problem was that I didn't understand what that had to do with making music.

Why was I problematic, a "bad influence?" I never understood that one completely. Granted, I was a "take charge" guy who loved being in recording studios, always scheming to make another record, because I liked to see cool stuff happen. You can only offer a budget of $300? No problem, I'll make a record for you.

I made records at a steady pace for small labels who offered moral support but very little input to the creative process. Most of these folks were great allies, such as Danny Beard at DB Records, who was a master of album sequencing and to whom I could always turn for help there. He's also pretty gifted at coming up with album titles.

Like everyone else I worked with, though, Danny trusted me to make the records I wanted to make. So I got used to doing it that way.

Not that I never got any advice at all. When I was preparing to make my second solo album with Gene Holder at the helm, I sent him a bunch of demos and asked for his thoughts on song selection. He focused on a couple of the more low-key selections. During a phone conversation, Gene explained his thinking with an audible smirk, "Chicks dig slow songs, Tim."

Solid show biz advice there.

Being left to my own devices in the studio was the hand I was dealt. I collaborated with a lot of folks during that time, but no one from the label side of things got much involved.

I guess from the outside it appeared that I only did what I wanted, didn't listen to others, hence problematic, a bad influence, and certainly no star-seeker.

I loved the work, but never fully committed to playing the game. Hell, I never even saw the rulebook. I just wanted to make some cool racket.

Eventually, the fun began to fade. As time passed, I began to wonder if I even had a place in music. I felt more and more like an outsider in the world I'd so wholly embraced.

During later tours, I began to withdraw a bit in the van. There was always somebody who wanted to drive, so I spent a lot of time in the passenger seat, staring out the window and listening to my Walkman, watching the landscape pass by, getting lost in the world of my favorite records and wondering what the future held.

One can only see a dozen faces and find the wherewithal to rock each of them so many times before you start to wonder about the cost of it all. Being gone from home and Susan for long periods of time, while seemingly gaining nothing from my work, was wearing on me.

On one 1987 tour, we played shows with L.A. band Divine Horsemen, fronted by Chris D. and Julie Christensen, who were married at the time. They quickly became one of my favorite bands, and I loved watching them every night.

After gigging together a couple times, the two bands were split up for competing gigs on a Monday night in Kansas City (yeah, kind of like Tuesday night in Pittsburgh). Our show was earlier, and I had a miserable time due to various circumstances, so as soon as it was over, I got the promoter's assistant (the promoter was too busy to attend) to drive me over to the club where the Divine Horsemen were playing.

I was pretty hammered by the time I got there for their last couple songs. Sitting with Julie and Chris at a table afterward, I started moaning to them about how jealous I was that they got to do this music thing together, that I was hundreds of miles from my wife, blah, blah, blah. I'm sure it was pretty pathetic. But they humored me until the rest of my band showed up to whisk me away.

Years later, Susan and I got to know Julie after we crossed paths a few times in her adopted home of Nashville. The first time we talked, I asked her if she remembered that Kansas City episode. Fortunately, she didn't.

I never want to make it sound like there wasn't a lot of joy in my journey; there was tons of it. One of my favorite moments came at the end of a week of recording **The New Thrill Parade,** *the theoretical follow-up to* **What Time Will Tell,** *again at Water Music in Hoboken.*

We'd finished the sessions a day early (talk about your trends), so we took the final day's allotted budget and invited everyone involved out to dinner at an Italian place in Manhattan.

by Tim Lee   171

The core group — myself, bassist/producer Gene Holder, drummer Will Rigby, and engineer John Rosenberg — had busted ass during the previous days, tracking, overdubbing, and mixing 11 songs ahead of schedule.

Despite the nose-to-the-grindstone 12-hour days, we had a blast. Gene was again the perfect foil for me: sardonic, hilarious, and full of great ideas. We argued good-naturedly every step of the way, and that verbal sparring kept us moving forward, fueled by the 10-ounce Budweiser cans we purchased in eight-packs at the deli downstairs from the studio. Naturally, we dubbed those smaller cans our "little Buddies."

Over dinner that night, engineer John, normally a pretty quiet guy, cleared his throat, raised his glass of wine, and spoke up.

"All I remember from the past week is sitting around, telling jokes, and drinking beer," he said. "But I think we made a damn good record at the same time!"

That's the deal: it shouldn't look like work.

As the 1980s began to wane, the independent scene as I'd known it began to fade with the times. The major label associations didn't seem to work for most bands or labels. I watched many of my friends' combos break up or slowly dissolve. They'd seen their Warholian fifteen minutes come and go on MTV's "120 Minutes."

For most, it appeared to be time to pack up camp, piss on the fire, and go home. In spite of its ultimate long-term influence, at that moment the revolution was largely a failed coup for those of us who'd joined the fray early on.

Rock and roll wasn't going away. For someone like me, though, who'd been around the block a few times and kept running into the same brick wall, the possibilities didn't seem so endless anymore.

The future was no longer wide open.

23. THE UNRAVELING

"Um, Tim, I've got some bad news."

Steve Fallon, the head of Coyote Records, was on the phone.

"The label's done; I'm shutting it down."

I looked over at the test pressing for *New Thrill Parade* and the proof for the album art that Susan had put so much work into and got a sick feeling in the pit of my stomach.

The reviews for *What Time Will Tell* had been good, and it felt like we'd paved the way for the follow-up. After all those records and tours, I felt like I was developing as an artist, maybe I was really a songwriter, not just a hack who could talk people into putting out his records.

The summer before we recorded *New Thrill Parade* had been particularly creative. I hit my stride and wrote a bunch of inspired tunes that actually hung together, concept-wise. I was particularly confident when Gene Holder and I reconvened in early 1989 to start work, returning to Water Music in Hoboken, where we'd done *What Time Will Tell*.

As noted elsewhere, the *New Thrill Parade* sessions were both productive and hilariously fun. My friend Will Rigby played drums and sang some "Johnny One Note" backing vocals, as he and Gene called them. Janet Wygal, who'd participated in the *What Time Will Tell* sessions, was back to provide vocal harmonies, and my Mississippi homeboy George Cartwright, who I'd first seen play with Ars Supernova and was currently fronting his band Curlew in New York City, signed on to play sax on a song or two.

It was an inspired seven days, and I was thrilled with the results. I still am to this day.

The finished product was on the verge of release on Coyote when I got Steve's call. I'm sure it was hard for him, but it was devastating for me. Not only was the rug pulled from beneath an album I was so proud of, but also, it felt like all the momentum I'd gained from the previous seven years had come to a screeching halt.

That *The New Thrill Parade* didn't get its due, never got a chance at a release when it should have, was a tough pill to swallow. It still is. Initially, Coyote wanted to recoup their investment before allowing another label to pick it up and run with it, but their investment was a bit higher than anyone I knew was willing to cough up. After a year or so, they just released it to me, and my pal/entertainment lawyer Trip Aldredge got a licensing deal with a French label. To this day, that record has never come out in the U.S.

At this point in time, my so-called career was already pretty tenuous. I wasn't making any money for anyone, let alone myself. Every gesture of assistance began to feel more akin to charity than a business decision. I received my share of lectures from the "grown ups" in the biz. Booking agents told me I needed to be on a bigger label. Club owners reminded me that I didn't draw enough people to justify their continued bookings of my bands. Would-be managers told me I made too many records.

It was like being back in junior high school when the math teacher asked me to stay after class to "discuss my attitude" ... more than once.

I knew I could only keep it going at this level for so much longer, but I believed I had more good work in me.

Any reasonable person would have already pulled the plug on the operation.

Susan and I were living in Atlanta, and rather than face my disappointment, I dove deeper into playing, joining up with anybody who would have me. A three-week tour filling in on bass with the Swimming Pool Qs turned into a two-year tenure with the veteran band (guitarist Bob Elsey dubbed me the "new wave journeyman," my favorite nickname ever). After running into Linda Hopper shortly after moving back to town, I offered to play bass with her and Ruthie Morris' new band Homemade Sister, which also included Linda's Oh OK bandmate David McNair on drums (you may know them now, with the addition of bassist Shannon Mulvaney, as the excellent Magnapop). I talked my buddy Dave Weil into letting me play guitar with his roots-rock combo the Paralyzers, which we eventually morphed into the Cosmonecks.

Despite the tenuous status of my so-called career, I was lucky enough to be playing with people I admired. I was big fan of the Swimming Pool Qs and had become pals with singer/guitarist Jeff Calder when I lived in Atlanta earlier in the 1980s.

I used to listen to their records and think they would be a cool band to play bass in. So, naturally, I jumped at the chance when Jeff called to tell me that bassist J.E. Garnett was leaving to join the Atlanta Rhythm Section and ask if I could fill in on the upcoming East Coast tour for their fourth album, *World War 2.5*.

Playing with those guys was fun, so I stuck around as long as I could. As I'd suspected, Billy Burton was a great drummer with whom to play bass. He's one of those guys who can drive the groove home in such a solid and simplistic fashion that when he does something fancy (or even hits a crash cymbal), it really catches your attention. Bob's a killer player and comedic presence, Jeff was an engaging and spontaneous front man, and all three of them were good hangs.

> *During one weekend jaunt, Bob, Billy, and I decided to start an imaginary band called the Van Dykes, named after actor Jerry, "the lesser Van Dyke." Our plans for the combo never extended beyond choosing an album title (***Which Way to the 19th Hole?***) and buying matching outfits. From a Kmart in Birmingham, we purchased V-neck white t-shirts (the better to display au jus stains), powder-blue Sans-a-Belt slacks (with cuffs), and imitation leather zipper boots.*
>
> *The next night at a frat house in Athens, Georgia, we took the stage for the Qs' set in our uniforms, walked to the center of the stage and struck a pose with one foot on the middle monitor wedge. Kids immediately came forward and started tugging the zippers on our footware up and down in a ritualistic fashion. The one and only appearance of the Van Dykes went down a smash without us playing a single note.*

With Homemade Sister, I was able to help Linda, of whom I'd been a big fan since her days in Oh OK and Holiday, get a new band rolling. Ruthie and David quickly became good friends as well. It's been gratifying to see all they've accomplished with Magnapop in the years since. One can't help but feel a bit of pride for helping launch that project.

I was having trouble putting together a band of my own, though, regardless of how musically active I might have been. Maybe that's when I should have noticed the rather large font in use for the writing on the wall.

by Tim Lee   175

The travel was getting out of hand. I worked during the week for my friend Charlie Kerns at his popular Tortillas restaurant, the first mission-style burrito joint in the South. I'd get up early most days and head into the kitchen on Ponce De Leon Avenue for a few hours of food prep. Starting Thursdays, though, I usually climbed into whoever's van had my gear in it for two to four days of gigs around the Southeast.

Like ol' Ponce and his fountain of youth, I was on the hunt for something that didn't exist.

I knew it was all getting to be a bit much the weekend I loaded my guitar and amp into the Paralyzers' van to play Thursday and Friday shows in east Tennessee and North Carolina. Saturday afternoon, on the band's way back to Atlanta, they dropped me and my backpack off at a pre-determined truck stop on the interstate where an hour later the Swimming Pool Qs arrived with my bass gear and picked me up en route to a South Carolina show. Mind you, this was before cell phones or internet, so I'm amazed to this day that we pulled that off. If I'm not mistaken, Homemade Sister was on the Saturday night bill as well.

It was getting crazy to say the least.

Eventually, Susan sat me down at the dining room table and said, "I want you to quit going on the road."

The words hit me like a ton of bricks, but I knew she was right, whether I was ready to admit it or not. We both needed a change in our lives. They say you can't keep going back to the same well, and I was beginning to suspect I'd been there a few times too many.

They also say that the very definition of insanity is doing the same thing over and over, expecting a different outcome.

Guilty as charged. As Kinky Friedman says, I was in need of a "check up from the neck up."

Kinky also says you've got to know when it's time to "bug out of the dugout."

Once the shock of the whole idea wore off, I began untangling myself from my commitments as Susan and I tried to figure out what our world would look like without half of us wasting his time chasing some crazy dream. Ultimately, it was the wake-up call I needed.

At the same time, though, Susan began to have doubts about the whole thing: me, her, us.

That was understandable. It couldn't have been easy living with someone who put so much time and energy into pursuing

I Saw A Dozen Faces...

some elusive ideal, only to fall short time and time again. Susan had been the rock who kept our household together while I traipsed about, searching for some non-existent pot of gold. Something had to give.

We went through a really rough patch for the following months. I was hurt, but I also had to face the fact that I'd not been a particularly good partner. I wasn't abusive or unfaithful or anything like that. I was just selfish.

Self-absorbed, the way artists can be.

There was a lot of self-reckoning to be done on my part. And it's taken a lot of years to feel like I've begun to make up for it.

Of course, I managed to eke out one more solo album before closing the door on that chapter of my life. While working through mine and Susan's problems, Coolies guitarist Rob Gal and I met weekly at his Not Bad for 8-Track Shack and put together the *Crawdad* album, which featured members of his band and Ann Richmond Boston, as well as folks from the Qs, the Paralyzers, Right as Rain, Lava Love, and other Atlanta acts. Rob was staring down the end of his own marriage, so we dubbed our meetings the "Wednesday Afternoon Therapy Sessions," and ultimately talked Danny at DB into financing the low-budget record. *Crawdad* came out in 1992, alongside *The New Thrill Parade*, which was finally released in France only and with no fanfare at all.

The French label never even acknowledged to me that *The New Thrill Parade* had been released. If Danny hadn't given me a copy from Wax n' Fax's stock, I would have never gotten one.

In the past, I've made the mistake of marginalizing **Crawdad***, mainly because it came out "after the fact" and there was no tour and very little follow-up. I recently listened to it for the first time in years and was surprised at how personal so much of the material was. When I hear those songs now, I hear one seriously hurting dude who was in fear of losing everything. Even the songs that don't sound sad seem kind of desperate to me. I think it holds up.*

Following a particularly hard time involving tough decisions and aching hearts, Susan and I figured out how to heal the wounds and we started making a plan for a new life.

I Saw A Dozen Faces...

PART 5: SLEEPWALKING

I Saw A Dozen Faces...

24. OXFORD TOWN: THE NEW WORLD

"She said the photos fade too fast, and the feeling never lasts"

That was odd, I thought. On moving day in our new home of Oxford, Mississippi, I made the first of what would be several trips around town, going to the hardware store, the grocery, and all the joints you're likely to visit when settling into a new place.

Shortly after I dialed in the University of Mississippi campus radio station, I heard the Windbreakers song "All That Stuff." Quite a coincidence, I figured, as I went about my errands.

A few hours later, I made my second trip out, and I heard "All That Stuff" again. Hell, maybe I was famous in this town!

Sure thing, big shot.

When I heard it again on my third outing late in the day, I realized that, since the school semester had not started yet, the station was broadcasting a three-hour loop of music. There was no DJ picking out tunes on the air.

"All That Stuff" was just going to keep popping up every few hours until the student record-spinners returned and took the airwaves back.

Susan and I settled into Oxford, a small college town touting a strong literary tradition, with the notion that we'd both go back to school. Susan planned to pursue a masters in Southern Studies, while I'd work toward an undergrad degree in Elementary Education.

A couple years before, I'd played in Oxford with the Swimming Pool Qs and had fallen in love with the little burg in the north quadrant of the Magnolia State. That trip marked the first time I'd visited Oxford since my high school cover band played there in the late 1970s. It was nothing like I'd remembered it.

by Tim Lee   181

Susan and I later made a visit and she agreed it was the place for us. There was so much more to the town than just being a renowned party college of the Southeastern Conference.

We only knew a couple of people in Oxford before we got there, mainly John Stirratt, who I'd met when I saw his band the Hilltops several years earlier at W.C. Don's, but we were excited to undertake a new life in a new place.

As for music? I had no plans either way. I'd sold much of my gear, but still had my beat up old Telecaster, a small amp that worked if I pounded the top with my fist in just the right spot, and a battered Tube Screamer pedal.

We had only been there a couple weeks before John called and asked if I wanted to come play guitar on a gig with his side band, the New Boozoo Review. Sure. I was in. Why not?

On our way to the Saturday afternoon party out in the country, I rode with John in his old Ford with my guitar and amp in the back seat, feeling the breeze through the open windows on a late summer day. I'd agreed to play without seeing a setlist or really having any notion what we were doing. I liked that idea. It reminded me of the impromptu bands my friends and I would patch together whenever there was a need for a couple sets of old rock and roll songs when we were younger. There was a group of us in Jackson who had a shared knowledge of Beatles, Stones, Kinks, Chuck Berry, and rockabilly tunes that we could whip out without rehearsal. When the occasion called for it, we could produce a pretty good party band out of thin air.

John and I arrived at the venue, a fancy term for a rustic covered outdoor stage that looked like it was more accustomed to hosting local rodeos than college parties, and I met the rest of the band. We played a couple sets of covers, mostly old blues and rock and roll songs, straightforward three-chord tunes like the ones I'd played since I was a teenager. I was even coerced into singing a couple: "Shake, Rattle, and Roll," and "Roadrunner" (based on the Gants' version of the Bo Diddley number … pardon my fansplaining).

From there, I fell in with the Boozoos for their Monday night residency at the downtown bar Sid & Harry's. It was a good gig for a guy who loved playing guitar but had jettisoned all ambition: two sets of three-chord blues rock, almost no singing, free beer, and we got paid.

It made the transition to my first year back in school a little easier.

Somewhere along the line, the piano player and drummer moved on, and John, Boozoo guitarist/singer Jimmy Phillips, and myself resurrected a version of the band under the name Mercy Buckets.

The lineup was made complete with the addition of John's drummer friend, Charles David Overton, with whom I soon became good buddies.

One could write an entire volume about Charles David. He was almost always late to Mercy Bucket shows, but always had such a good story that it was worth the wait. The first one I remember involved a trip he and a buddy made the day of our show to the Gulf Coast to buy a quantity of fresh shrimp. Their car broke down on the return trip, and CD's mom, the lovely and long-suffering Dottie, drove down and picked him up to deliver him and his drums to the club, presumably leaving CD's pal behind with a broken down car and a couple hundred pounds of raw shrimp in the middle of August in Mississippi.

Despite his predictable tardiness, CD was a joy to be around, with his sly grin, "aw shucks" demeanor, and wicked sense of humor.

Oh yeah, he's also one of the great natural rock and roll drummers of all time: comes down on the snare like he's trying to kill a snake with a stick, as Fuzzy said.

The first sentence he uttered to me when we met was, "Hey, I'm Charles David. John tells me you hate drummers."

"Just the ones that suck," I assured him.

If you ever meet Charles David, ask him about me. He tells much better tales about me than I ever could. How true they are might be another thing, though. Like all good raconteurs, he'd never let the facts get in the way of a good story.

One time, several years later, Susan and I were traveling back to Oxford to play a show with Charles David. En route, Susan rang up CD on the cell phone to confirm our meet-up plans.

"Charles David, what're you doing?" she said into the phone.

"Just riding around, drinking beer, and shooting snakes," was his reply.

by Tim Lee

Mercy Buckets mostly played at Ireland's, a dive bar right off the downtown square. Among the joint's more interesting features were the framed photos of the Manson girls posted above the stairs that led down to the basement restrooms. Nothing like Susan Atkins' knowing smirk staring you down on your way to the pisser. At happy hour, the bar was usually populated by construction workers sharing nail gun horror stories, but later in the evening the grad students and authors came out.

We were a pretty good bar band. Larry Brown mentioned us in the liner notes to an early Blue Mountain record; said we played the "damnedest" version of Chuck Berry's "Nadine" he'd ever heard. Folklorist/future NEH head Bill Ferris, who is no stranger to hyperbole, saw us at Ireland's once and said my guitar playing prompted an "out-of-body experience" for him; said I made him think of Billy Gibbons.

I must have hit that old amp in just the right place that night.

During our time in Oxford, I finished my degree and taught school for a few years, trying my hand at the straight life.

Susan and I made a lot of life-long friends there, and I played music with a variety of good folks during that time. John, Charles David, and I started a separate band called the Gimmecaps to play John's songs. I played bass in the Gimmecaps, which is funny considering John's a pretty famous bass dude these days.

For a while, John and I also had an every-other-Tuesday-night acoustic gig at the Harvest, a vegetarian restaurant and market on the square. We played a couple sets, trading weekly turns with the Blue Mountain duo, in exchange for food credit.

When Harvest owner Joan announced she was moving away and the restaurant was closing in the fall of 1996, a final night of music was planned. John and I kicked off the evening with a short set, and I was about to go home when Cary and Laurie from Blue Mountain asked John and me to play a couple songs with them.

From there, the end of the room that was acting as the "stage" filled quickly. Soon, the four of us were joined by bassist Dave Woolworth, guitarist George McConnell of the Kudzu Kings, Beanland, and Widespread Panic, and dobro-player Ed Dye. You couldn't have crammed another guitar in there as we strummed and sang our way through a bunch of Bob Dylan, Gram Parsons, and Hank Williams songs.

It was another one of those magical musical events, during which spontaneity trumps order, where anything can happen and the best stuff does when you least expect it.

Later, as we were putting away our guitars, somebody remarked, "We ought to plan to do this more often."

I laughed and said, "You can plan this kind of thing all you want, but you can't just make it happen."

Only magicians conjure magic on demand. The rest of us are just lucky to be present when it appears.

John eventually went on the road with Uncle Tupelo, but we usually scrounged up some kind of gig whenever he was in town. He invited me up to St. Louis to open one of the last Uncle Tupelo shows with an acoustic set. We stayed in close touch, but John moved to Chicago when Wilco got started, and we didn't cross paths so much. We still hang out whenever he comes to my town these days.

> *Thanks to its reputation as the home of William Faulkner, Oxford had its share of authors, and I was fortunate enough to befriend two of my all-time favorites, Larry Brown and Barry Hannah, while there.*
>
> *One Saturday afternoon, I was working for a friend at the local music store CD Alley, when Barry came in to browse. We chatted a bit, mostly talking about his son Barry "Po" Hannah Jr., a gifted guitarist.*
>
> *At one point, Hannah picked up a Jimi Hendrix record and turned it in his hands, admiring the artwork.*
>
> *"The way I see it," he pronounced in his gruff nasal tone, "is to write a good pop song, you've either got to be really stupid or really fucked up on drugs."*
>
> *I nodded, laughed, and went about my business.*
>
> *Several years later, I got a kick out of telling that story to Po, who had moved to Knoxville and become a good pal and occasional collaborator.*

A lot of cool music folks were in Oxford then, either attending the university or just hanging out while it was still cheap to live there. In addition to John, CD, and Jimmy, I played with Laurie and Cary, who had moved back to town after a brief stint in California to start Blue Mountain, as well as Neilson Hubbard, Clay Jones, and Garrison Starr. I was pals with Tyler Keith from the Neckbones and the Preacher's Kids and Scott Rogers from the Dutchmasters, the Cool Jerks, and others.

Thanks to local up-and-coming music promoter Jim Green, I played a good many solo acoustic sets opening for touring acts of all sorts. In the span of a year, I opened for everyone from Jonathan Richman to David Allan Coe, including memorable shows with Roger McGuinn and Guy Clark.

I was scheduled to open for Warren Zevon, but a week before the show his management called Jim to let him know they were bringing their own opener. So, I stayed home... wish I hadn't.

It was a great group of players to fall in with, but my heart wasn't completely in it. I was still trying to find my footing away from a concerted effort at a music career, an endeavor that proved to be harder than I'd imagined. I enjoyed the people and the playing, but ultimately I was sleep-walking through a lot of it.

As odd as it seems, I was involved in music, although I was not committed to it. Famous moonshiner/stock car racer Junior Johnson once explained the difference like this: "When you sit down to eggs and bacon for breakfast, the chicken is involved. The pig is committed."

It was a strange head space to occupy after all the years of single-minded obsession.

I'd go see my friends play when they came through town on tour, but that usually just led to second guessing and an empty feeling in my gut. I'd wonder, "What would it be like to still be doing that?" If I thought too hard, the answer would always come back, "Nothing would be any different than it ever was, except that you're older and the world has changed. There would be a lot more Tuesday nights in Pittsburgh than Saturdays at CBGB."

The gut rarely lies.

During my Oxford days (daze?), our friend Mark Roberts started a local label called Fishtone Records and released a couple CDs. He wanted to put out a collection of my material from the previous ten years, so I pulled together the 30 some-odd songs that comprised the double-CD *All That Stuff: 1983-1993.*

I Saw A Dozen Faces...

The collection that resulted included plenty of previously released material, along with outtakes, remixes, a B-side, and a handful of new songs I'd recently recorded with Oxford friends. In all, it covered a good bit of ground from the Windbreakers and Beat Temptation through my earliest solo stuff and oddball collaborations.

You'll never guess what happened then. Mark shut down Fishtone Records before *All That Stuff* was released.

Did somebody say something about recurring themes?

Fortunately, Fundamental Records founder Richard Jordan lived in town at the time and expressed interest in picking up the ball and running with it.

So, some time in the mid-1990s, *All That Stuff: 1983-1993* was released on Fundamental. My friend, rock critic/author/poet Karen Schoemer was kind enough to pen the liner notes, which included such keen observations as:

> "Tim Lee has always worked utterly outside of fashion. Where he lives, fashion doesn't even come to call. He has his own well-defined, slightly belligerent notions of what constitutes good music, and he will stand by those notions long after the show has ended … even among [postpunk indie-rock artists], Tim stands out as something of an iconoclast, a guy anxious to set right something that has been wrong for too long."

Yeah, Karen totally understood young Tim, the boy who didn't want to be a rock star.

25. GETTING THE BLUES ... OR HOW I LEARNED TO STOP WORRYING AND DIG THE GROOVE

"Well, well, well."

The great Hill Country bluesman R.L. Burnside commanded the tiny bandstand at Junior Kimbrough's juke joint on a Sunday night. The crowd danced and hooted while R.L. and his trio laid down their thing with a loose groove that was deeper than quicksand.

The gutted sharecropper's shack sat on the edge of a cotton field, which glowed white under a near-full moon in autumn. Situated along Highway 4, just south of Holly Springs, Junior's was the place to be if you wanted to dig the real deal in north Mississippi.

Susan and I had taken that ride some 20 miles north of Oxford with David "Fuzzy" Nelson, my oft-quoted pal who was the editor of *Living Blues*. David was our neighbor, and Susan was the art director for the magazine. He'd told us we needed to check out the Hill Country blues scene, particularly the sounds that the Burnside and Kimbrough families produced.

This was the early 1990s, prior to Fat Possum Records and that label's push to familiarize the rest of the world with the likes of R.L., Junior, T-Model Ford, Asey Payton, Paul "Wine" Jones, and others. The elder statesmen of the region's unique musical heritage were barely known outside the area, except to folklorists and deeper-digging blues aficionados.

During our time in Oxford, I got an official educa-tion courtesy of the University of Mississippi, but that era also provided a whole other schooling courtesy of Junior Kimbrough and R.L. Burnside.

Having grown up in the deep South, I was no stranger to blues music. I definitely knew of it, certainly through its influence on the rock bands I'd grown up on in the 1970s. I'd been lucky enough to see my fair share of blues artists: Sam Chatmon, Jack Owens, and the great Jesse Mae Hemphill at local festivals. Albert King at a popular Jackson bar. Shows by Albert Collins, B.B. King, and homegrown Jackson acts such as King Edward, Blind Sam Myers, and Big Daddy (500 Pounds of the Blues!), so I knew how good it could be.

But it just hadn't really been my thing. I wasn't ignorant of the form, just a bit stand-offish, you might say, for a couple of reasons.

Most of the blues I was exposed to in my upbringing was of an athletic nature, filtered through its white practitioners to resemble an olympic event for show-off soloing. While there's nothing wrong with that, there's very little of that branch of the blues tree that I find interesting, however authentic it may or may not sound.

More than anything, I was too young to "get the blues," and I knew it. I mean, I nearly lost my mind when I saw Muddy Waters on some PBS show as a young teen in the early 1970s, playing a wild slide style on a red Telecaster, but somehow I was self-aware enough to know that this was music I would have to grow into. I bought a few blues records along the way, particularly the prerequisite Robert Johnson collections, but I was somehow cognizant that this was music I was filing away in my brain until the day came that I was ready to embrace the blues. It was lurking in my background, waiting its turn to come out in the light.

That night at Junior's Juke Joint, the metaphorical door burst wide open.

We pulled up to the place just before 8 p.m., well past dark in the fall, and stepped in through the front door (in subsequent years, after the hipster quotient rose, they charged two bucks to get in). The bare bones abode was filled with folks drinking, dancing, smoking, swaying, laughing, and celebrating. One certain truth hit me right away: this blues was not for cross-armed guitar students investigating "awesome riffage," this music was all about the party. The stories the singers told may have run the gamut of emotions, from happy to sad, but the spirit was pure house rocking.

I've rarely encountered so much unabashed joy in one place. This was the last gasp of the weekend before the work week rolled back around, and there was no time to be wasted on anything less than a good time.

Junior and his Blues Boys kicked things off shortly after we arrived, digging into their wild modal one-chord version of the age-old genre. My mind was immediately blown by this sound that felt as much Saharan in origin as Mississippi Delta.

Junior sang about getting old, not being able to do what he used to. Still, he was perfectly capable of inciting his Hill Country folks to dance and party and put off their problems until Monday morning, because Sunday night was for celebrating.

This was life-affirming music, and it was unlike anything I'd heard before.

After a while, Junior yielded the stage and wandered off to sell $1.25 Busch beer cans from the well-worn kitchen refrigerator behind the crude bar.

R.L. ambled up to the grandstand, accompanied by some combination of his kids and grandkids, and kicked up a mighty ruckus that sent the dancers into overdrive. This was a style of blues I could get behind. There were no formal activities like choosing a proper guitar and tuning it up. They just grabbed whatever instrument was handy, adapted to its particular state of tuning, and dove right in with spirit and abandon.

And with nary a flurry of pentatonic gnat-notes to be found.

Susan, David, and I were the only white faces in the place. Some of the locals knew David through his work with the magazine, and a couple of the older men asked Susan to dance. One of the regulars politely offered me a sip of something from a Mountain Dew bottle. Being a good guest, I took a small swig. This particular potion possessed a nose of fire that left a bouquet of radiator rust in its wake. I guessed it was of recent vintage.

I leaned against the back wall and let the music wash over me, falling in love with the droning sound that flowed from the stage filled with cheap instruments and inspired players. It was exciting. It was primal. It was simple and basic, but it was way over my head. The experience deeply influenced how I thought about music going forward.

Most of the music I had previously known featured form and structure: verses, choruses, perhaps a bridge section (or "middle eight," as per the Beatles). This Hill Country blues was pure groove, repetition, and soul.

As much as I immediately took to this music, it still took years for me to wrap my head around it. Don't even bother to ask if I can play it, the answer is a solid "no." But I can listen and dig it deep.

One of my favorite afternoons of all time was a Sunday when I rode along with Fuzzy back up to Holly Springs to run a couple errands. First off, we dropped in on R.L. at his apartment to deliver copies of a recent issue of *Living Blues* with him on the cover.

We sat in R.L.'s living room and chatted a bit as Burnside admired the magazine. It was interesting to watch the elder statesman take in a symbol of his newfound status in the blues world amid such humble surroundings. I can't imagine that the thought of being on the cover of a glossy publication would have seemed remotely possible to R.L. when he started out playing house parties and jukes several decades earlier.

From there, we dropped by Junior's home, where his wife informed us he was at the K&B Drug Store, buying beer for the Sunday night show. Fuzzy had an old couch he wanted to donate to the juke joint, so we made our way there, where we found Junior stocking the fridge in the late afternoon.

He was glad to have more seating for the club, so he offered us beers. We hung around for a while, discussing a wide range of topics, including Kumala the Ugandan Giant, the character played by a local hero who'd made it big in professional wrestling.

"He's not from Uganda," Junior explained. "He bought his mama a house just over there a few miles."

We returned to Kimbrough's joint a few times, but as amazing as it was, there was no replicating that first time. Soon thereafter, Fat Possum Records launched the Burnside and Kimbrough legacies into hyperdrive, presenting them to a younger crowd who were happy to dance to remixes of the masters of the form.

Somewhere past the mandatory retirement age, R.L. and Junior got their hard-earned due.

That first trip to Junior's Juke Joint allowed me a glimpse into the heart and soul of the blues, what that escape from reality means to its intended audience. That experience changed my views of the genre at its foundation.

In other words, I learned to stop worrying and just dig the groove. In time, I would learn to adopt that philosophy toward my own life and music.

by Tim Lee

I Saw A Dozen Faces...

PART 6:
A NEW MISSION

I Saw A Dozen Faces...

26. THAT GIRL: SECOND ACT

"I want to learn how to play bass."

One sunny Saturday morning early in the 21st century, some 20 years into our marriage, Susan woke to an epiphany and uttered the preceding pronouncement.

As she tells the story, I got out of bed, went straight to a local pawn shop, and came back with a Danelectro bass for her. That sounds close enough to the truth.

What's important to me is that six months later, she was on stage.

Susan's decision to take up an instrument dovetailed rather nicely with my own renewed interest in making racket after several years of relative inactivity. Like a lot of folks, she was given piano lessons as a kid, but never really took to it, thanks to the boring songs she was forced to learn. But she was right at home with the bass and had a feel for it from the get-go. The first time she played along with a record, she landed on the first and third beats of the measures with the bass drum, a skill that some players never develop. It was damned impressive.

The more she improved, the more inspired I became. And she got better quickly, developing a solid low-end style that I soon grew to appreciate. It was the perfect approach for the music I wanted to play.

Besides, we were the couple who took a side trip to see Mission of Burma on their honeymoon in 1981. Of course, we should be in a band together.

Around the turn of the century, Susan and I settled in Knoxville, Tennessee, after leaving Oxford in 1997 and spending a couple of years in western North Carolina pursuing careers in auto racing journalism.

Through some acquaintances I made shortly after moving to Knoxville, I'd gotten back into recording. In collaboration with

Jim Rivers and John T. Baker of the local band French Broads, I made **Under the House** in 2002, which feels a bit shaky in retrospect, but it was a good start to my second act, of which Susan was destined to be a large part.

Maybe it was my third act? Perhaps second childhood is more appropriate.

In time, I also fell into playing guitar with new friends and local stalwarts Todd Steed and Leslie Woods and their respective bands, the Suns of Phere and Black Mountain Orchid. That activity introduced me to an ever-widening group of local music folks.

With Susan fully on board, we set out to make **Under the House**'s follow-up, **No Discretion**, which came out in 2004. We recorded a few songs with Jim and John, but also branched out, working with Mitch Easter at his new Fidelitorium studio, as well as with our Oxford buddy Bruce Watson at his space in Water Valley, Mississippi, where many of the Fat Possum blues records had been made. We tracked a song in Neilson Hubbard's apartment in Jackson, and another in Todd Steed's spare bedroom studio.

During that time, I became friends with Don Coffey Jr., who had just come off the road with Superdrag and was establishing himself as a recording engineer/producer at Studio 613 in town. Don and I hit it off pretty quickly, and he played drums on and tracked several songs for **No Discretion**.

My old friend Mark Wyatt, a recurring theme unto himself amongst these scribblings, made a trip down to Knoxville from Ohio to play on a handful of songs, marking our first collaborations since the final Windbreakers album, **Electric Landlady**, in 1990.

Working in six different studios made for a sprawling collection of recordings, but one of which I remain particularly pleased. It was a real cool time, hanging out and working with a variety of friends, new and old, and doing the thing I'd always loved. Susan's involvement was icing on the cake. She played bass on all thirteen songs, garnering a whole lot of recording experience in a brief period of time.

All of this activity eventually added up to a pretty serious re-immersion into the world of bands and music. I don't remember how much of a conscious decision it was to return to that path, but as long as Susan was up for the ride, it just felt natural to follow wherever it took us.

Her participation gave me a reason to pick up where I'd left off and make an effort to get back out into the world. On my own, I wasn't particularly motivated to return to the grind of having a band (particularly the headaches associated with keeping one together). I'd already accomplished pretty much everything I was ever going to do with music. But being in the position to provide Susan the opportunity to do all the things to which she'd previously just been an interested observer allowed me to experience it all anew through her eyes.

In short, Susan brought the fun back into the equation. There is great joy in looking across the stage to catch her eye while playing. Our bond adds something special to what we are doing. It's a cool thing.

In the beginning, it was my band performing my songs, and Susan was the bass player. Then one day, she laid a piece of paper with some words on my desk and said, "See if you can do something with this."

That simple gesture changed our entire musical dynamic.

We immediately put together the song "Real Bad Habit" and recorded it for what became the *Concrete Dog* album, which was released in 2005.

From that simple beginning, she and I continued to collaborate on songs.

During one session with Don (whose studio had moved around the corner and was renamed Independent Recorders), we felt we needed some backing vocals for "Real Bad Habit."

"You should go out there and give it a try," Don said to Susan, pointing to the tracking room where the vocal microphone was set up.

Susan had never tried singing before.

"Do you think I can do it?" she replied.

"There's only one way to find out," he said.

As it turned out, not only could she do it, but she could do it quite well.

By then, we'd settled the line-up of the band to Susan and me with Don on drums and Greg Horne on guitar. Greg is a multi-talented guy, a singer and songwriter who can play most any stringed instrument you put in front of him (as well as a few with no strings attached).

We first met Greg in Oxford, where he'd lived for a brief period during our time there. Reconnecting soon after we moved to Knoxville, Greg and I have worked together a great deal over the years. I've played with his band; he's played with mine. We've played together with other artists, live and in the studio. Together, he and I have pulled together several multi-artist tribute sets to the likes of Warren Zevon, Neil Young, Aretha Franklin, Lou Reed, Tom Petty, Ric Ocasek, and others, usually resulting in the types of magical evenings I've referenced so often in these pages.

> *My favorite is the set we put together for the 2017 edition of Waynestock, an annual winter benefit for which Susan and I have been on the planning board since its inception in 2011. For the seventh edition, Greg and I pulled together a wide-ranging tribute to the artists who'd died in the previous year, starting with Ralph Stanley and Guy Clark and winding up with David Bowie and Prince. It was an amazing night involving a wide variety of players and artists.*

Greg's a great guy to have as a friend and a collaborator, easy going and enthusiastic, with talent in spades.

On one of that band's road trips, we were in the Carolinas, playing with our friends Jane Francis and Jay Manley and their band Velvet. After a Chapel Hill show, Velvet's drummer Zsolt David offered to let us stay at the apartment of his girlfriend, who was out of the town for the weekend.

After stopping for fried chicken from a late-night restaurant, Zsolt got us settled at his girlfriend's place, where we eventually drifted off to sleep.

At 7:00 the next morning, there was pounding on the back door and shouts of "Police! We're coming in! Come out slowly with your hands up!"

Sure enough, Carrboro's finest were on the scene, shining flashlights in our eyes and peppering us with questions, which I tried to answer calmly through my barely-awake haze while mentally calculating how long it was going to take to get us out of this situation. I went to great lengths to explain why we were there, eventually giving them Zsolt's number. Fortunately, he answered the early-morning phone call and everything got worked out with no arrests.

It turns out that before our unknowing hostess left town, she contacted the police department and asked them to check in on her place, a service offered at the time in that college community. Of course, they saw a strange van in the drive and noticed the back door was not closed completely (our fault). You know what happened then.

In the late summer of 2006, Paisley Pop Records' Jim Huie invited Susan and I to come out to the Pacific Northwest for a couple of shows involving several old friends. Gigs in Portland and Seattle were slated to feature a reconstituted True West (Jim had been drumming with original TW members Russ Tolman, Gavin Blair, and Richard McGrath), Don Dixon, a Windbreakers set (Bobby, Susan, Jim, and me), and a set of my solo material (with Jim, Susan, and Matt Piucci, who came up from the Bay Area to join in the fun).

We all flew out a few days early, providing ample time for hanging out and practicing together. Jim's basement was a flurry of activity as we sorted out our various sets. It was a great weekend of rock and roll fellowship.

One of the funniest moments came after the Seattle show, when several of us rode in a mini-van back to the hotel. Although our lodgings were a mere two miles from the club we'd just played, in those pre-GPS days, it took nearly two hours to make it back after all the false turns and one-way streets that stymied our progress. Dixon was at the wheel. Susan and I sat in the back and tried not to laugh too hard, as this was not out of the ordinary for us. Before smart phones, we were really good at finding our way to a venue, but not necessarily so good at finding our way from said venue to wherever we were headed. We were just happy it wasn't one of us driving. Under those circumstances, it might have taken three hours.

by Tim Lee

In addition to my own band's activities, I spent a lot of time working with Don Coffey on various projects. It started with him calling on me to help younger bands set the intonation on their guitars, loan them instruments for specific sounds, or assist them in getting the best tone possible out of their gear. From there, I began playing on a lot of the records he was producing.

Doing studio work was fun, especially with Don. His recording history was quite different from mine, and I enjoyed his perspective. He was much more of a stickler for performances that were as close to perfect as possible than me, but we were a good team in the studio. I'd always loved recording, and I found that I was pretty good at coming up with parts and sounds that worked well and made everyone happy. As I'm not much of a technical player, it was funny to think of myself as a "studio guitarist." But I do have a good sense of how to use a variety of gear for different sounds, and I'm not afraid of a challenge. I loved being given vague instructions for a sound someone was looking for and figuring out the best way to achieve it. It was a cool experience.

After a good run together, that band ended. Don's studio responsibilities made it harder for him to play out with us, and Greg was heading out for a month or so to teach at a guitar workshop. Besides, he was itching to get another band of his own in action.

During that four-year stretch, I'd returned to music with a renewed enthusiasm and Susan had gained recording and band-life experience. All of that cemented our musical partnership and gave us a solid footing as we moved forward.

27. JUST ONE MORE:
A LABOR OF LOVE

"Oh my god, did you hear? Larry Brown died."

Thanksgiving 2004. I was in Jackson, visiting my parents, when Susan called from home with the sad news. Larry had been felled by a heart attack at 53.

Larry Brown was someone we'd been fortunate enough to know during our time in Oxford. I'd been a fan of his writing since I encountered his first collection of stories, *Facing the Music* at the Eudora Welty Library shortly after it came out in 1984. I sat down that afternoon in our little house on Duncan Avenue in midtown Jackson and read it cover to cover in one sitting.

There weren't many words of his I hadn't read by the time I made his acquaintance.

Susan and I met Larry and his wife Mary Annie soon after we'd moved to Oxford, and I always enjoyed running into him at the downtown bars, hearing him talk about whatever writing project he had in the works. He knew I played music, so he was usually keen to guide the conversation toward that subject as well.

Larry was obsessed with music. His favorite artists were often mentioned in his books, and as his popularity grew, so did the number of respected musicians with whom he became friends.

The night Susan and I met the Browns, we were invited to a small dinner party at the home of Richard and Lisa Howorth, who own Square Books, a national treasure located in the center of town. We hadn't been in Oxford long, so I have no idea how we were involved, but the other two couples in attendance were Larry and Mary Annie and this new author I'd heard about named John Grisham and his wife Renee.

by Tim Lee

I was beside myself at the prospect of hanging out with Larry and probably peppered him with questions and praise all night. Can't say that I paid much attention to that other writer.

The snot-nosed punk runs deep in this one, Obi-Wan.

One night, not long after that gathering, I ran into Larry in the parking lot of the Gin, a bar located in an old cotton facility that was a downtown Oxford institution. He was sitting in the cab of his small pickup truck with the windows down, a cigarette dangling from his fingers.

"Hey Tim, come over here, check this out."

He was listening to a cassette of a local group that used to play at the Days Inn lounge out on the bypass. Larry said he used to like to go see them play, that they were really good.

I have no memory of the band's name or what their music sounded like, but I remember well the way Larry's eyes lit up when he talked about music that meant something to him.

In time, he penned liner notes for Blue Mountain and the North Mississippi Allstars and wrote a feature story for *No Depression* magazine about singer/songwriter Robert Earl Keen, one of his favorites.

After getting the word from Susan that sad November morning, I decided to stay an extra day in Mississippi and drive up to Oxford for Larry's visitation.

Upon my arrival, I met up with our good friends Ron Nurnburg and Joe Osgoode for a quick dinner and drinks at Ajax Diner before we headed over to the funeral home, where there was a line out the door.

Dozens of us stood in the queue, still stunned by the idea that Larry no longer walked among us. His prized possession, a recently-purchased Gibson Hummingbird acoustic guitar, sat on a stand beside his open casket, and a mix CD of his favorite artists played overhead through the muzak system. The sounds of Lucinda Williams, Keen, Alejandro Escovedo, and others wafted through the stuffy halls of the parlor as friends and family chatted and consoled one another.

The following day, I struck out for home, taking Highway 7 north out of Oxford en route to Knoxville. I drove the two-lane route past churches, catfish houses, drag strips, and crude shacks. I'd barely made it out of Lafayette County into Marshall (where the laws of gravity don't even apply, Fuzzy once said) when the thought struck me: somebody needs to put together a tribute record to Larry Brown.

By the early 2000s, tribute records for popular or influential musical artists were pretty commonplace, but one dedicated to an author? It was a crazy idea, but I could visualize it.

I spent the next six hours on the road pondering the notion, and by the time I got home, felt a sense of urgency about the project. I was ready to start work. Immediately, I began reaching out to friends of Larry's and musicians I felt would be interested.

Not long into my enthusiastic dive into the idea, one of the artists I called on told me that somebody else had already started such a project.

Cool, I thought. I'm just glad it's going to happen. It doesn't have to be my deal.

After several months passed, though, it became apparent that, in fact, nobody was working on a Larry Brown tribute record.

I started over, more ambitious this time. A call or email to this person led to a phone number for that person. In time, it began to snowball. Pretty much every artist I talked to agreed to participate, with very few exceptions.

Originally, I got a little interest from a couple of smaller record labels, but nothing was really coming together on that front. I guess it was just too vague an idea. But it was one I believed in, so I was willing to figure it out as I went.

During one phone call, Alejandro asked if I'd approached Bloodshot Records, the "insurgent country" label based in Chicago. I said no, explaining that I didn't have any contacts there. Within a couple of days, he paved the way for me to pitch the idea to Nan Warshaw and Rob Miller at Bloodshot.

Nan and Rob were initially hesitant, but after a few conversations, they signed on to release the 18-song CD titled *Just One More: A Musical Tribute to Larry Brown, a Great American Author.* Among the artists involved were Escovedo, Keen, Blue Mountain's Cary Hudson, Greg Brown, Caroline Herring, Jim Dickinson and Duff Dorough, Vic Chesnutt, author Madison Smartt Bell, the North Mississippi All-Stars, Bo Ramsey, and Brent Best of Slobberbone. The last track was a recording of Larry singing a song he'd written called "Don't Let the Door Hit

by Tim Lee

You," accompanying himself on guitar with fellow author Clyde Edgerton picking along. Susan and I, in addition to our respective roles in pulling the compilation together (she provided the package design), contributed a song she'd written called "The Bridge," inspired by another Oxford writer Cynthia Shearer's book *The Celestial Jukebox*.

The tunes on the compilation ran the gamut from songs about Larry (Madison Smartt Bell & Wyn Cooper's "Going Down with Larry Brown" and Cary Hudson's "Song in C") to songs inspired by Larry (Caroline Herring's "Song for Fay" and former V-Roy Scott Miller's "Thirsty Fingers"), as well as songs dedicated to Larry (Jim Dickinson and Duff Durrough's cover of Dylan's "I'll Remember You"), alternate versions of Larry's favorite songs (Escovedo's live version of "Baby's Got New Plans") and songs that artists felt displayed some kinship to Larry and his work.

The title of the record came from a statement Larry was known to make, mostly late at night, usually when the evening was winding down. Just one more drink. Just one more song. Just one more cigarette. Just one more …

As an author of some note, it was rare that he couldn't find someone willing to go along with him.

Just One More was rush released to be available at the spring 2007 Oxford Conference for the Book, an annual event that was scheduled to focus on Larry's work that year. In addition to the 18 songs on the main disc, we put together a supplemental release for the Book Conference with the support of the Center for the Study of Southern Culture at the University of Mississippi and the Oxford Convention and Visitors Bureau. The second CD included another eight songs and a booklet with extended liner notes.

During the conference, several of us involved in the record took part in a panel discussion on Larry and music. In addition, there was also a live celebration at a club called Proud Larry's that weekend. Robert Earl Keen, Alejandro Escovedo, Cary Hudson, Brent Best, Ben Weaver, Vic Chesnutt, Duff Dorrough, and others came to town to play acoustic sets to a packed house at the venerable Oxford venue.

The record wasn't a huge success. It was a one-of-a-kind project that didn't seem to make a lot of sense to many people. Still, I'm quite proud of it and grateful to have been part of the team that made it happen and that proceeds from sales of the CD went to the Larry Brown Fund, an educational endowment to support the arts in Mississippi.

As far as I was concerned, *Just One More* was a project that needed to happen. Musicians loved Larry, as he loved them and their music.

In the liner notes to Blue Mountain's *Homegrown* CD, Larry explained his side of that two-way street.

"That's why I love and respect musicians so much. They've done the same thing I've done, practicing something over and over, for years, trying to get to the place that they want to be."

The pursuit of art is often based in the desire to be in some other place, whether physically or spiritually. Larry knew that journey well.

Sometimes you've got to make time in your travels for an occasional side trip, because the journey should be as interesting as the destination whenever possible. In June of 2015, Susan and I, along with drummer Chris Bratta, had a couple of shows lined up on the road with our pal RB Morris, including one in Oxford.

Larry's son Shane, who I'd met during the book conference, had contacted me to say he and some friends were coming to the show. He also invited us stop in and visit the piece of property his dad had bought in the community of Tula, just east of Oxford. On that seven acres, Larry spent days and hours expanding the little pond, shoring up the levee, and building the Shack, which was to have been his new writing space, replacing the Cool Pad he'd established in the carport storage room of the family home in nearby Yocona.

We accepted, and Susan, Chris, and I looked forward to the visit. RB and our buddy Greg Horne were traveling separately, but they were down for the adventure.

After driving across north Alabama and passing through Tupelo and Pontotoc, we turned westward on 334, through an area that Susan and I know well from visits to *Living Blues* editor Brett Bonner's house in Toccopola, our friends Ron and Joe's place in Yocona, and rock and roll lifer Tyler Keith's pad near Shane's brother Billy Ray's dairy farm.

Upon our arrival, we turned into a long dirt driveway through an open iron gate that read "A Place Called Tula." Larry wrote extensively about this land in his nonfiction book: *Billy Ray's Farm: Essays From a Place Called Tula,* so I felt like I knew it, although I'd never been there before. I have a photo that Mary Annie sent me along with a nice letter after **Just One More** came out. In the picture, you can see Larry from behind as he sits on the dock he built overlooking his little pond. I keep both together in a frame in our home.

Arriving a few minutes before Shane, we got out, stretched our legs, and took a look around. The first structure you notice is a cabin that was built after Larry's death, with an outdoor cooking area, close to the pond. That's where Billy Ray's and Shane's kids gathered nearly every weekend to play, fish and "just be kids," Shane said. Thick stands of pine trees surround the property, and there's an old barn up on the hill to the north.

It is very quiet there, and it's easy to understand why someone would choose this as a place to write.

Shane showed up, and immediately pulled a beer from the cooler in the back of the Toyota pickup that once belonged to his father. Larry usually had a full cooler in the back of that truck, too.

At 35, Shane looked a lot like his daddy, talked like him too. He was showing promise as a writer, as well. On the day we were there, he'd just worked out a deal to start publishing his stories on a local website.

We walked up a small incline to the spot where Larry is buried. The back of his tombstone is engraved with the names of his children and grandchildren, as well as the phrase, "The Road Goes On Forever …" in reference to a Keen song of which Larry was particularly fond.

Shane led us around the pond to see the Shack. The construction of the small building is covered in great detail in Larry's piece "Shack" from *Billy Ray's Farm*. Larry did nearly all the work himself and took great pride in it. Sadly, he only got to use it briefly, writing the bulk of his unfinished final novel, *A Miracle of Catfish*, in long hand on legal pads there. He hadn't even moved his typewriter.

Shane had recently come across Larry's typewriter in the barn and placed it in its rightful spot on the small desk facing the crank windows that looked out over the pond from the east.

Under the cover of an outdoor cooking area, Shane told stories about growing up around the place, expressing pride in the hard work Larry put into it. He's a natural-born storyteller. I looked up and saw a sign that read "Life is Good" nailed to a tree on the edge of the pond.

Shane later reminded me that those were Larry's last words to Mary Annie the night he died.

28. GOOD2B3, THEN TWO

"We're gonna push it 'til the roof caves in."

At the end of 2006, after our band with Don Coffey and Greg Horne came to its natural conclusion, Susan and I made the decision to give it a shot as a trio, bringing in drummer Rodney Cash, who'd played with us a few times previously. Susan was singing and writing more, plus she'd had a good taste of what makes one want to climb in the van, so despite the Tim Lee 3 moniker, it naturally became "our" band instead of "my" band.

Rodney is a sweet guy and a hell of a basher, another one of the purest rock and roll drummers I've ever played with. He and Susan combined to make a solid, rocking rhythm section, and I quickly adapted my playing to the three-piece lineup. It was ferociously rocking and I couldn't have been happier, playing loud guitar and trading vocals with Susan.

Many of the Tim Lee 3's earliest shows were at the Corner Lounge, an aging dive bar in the Happy Holler district of Knoxville that dates to the early 1900s and is featured in Cormac McCarthy's book, Suttree, *as one of the title character's regular hangouts. The photo of the three of us on the cover of the first TL3 release,* **good2b3**, *was taken at the Corner's bar.*

Coincidentally, Rodney's late father, the very real Henry Lee Cash, makes an appearance at the Corner Lounge in McCarthy's work of fiction. He's the man standing in the corner reciting the "Signifying Monkey" as the Suttree character walks in one night.

Over ten years with that band, we released five studio albums, as well as a couple of live recordings, and built up a small fan base (a dozen faces at a time), many of whom were not familiar with the Windbreakers or my other early pursuits. It was cool and gratifying that the Tim Lee 3 was able to develop an identity apart from my previous history.

During my so-called career, I've been lucky to have recorded in a range of cool studios with a lot of cool people, and that streak continued with our trio. A good chunk of the Tim Lee 3's recorded output was captured at WaveLab Studio in Tucson. Susan and I became friends with studio owner Craig Schumacher in 2005 through his involvement with the *TapeOp* conferences in New Orleans and were soon working with him on his own Pot Luck recording conferences in New Orleans and Arizona.

When the conferences moved to Tucson, we would fly out for several days to assist Craig. The gatherings were always fun, and we'd get to spend a lot of time with studio friends from around the country in between panel discussions and gear demonstrations. Once Pot Luck wrapped up, we'd move over to WaveLab and hang out for a week and record with Craig and house engineer Chris Schultz, a quiet guy with a lot of ideas whose eyes would light up whenever it was suggested that we "put something fucked-up sounding here," as it often was.

There were no shortage of sonic adventures there.

WaveLab is a cool space with tons of desert rock vibe located in the center of downtown Tucson. Packed with wall-to-wall instruments and gizmos, the studio has a great clubhouse feel that fosters creativity and spontaneity. Although we always showed up with plenty of songs in hand, on several occasions there, we concocted or learned songs on the spot and got good takes on the first, second, or third time we played them all the way through. On "Mile Long Midway" from *good2b3*, I just started playing that simple riff one day and Susan and Rodney fell right in. I wrote words that night and we tracked it the following morning. During another session, we were setting up when Susan started playing a pulsing bass line. Our drummer at the time, Matt Honkonen, and I fell in and she started singing a song she'd been working on called "Dig it Up." We followed her lead and nailed it on the third run-through, improvised ending and all. Another time, when recording songs for our *Devil's Rope* album, I was strumming some chords on the studio's 12-string acoustic. Something I played caught Susan's ear and she urged me to keep it going, listening intently and eventually singing along. We took a few minutes to sort out the song's changes, and "Alibi" was born. We worked it up with drummer Chris Bratta and recorded an elaborate version including drum machine, mellotron, and e-bowed guitars later that day.

That kind of spontaneity is one of my favorite aspects of playing music.

Oh yeah, and WaveLab is located within easy walking distance of many great happy hour opportunities, which only added to the relaxed approach to recording we undertook there.

We were recording fools, hitting the studio any chance we got. In addition to WaveLab, we also tracked TL3 material with Mitch Easter at the Fidelitorium in Kernersville, North Carolina, Bruce Watson at Dial Back Sound in Water Valley, Mississippi, and Mary Podio and John Harvey at Top Hat Studio in Austin (and later in Knoxville after their move east). We also recorded with our old pal John Baker at his Arbor Studio and Scott Minor at Wild Chorus in Knoxville.

I'm proud of that band's catalog. We accomplished a lot in the studio, including our second release, *Raucous Americanus*, a sprawling double-CD featuring 21 songs recorded at three different studios. Despite its length, surprisingly, the reviews for *Raucous* were great.

The fact that so few people will ever hear those records reminds me of the smart-ass kid I was in 1985 when interviewed by Rolling Stone *for the piece in which they proclaimed the Windbreakers one of the best unsigned bands in the country.*

"We're probably destined to be a cult band," I told the writer presciently, although in retrospect even that might have been a bit of a reach.

We did a lot of good work with the Tim Lee 3, but more importantly, we had a lot of fun.

There was one winter during that era when it seemed to snow on any day that we had a show lined up. Each time, we just resolved to show up and play, regardless of the circumstances.

One Friday night, we had a show slated for the Downtown, a cool little restaurant bar in the middle of Morristown, an hour north of Knoxville. It started snowing early in the day, and the Downtown's owner Alan Herbst called to let us know that the other band on the bill had canceled. I told him we'd be there either way. The Downtown served excellent burgers and fries, so it could've been my stomach talking as much as anything.

By the time we showed up, the snow had intensified and we played a set to three people plus Alan (who ran sound) and his wife/partner Patti (who minded the bar). Yes, we saw just less than a half-dozen faces, but we did what we set out to do.

At the end of our set, the three listeners said they were leaving as they feared the roads would get worse as the night progressed. I asked Alan if he wanted us to play another set or pack up and go home (hey, we aren't quitters!). Before he could answer, the bar's phone rang. A voice on the other end of the line asked if the Downtown was still open, said they were bringing a group of ten or so people down.

That settled it, we started up again as the new crowd, mostly members of a German documentary film crew who were working in the area, arrived, bringing the assembled group to the appropriate dozen. The foreigners were ready to have a good time, so they bought drinks and hit the dance floor. One of the women used her limited knowledge of the English language to repeatedly request, "Sweet Home Alabama." In the spirit of the evening, we obliged but substituted the words to "Werewolves of London." It's all the same three chords.

The night ended with us all outside in the middle of Morristown's Main Street engaged in a spirited midnight snow-ball fight, rock band versus Germans. In the end, both sides claimed victory and we made our goodbyes. Then we hit the road for a particularly slow and precarious drive home down Interstate 81.

Another time, we drove through a heavy snowstorm to a gig in Whitesburg, Kentucky, a small town with a thriving arts community smack dab in the center of coal country, for a return engagement at the Summit City, a happening coffee shop/ bar on the main drag owned by our friends Joel Beverly and Amelia Kirby.

By the time we arrived, there were several inches of snow on the ground, so we figured the turnout would be light (hey, we had an excuse this time!). Susan and I were sitting near the door, chatting with Amelia, who was collecting cover charges, when a middle-aged guy came in. There was nothing unusual about him beyond the fact that his clothing resembled a mail carrier's uniform minus any identifying patches. He looked like someone whose neighbors would later say, "He seemed nice enough, but he was quiet and kept to himself."

He asked Amelia who was playing, and she pointed at us and said, "Them."

"Do you think they'd let me sit in?" he inquired, as if we weren't sitting right there.

"Ask them," Amelia replied.

He introduced himself, adding, "Everybody calls me Maestro," and said that he played trumpet. He asked what kind of music we played, and I tried to downplay it. I mean, original bands like ours are not exactly looking for complete strangers to join in without them being asked.

"It's just rock and roll, you know," I said. "Kinda three chords and a cloud of dust."

"Three chords and a cloud of dust," Maestro chewed on the words, parsing the concept internally.

He asked to sit in, and I put him off, figuring he wouldn't stick around after actually hearing us. I told him we'd play the first set and get everything situated, and if it worked out, he could play a song with us in the second set.

When we finished the first set, Maestro was still sitting at a front table, nursing a Pepsi and smiling. "Should I get my axe out of the car to warm it up?" he asked.

Sure, I said, and told him we'd bring him up for the last song of the second set.

At the time, we were in the habit of ending our second set with an extended version of R.L. Burnside's "Snake Drive," the closest thing to a jam song we played. When we reached that point, we introduced Maestro, who brought his horn up. We told him the song was in the key of A, and we started the quiet buildup we always used to start the song.

Maestro stood probably ten feet behind the microphone and let loose with one of the purest tones I've ever heard. Magic sound issued from the bell of his trumpet. We all looked at each other in disbelief. The guy was fantastic, laying down really cool solos in the right spots and comping appropriately in the others.

We finished the song, excitedly telling Maestro how good he sounded. He was largely nonplussed as he quickly and quietly put his "axe" back in its case and made his way out the

I Saw A Dozen Faces...

front door, disappearing into the snowy night. We never saw him again.

Bo Diddley was right: you can't judge a book by looking at the cover.

After all the years of patching together combos for tours that would end with all the members going different directions, it felt good to actually be part of a real band, even if it was one that went through four drummers in a single decade. Throughout it all, Susan was the rock I could count on to help hold it together.

We often took advantage of the three-piece lineup's flexibility to include friends of ours when the spirit moved us. Guitarist friends Greg Horne and Kevin Abernathy were often invited to sit in. Another pal, Christina Horn, played keyboards with us some and I, in turn, played guitar with her band Hudson K on occasion.

One night, early in the TL3's existence, we were playing a benefit for the local roller derby team at the Corner Lounge. Local rapper/poet Black Atticus was on the bill as well and I ran into him when he entered the crowded club. Atticus is a master of free style, so I asked him if he wanted to join us for a song in our set. Although we barely knew each other, he agreed, and we came up with a plan.

When we got to the midpoint of the last song in our set, Atticus took his cue and hit the stage blazing, bringing his buddy Star up to join in as hype man. The energy was off the charts, and the fun meter was pegged. They killed it and the audience loved it.

To me, there are few things more fun than pulling off the unexpected, especially when bringing disparate folks together in the name of a real cool time.

A few years later, we were playing in Jackson, where we hung out with my nephew, Garrad Lee, who was involved in local hip-hop promotions. He told us about a series he'd put together with his friend Cody Cox, a local indie rock musician, called Blenders. Their concept was to pair up rock and roll bands with rappers and DJs for gigs that showcased the acts, but also provided some cross-pollination between genres.

I got excited about the idea, and we immediately planned a couple of Knoxville/Jackson Blender collaborations. Initially, Cody's band Liver Mousse and rappers 5th Child and James

Crow traveled up to Knoxville to join the TL3 and the Theoritz (Atticus' project with Jarius Bush) for a show. Another time, we loaded up with Atticus and hit the road to Mississippi for a show in Jackson, where we shared the stage with DJ Young Venom and rapper 7thirty.

The exchanges were fun for all involved, and it was cool to work with Garrad and Cody. As usual, it's the unexpected combinations of folks that make this music thing magical.

The Tim Lee 3 kept busy, but Susan and I started our new duo band Bark in 2014. After a couple years of going back and forth between the two combos, it became a lot of work to juggle the booking and maintaining of two bands so we ultimately decided we should do one or the other.

In 2016, the Tim Lee 3 released our fifth full-length recording, *Tin, Man*, and went on indefinite hiatus, allowing Susan and I to focus on Bark.

I talk a lot about chemistry and the joy of interacting with fellow players amongst these scribblings, but there is nothing that compares to the Bark experience for me. Susan is my soul mate, my best friend, and when we lock into our thing, the feeling is sublime.

Playing together with other people is great, but with Bark, it is stripped down to just the two of us. What you get is the essence of who we are: the good, the bad, and everything else. There's just not much to hide behind in a two-piece band.

Susan took up the drums out of the blue, after we got a kit for our basement practice space in early 2014. Initially, latter-day TL3 drummer Chris Bratta showed her a few things and wrote out some charts to get her started. Susan took to it immediately, and within a couple weeks I'd hear her downstairs, banging along with Creedence Clearwater Revival records, hitting all the snare fills and cymbal crashes without missing a beat (so to speak).

In time, I ventured down and played some guitar riffs along with her drumming. We started making up a group of songs for a duo format. It really came together when I got my hands on a Fender Bass VI, which is a six-string instrument tuned like a guitar but an entire octave lower. The VI gave me the tonal range to come up with parts that amounted to essentially playing bass and guitar at the same time.

Susan quickly figured out that she could sing while drumming, and Bark was born. It's a fun mixture of groove, grit, and melody, a fun rocking kinda post-punk swampy thing.

It's always a trip to hear people try to describe what we do. One night, a young guy in Charlotte told me that he and his friends had spent our entire set trying to come up with a genre description for us. "We finally decided on stonerbilly," he said proudly.

"That's swampedelic stonerbilly to you," I shot back, with a laugh.

Bark had only been a thing for about six months when we went into Top Hat Studio with engineers John Harvey and Mary Podio to record our first record, a self-titled eight-song CD (we knew a total of nine songs at the time). Susan had only been playing drums for seven months and initially protested that she wasn't experienced enough with that instrument for recording, but I talked her into going through with it.

We recorded everything pretty much live, no headphones, and with minimum fixes, and the results are quite good. After years of making records with all manner of approaches, I enjoyed the primitive garage band-type approach. John and Mary were great fun to work with and got into the stripped-down vibe of the project. It was impressive to watch Susan record her vocals live as she tracked drums, which is no small feat.

I've long been a fan of the male/female vocal dynamic of X, Gram Parsons and Emmylou Harris, Richard and Linda Thompson, Buddy and Julie Miller, and the Divine Horsemen. I tried for a long time to find my own version of something like that, and I've had in small doses here and there, so I'm really grateful (and lucky) that Susan has turned out to be such a perfect musical partner. When we sing together, something magical happens. When working on a new song, our voices tend to find their places in a natural way. I would have never guessed it would turn out this way, and I don't take that for granted.

Looking back, it seems that I tend to thrive when working with a musical sparring partner (or partners). Starting with Barron Sartin or Benny Douglas, through Bobby Sutliff or Beat Temptation, Gene Holder or Randy Everett, John Stirratt, Mitch Easter, or Don Coffey, there's something about the give-and-take of that type of relationship that works for me.

by Tim Lee   215

Despite our late start as a musical team, Susan and I have created our own world, first through the Tim Lee 3 and now with Bark. I couldn't ask for a better partner, both in life and in rock and roll.

Over the past couple decades, we've traveled the majority of the country to play music, both ours and that of our various friends and collaborators such as Knoxville's RB Morris, a renaissance man of sorts: singer-songwriter, poet, playwright, author. We've continued to work with Black Atticus, both live and in the studio. There have been occasional recordings, tours, or one-off live shows in collaboration with the Silos' Walter Salas-Humara, Austin stalwart Jon Dee Graham, our old Rain Parade pal Matt Piucci, Steve Wynn of the Dream Syndicate, Judybats singer Jeff Heiskell, Appalachian singer-songwriter Angela Faye Martin, my Knoxville buddies Kevin Abernathy and Greg Horne, former Tenderhooks front man Jake Winstrom, Arkansas singer/songwriter Jim Mize, DJs Young Venom and Bric a Brac, improvising composer/electronic guitarist Mike Baggetta, Bruce Golden and Sherry Cothren, and others.

It's pretty safe to say we don't back down from a collaboration.

You can do that when your bond is strong.

The two of us have been through a lot together: ups, downs, and all points in between. They say that what doesn't kill you makes you stronger. In the case of Susan, I'd say it's *who* doesn't kill you that makes you stronger.

29. WHAT MAKES A MAN START BANDS?

In 2015, the Tim Lee 3 were in our ninth year of existence. Chris Bratta was the fourth drummer to join up with Susan and I in this particular endeavor, and he'd been on board for four years at that point.

I was in my mid-50s, and the TL3 was the umpteenth band I'd been in over the previous 40 years.

June 6, 2015

What makes a grown man climb in a van and drive long distances just for an hour (or less) of being on stage, playing rock and roll?

That's what I asked myself as we pulled onto I-85, headed back to Knoxville from Charlotte on a beautiful spring morning. We were on the cusp of summer, and most middle-aged guys were washing their cars, mowing their lawns, or getting ready to cook out with the family and friends.

I was driving the van.

My band and I had just fueled up: gas for the van and coffee for the body and soul. With our usual NPR radio fare on the box, it was time to roll home.

I considered the four-hour drive that we faced, and I thought about the question I posed at the opening of this bit of scribbling. I knew the answer, and frankly I was quite comfortable with my choices.

The previous night, we played a show with two of our friend bands at a great rock club called Snug Harbor. It was probably our fourth show in Charlotte over the past couple years, and it had been the best. We kicked off the evening with a short

by Tim Lee

set, played well, and the 45-minute affair felt well-paced and rocking. The room had a great vibe, a lot of energy, and the three of us had a blast.

The audience was responsive, and we made some new friends and fans from those who were mainly on hand to see 6 String Drag, a killer roots-rock band from Raleigh, and local rockers the Temperance League.

We saw at least a couple dozen faces, and we rocked them all.

The Temperance League featured our pal, Shawn Lynch, who was also kind enough to put us up for the night at the house he shares with his wife Kat Babbie. We met Shawn several years ago when he was playing bass with Mitch Easter, who made the drive down to Charlotte from his home in Kernersville to see the show and hang out.

It was great to share a few moments with Mitch. It had been a while. He's a relatively private person, so we enjoyed seeing him out. He's also a hero to many people, and occasionally our conversation was interrupted so he could pose while people had their picture taken with him.

The miles clicked off as we drove west toward the Smoky Mountains that separate our home in the valley from the Piedmont region of the Carolinas, and I thought about the set we played the night before, the chemistry we enjoy as a band, and the sheer joy I derive from playing electric guitar with the two other people in the van.

It's a funny thing, this band business. You can spend years playing with different people and never find that chemistry that makes a combo special. That undefinable communication that separates a random group of musicians from a true band, a living, breathing entity. Some folks find it pretty early. Look at combos like R.E.M. or the Who. Those original groups of four individuals found each other early on, and together they created something akin to a force of nature. They just had it. Each member's strengths supported the others' strengths, and also covered any potential weaknesses.

I've played in my share of bands over the years, from various ragtag collections of misfits to well-rehearsed professional outfits. On occasion, I've experienced that collective chemistry, and it is among the most thrilling experiences there is for those who have been fortunate enough to feel it. When it happens, it's an electricity of sorts, a bond that tugs at the soul, and in the best circumstances, pulls the body along. Time stands still, conscious thought leaves the room, and the groove carries you along.

I experienced it for the first time at 14, when a friend of my older sister found out I was learning to play guitar. He was looking for someone to accompany him while he cranked out some solos, so he invited me over one day.

David Bowling was a skinny red-headed high school student with a Fender Mustang he played through the family stereo in the den of their house. I was a skinny dark-haired kid who had an old Kay hollow-body with ridiculously high action, the knowledge of a few chords, and a tiny Silvertone transistor amp.

Somehow David had the patience to teach me to play barre chords and the riffs to "Johnny B. Goode" and "Jumping Jack Flash." But the moment I could suffer through the pain of pushing down on that old Kay's strings to follow along while David reeled off solo after solo, I was hooked. It was thrilling to hear (and feel) the meshing of two musical instruments in some sort of synchronicity. I'm sure we were terribly out of tune and time both, but it felt amazing.

I've never forgotten that feeling. I still chase it every time I pick up an instrument.

We kept pretty quiet as we rolled down the road, now on scenic state route 74, past green fields and older farm homes, and a rare still-functioning drive-in theater, which was showing a double bill of *Poltergeist* and *Mad Max*. I wondered aloud if this was actually 2015 or 1985.

Regardless of the decade, I was still in the van, making miles and bad jokes, on the hunt for a reasonable cup of coffee.

A traveling band spends a lot of time together. Between road time and practice, even a part-time combo is together for a lot more time off stage than on. It helps to enjoy the company of your companions. I've certainly spent time in vans, dressing rooms, and studios with people who were hard to get along with or just unpleasant on one level or another. Hell, I'm sure I've been that person at times. In my world, though, those folks have proven to be the exception rather than the rule.

With Susan, there is the obvious chemistry that has kept us together as a couple for more than 30 years through thick and thin, and we've experienced plenty of both. When she started playing music, I wondered what it would be like to be in a traveling band with her. Sure, we'd covered lots of miles together over the years, but there is a difference between being half of a couple and being part of a larger contingent, a band, for instance. Fortunately, she's a trooper who just wants to go places and play rock and roll. She calls herself "one of the guys" on the road. Sure, she appreciates a clean place to change clothes and "be a girl," but she rarely complains about the accommodations, unless they're bad enough that we all grouse.

Chris shared her passion for going places and playing music, so as the de facto ringleader my job was pretty easy.

At some point, one of us brought up the previous night's show, and we all agreed that it was a high point, recounting various reactions from people. It never hurts to remind yourselves, collectively, of the positive aspects of this crazy thing we do.

It gets back to that reason for climbing in the van in the first place. If you love the buzz that you get from playing music with your friends, it's worth all the hours on the highway, the lack of sleep, the crappy truck stop coffee, and occasional inconveniences. It just is.

This is our fun. It's our version of fishing trips, family vacations, beach visits, and golfing excursions all rolled up into one with an added dash of art on top. And we do it more weekends than not. It is a joy, not a labor.

Is it work, though? That's a good question. My best answer is that it shouldn't feel like it.

Much as it was during my original so-called career, my latter-day bands exist in a funny spot. We play music because we love the experience, the travel, the buzz of our chemistry, the fellowship with other bands, the fun, and the element of the unknown that awaits you every time your tires hit the pavement. We write new songs and make new records that we want to be heard. So the work is there, but so is the joy.

We played 50-something shows in 2014, going as far west as St. Louis, as far south as Hattiesburg, Mississippi, and as far north and east as Boston. Not bad for a group that books it own shows. We jokingly referred to ourselves as "the world's busiest part-time band."

The gig at Snug Harbor was based on a door deal, meaning a percentage of the collected cover charges goes to the bands to split. It's rarely a super-lucrative arrangement, but it can work out. That night, we received a reasonable amount, considering it was three acts. Not quite enough to break even on the trip, but we also sold a handful of CDs, albums, and coozies, which put us over the top. We were able to pay Chris, cover gas and food, have our dogs boarded overnight, and Susan and I managed to take home a few bucks.

Nothing great, but honestly, I'd have gladly paid for the experience. Playing a fun show, seeing good bands, meeting new people, collecting a few stories to tell, and spending time with old pals … you can't put a price on that kind of thing.

> On a recent road trip to Mississippi to visit my dad, I listened to a pretty successful singer-songwriter being interviewed by a popular podcaster. Discussing their career's origins, the artist described an early band, pointing out that "we'd drive five hours to play a show for $100." Both interviewer and interviewee marveled at the notion of such craziness.
>
> All I thought was, "Big deal. I do that all the time."

Make no mistake, there are plenty of time-consuming tasks that go into this stuff: band practice, songwriting, booking, planning, coordinating schedules, and working out logistics all take up a fair amount of your day. Plus all of that happens during the time that you aren't working a job, having normal relationships, grocery shopping, cooking, cleaning, taking care of pets, and all the requirements of everyday living.

Because we're gone a lot, we miss out on events that we'd otherwise attend, but being out in the world, experiencing new things, making memories, and interacting with different people is a life-affirming activity, one that some of us crave.

Eventually, we lost the NPR station signal and Susan hooked up her iPad and "put on some jams" as she says. Her iTunes holds a few thousand songs, so she just puts it on shuffle and we listen to whatever comes up.

by Tim Lee   221

On this morning, it was the usual blend of old and new. Howling Wolf followed Thin Lizzy, and then our pals Wussy popped up. Soul singer Howard Tate segued into Sleepy Kitty, a guitar-and-bass duo I saw at the Pilot Light one night on a whim. A song from our friend Dan Montgomery, a singer-songwriter in Memphis with a shit-hot band and new record, popped up. I'm always happy to hear an old friend continue to produce their best work. The Saharan band Tinarewin met British punkers the Buzzcocks, while R.L. Burnside, Cheri Knight, the Dirtbombs, Buck Owens, the dB's, Big Chief Monk Beaudreaux, and Jimi Hendrix all had their turn in the queue.

I took in the various musics, felt the road buzz beneath my feet, worked through the traffic that moved with and away from us. I prefer driving to riding these days, due to my generally fidgety nature, so the steering wheel is no stranger to me.

Sometimes the digital listening device seems to sense your mood and provide the proper playlist. I'm not a particularly sentimental or nostalgic person, but what's left of my mind is packed with good memories from all the years I've done this music thing.

Picking up on my musings, the iPad offered up "Don't Go Away" by the Primitons, a band that came out of Birmingham in the 1980s who were close friends of mine. I always thought of them as the Windbreakers' brother band. We played many shows together, arguing good-naturedly over who had to play last at the notoriously late Nick in their hometown, or who had to play first at W.C. Don's in our town, where the bars closed at an earlier hour. Jon Byrd and David Minchew both did stints with the Primitons after their tours of duty with the Windbreakers.

Primitons front man Mats Roden was a lovable bear of a Swede, a massive guy with the voice of an angel and a melodic sense that produced "more hooks than a tackle box," as Susan says. Sadly, Mats passed away just over a year ago. He'd suffered a stroke and had some rough times in recent years. I regret not seeing him during that time, but we emailed a bit, and his spirits seemed to be good.

Such a sweet soul, such a killer talent.

I thought about his longtime bandmate, drummer Leif Bondarenko, a ridiculously handsome guy of Russian decent, who'd played drums on a tour with me once. I considered him the Southern Max Weinberg, solid as a rock with the "open style" of stick handling, a completely instinctive player. One of the best I ever heard. (Um, it might be obvious, but I've been blessed to play with a lot of great drummers.) I hoped he was doing well.

Tunes by Game Theory and Let's Active followed, reminding me of more friends who have left us in recent years. Game Theory's Scott Miller and Let's Active's Faye Hunter died by suicide just a couple months apart two years ago, devastating us, their friends and families. I knew Scott from playing shows together on the road and from the time Game Theory stayed at our house in Jackson. Faye was a closer friend, someone I'd collaborated with on record and played alongside on stage during the Let's Active tours. We last saw her just a few weeks prior to her death, when she and a friend came out to see us play in Winston-Salem.

She and Susan had a long conversation that night, and Faye looked well. It was no secret that she was having a tough time as full-time care-giver to her aging mother, but she seemed to be doing better. As the evening wound down, she gave me a hug, one that lasted noticeably longer than the usual hugs between friends.

I'll never forget that hug. It haunts me still.

In August of 2006, Mitch put together a band called Gravel Truck, which he billed as a Let's Active cover band (claiming "we don't like them enough to be a tribute band"), to open for Pylon at an event in Winston-Salem. He asked me to play bass and Susan to sing. She and I figured it took the two of us to play the part of one Faye.

It's a drag getting older and losing some of your contemporaries. For me, though, that's just impetus to keep moving forward. No time to rest on one's flimsy laurels; not enough hours in the day to slack off. Rock and roll ain't gonna make itself, you know?

A recent Dan Stuart song played, and I thought about our old pal, who we've known since Susan and I booked Green on Red in Jackson about 4,000 eons ago. They stayed at our house for a couple days, and we've remained friends. Recently, we've been fortunate to reconnect with Dan and play a couple shows together.

by Tim Lee

I recalled a week maybe four years prior, when a bunch of us gathered in Tucson to play the HoCo Fest to help raise money for our mutual friend Craig Schumacher, who was fighting head-and-neck cancer and trying to keep his WaveLab studio open during his draining rounds of radiation and chemo. Susan and Dan and I closed down the bar at the Hotel Congress several nights in a row with bassist/producer J.D. Foster and singer-songwriter Richard Buckner. It was a helluva time, one of those memories that sticks with you.

Buckner played a killer set that weekend, backed by Calexico along with J.D. and steel guitar wizard Jon Rauhouse. Susan and I played a TL3 set with our Tucson pal Winston Watson on the skins, and we ended up joining Dan and J.D. and Jack Waterson to play a set of Green on Red songs, which was just an insane amount of fun. After that, I sat in with Saint Maybe, which featured Craig on keys, former Patti Smith guitarist Oliver Ray on lead vocals and guitar, local guitarist Naim Amor, and Winston on drums.

It was a good time. A real good time. Another one of those magic nights. I sometimes pinch myself and wonder if I really get to do the things I do.

As the last note of the song trailed off, Jon Dee Graham slipped the headphones off his head and looked around at the players on his right and the recording engineers on his left.

"That was pretty magical," he said with a grin.

Those of us gathered at Top Hat Studio for the occasion nodded our heads in agreement. We'd just nailed Jon Dee's song, "The Ballad of Dan Stuart," in a single take, not bad considering we'd never played together before that week.

It was early February of 2016, but strangely warm outside, when Susan, Chris, and I set up for the inaugural session at the new Top Hat Studios, which had relocated from Austin, Texas, to Knoxville.

Singer/songwriter/guitarist Jon Dee Graham had come from the Lone Star State to lay down tracks with his friends and longtime collaborators, Top Hat proprietors John Harvey and Mary Podio.

Jon Dee asked the Tim Lee 3 to be the backing band for the sessions, which yielded five songs for eventual release under the title *Knoxville Skyline*.

As a fan of Jon Dee's dating back to his tenure in the True Believers, it was gratifying to be involved in the project, especially on a wryly humorous song that paid homage to a mutual old friend. It was also great fun to christen John and Mary's new studio, where Susan and I have made many recordings since.

Jon Dee came back to town in early August 2017 at John and Mary's invitation to play their "T 4 Texas, T 4 Tennessee" series, for which they paired one of their Lone Star State friends with a Knoxville artist at the Pilot Light every Thursday for a month. Jon Dee shared the bill with RB Morris for what promised to be a great show.

It didn't disappoint.

Unfortunately, Susan was out of town tending to her parents, but John, Chris, Mary, and I backed Jon Dee on the opening set, and it was a scorcher. Chris, Greg Horne, and I were slated to be RB's band as well, and his set came out of the gate smoldering in a slow burn. Halfway through, we turned up the heat by inviting Jon Dee to join us, upping the guitar muscle (and the volume) considerably.

We closed out with RB's song "Distillery," which the TL3 had covered with Black Atticus for a local compilation a few years previous. We drew the ending out as Jon Dee and I traded solos behind RB's testifying. I looked up to see Atticus in front of the stage. Apparently, he'd just been walking past the door of the club when he heard what was happening and came in. I motioned him to the stage and he took the mic and started freestyling, playing off of RB's words, taking the whole thing to yet another level.

It was a wild climax to an already amazing evening of music, another one of those instances of disparate folks getting thrown together to spontaneously create magic.

30. ENCASED IN AMBER

"That was great, but I was hoping you'd play some older stuff."

The stranger put his hand out to shake mine as I stepped off the stage.

The Tim Lee 3 had just finished our set at Piano's, a small showcase venue in Manhattan, where we'd just seen roughly a dozen faces and rocked them all. Okay, I thought, here's one of those record collector guys who wants to ask why we didn't play "Changeless" or "Glory."

"Yeah," I replied, in my most diplomatic tone, "I haven't really played the Windbreakers stuff in a long time."

"I actually meant your early solo stuff," he explained, catching me off guard.

It was well into the 21st century but, prior to that moment, I had never thought about the fact that I actually had several different eras of "older stuff." To my mind, there were simply two things: what I was currently doing and the stuff I'd done in the past. That was it, just two categories.

Over the course of almost 40 years, though, I've recorded three dozen or so records and have had some involvement with easily that many again. There are plenty of folks who've created larger discographies, but mine is pretty deep for a rock and roll kid from Mississippi.

At this late stage in the game, I still don't really know how to relate to my back catalog. But I've learned to accept that it's akin to George Costanza and his recurring relationship woes. It's not the old material, it's me.

Recording a song is a funny thing. Once it's done and released, it's as if it is encased in amber, like one of those mosquitos in *Jurassic Park*. People can pick it up and admire it, but the object of their fascination never changes. That version of the tune is eternal.

If you or I hear an older song we like, it often takes us back to a different time in our lives when perhaps it had a specific

I Saw A Dozen Faces...

meaning for us. We can pick up that piece of amber and turn it in our hands mentally. Some new aspect of the trapped insect may emerge, seen by our eyes for the first time.

A songwriter might stick a needle into the center of the amber and extract a little DNA that is then used to come up with a whole new tune that bears some resemblance to the original.

Most folks, however, just admire the encased insect, appreciating its unchanged nature.

That's not to say that each individual doesn't bring their own interpretation to a song. Everybody gets something different from a piece of music, influenced by their own experiences or interests. For instance, when **Terminal** *was released, a good friend of mine told me they didn't really like the song "Changeless," said it had too much of a moon/June rhyme scheme happening. On the other hand, years later, another close pal told me of writing those lyrics down and sharing them with a family member with whom they were on the outs. They said the text put into words what they didn't feel they had the capacity to say directly and ultimately helped them patch things up. That's two pretty different interpretations.*

There are many ways to look at songs, but to my mind a song is simply words and melody. Everything else — instrumentation, the order of verses and choruses, backing vocals — is just arrangement (or production, in the recording process) and open to interpretation. I have friends who consider the arrangement as part of their songs, and that's cool too. Just a different way of looking at it.

For instance, the first song that Susan and I came up with for Bark was "Our Lady of the Highway," which is a moderately rocking, straight-ahead number. But we also decided to record it for the Tim Lee 3 album, *33-1/3*, but as a slowed down version showcasing the bass and drums while the guitars weave in and out of the mix, leaving lots of space between the notes for atmosphere. It was still the same melody and words, but the two versions sound nothing alike.

In 2012, we put together a side project to reimagine a few of our songs in a quieter setting. With Susan on vocals, me on acoustic guitar, our cohort Greg Horne on mandolin and guitar,

by Tim Lee

and our friend Cecilia Wright on cello, as Quake Orphans, we worked up quieter versions of several of our songs. We played a few shows and recorded a limited edition seven-song EP late that year. It was fun to explore some tunes in a completely different setting, to test them out in a new sonic space.

Sometimes you just need to jump up and down on a song to make sure it's a strong one.

In 2020, Matt Piucci and I took part in a podcast interview about the recording of the *Gone Fishin'* album we made together in 1986. Some of the questioning was specific to certain songs, with the interviewer asking about their origins.

Honestly, I was thrown off balance. I shouldn't have been, but I hadn't thought about some of those songs in any depth in so long I couldn't conjure words to describe their decades-old origins. I struggled to offer any kind of comprehensible answers. I mean, I knew what they meant, kind of, but I couldn't put it into words.

It wasn't the older material, it was me. While I was looking back through some imagined backwards telescope of time, the interviewer was holding a piece of amber, asking specific questions about the makeup of that prehistoric insect trapped within. I had nothing to offer in the moment. We were looking at two different things, and I felt bad for not giving meaningful, succinct responses.

It was then that it struck me how people view the songs they liked at different times in their lives. We change, our experiences transform us, and we grow in many ways, not the least of which is simply older.

But the song remains the same.

You may remember a Windbreakers song as part of the soundtrack to your college years, but as the guy who wrote the song I probably just hear it as the work of a kid who was learning the craft. But, trust me, the problem is not you. It's me. You remember the song as it should be. I attach a bunch of meaningless psychology to the memory, doing nothing but fogging up the lens.

For years, I hadn't really bothered myself with what other people might think about my catalog (or why they would even care). I knew that a handful of folks — you might say a dozen or so at a time — seemed to appreciate certain songs or records, but my focus has always been on that next thing peeking over the horizon.

I was pretty strident about it for a while, capable of being a real jackass. I didn't want to — and wouldn't — talk about the past, only whatever plate was presently laid on my artistic table. I was positively Chiltonian in my refusal to discuss the Windbreakers. It was almost as if I believed that acknowledging the past might somehow diminish the present.

In short, I was an idiot.

I'm in recovery now, though, even accepting of the fact that this body of work is mine, and I have to own it. And I'm cool with that. I mean, I dig most of it, but I'll always want you to listen to my latest thing.

I suppose every artist has to sort out their relationship to their past. Most of my friends and contemporaries seem pretty comfortable with it, mixing their older material with their latest in a seamless manner. Growing old gracefully is another one of those skills that doesn't come naturally to me. As with playing guitar or writing songs, I'll just have to work at it if I'm going to master it.

Still, I don't want to live in the past and/or feel that my best work is behind me. I have made my peace with much of this, but if I don't believe that my next album will be as good, or better, than anything I've done before, why should I bother to do it?

I'm coming around, though. I've learned to pull those old chunks of amber off the shelf, dust them, and show them off from time to time, not to just hide them behind the newer pieces.

Hey, wanna see my rock collection?

by Tim Lee

31. WITH FRIENDS LIKE THESE

"It's the second room on the right when you go down that hall."

I've never been comfortable in hospitals. Really, who is? This situation was no different.

Susan and I found the room and walked in through the open door. There was no one there, except the person on the bed who was hooked up to all manner of medical machinery. It was overwhelming, "Six Million Dollar Man" type stuff.

I didn't recognize the guy on the bed. This must be the wrong room, I thought, as I turned to go find the nurse and let her know she'd sent us in the wrong direction.

Before I made it to the door, though, I saw the name printed on a piece of paper and taped to the wall:

Robert Sutliff

It just didn't register. There was no way that banged up, unconscious being on that bed was my pal Bobby. It was June 2012. We'd been friends for more than three decades. I knew Bobby Sutliff, and this clearly was not him.

But it had to be. This was his room. His name was on the wall.

I leaned in and looked more closely, began to make out his features beneath the bruised and swollen face.

Yeah, this was my pal Bobby.

The realization took my breath.

Bobby had been involved in a horrific single-car accident a week earlier near his Powell, Ohio, home, just outside Columbus. He was still in a coma when Susan and I visited. We were in town to play a show and talked the initially skeptical nurse manning the station into letting us into the ICU.

I don't know what we expected, but it wasn't this.

Bobby couldn't hear me, but I talked to him, laid my hand on his arm and told him there were a lot of people pulling for him. There really wasn't much more to say. Coming from a long line of staid Methodists, I don't spend a lot of time telling people

I love them. That's not the way I was raised. In the absence of words, I trust that my actions will do the talking.

After a few somber moments, we made our way out of Bobby's room and out of the building into the daylight. The vision of what we'd just seen weighed heavy, and we quietly went about our business, heading out to load in for that evening's show at Ace of Cups.

As usual, there was a job to do.

Ace of Cups is one of our favorite venues for several reasons, not the least of which is that it was (until recently) owned by another old friend, Marcy May, guitarist and singer in the band Scrawl.

I first saw and heard Scrawl in the mid-1980s. The Windbreakers were on tour and played a date at Stache's, the longtime Columbus indie rock venue. Scrawl was booked to open the show. My pal Mark Wyatt assured me I would dig them. As usual, Mark was correct.

Scrawl consisted of Marcy, bassist Sue Harshe, and drummer Caroline O'Leary. They were scruffy and sassy, and they were great. I loved them from the get-go, and the first time Scrawl went on tour they came to Jackson and stayed with us for a couple days. So we go back a ways.

Hanging out with Sue and Marcy is always a treat. They've been best friends forever and apparently have never lived more than two miles apart in their adult lives. They still keep Scrawl going with a drummer named Jovan.

A few years back, Bark shared a show with the Scrawl duo at Rick Wood's Wood House Concert series outside St. Louis. Susan joined Marcy and Sue on drums for a good chunk of their set. As much as I love playing music with Susan, I also dig the rare opportunities when I get to hear her perform with others, especially when it's two of your favorite people from one of your favorite bands.

That's the beauty of this music thing: the friends you make. There's a lot of joy in traveling around and hanging out with old (and new) friends on a regular basis. We don't make much money or earn a lot of acclaim, but the friendships you develop make it all worthwhile, the ones that have lasted decades as well as the ones you've made in recent years.

That alone can be reason enough to drag one's old bones back into the van.

by Tim Lee   231

Initially, Bobby's prognosis was guarded and not particularly promising. Fortunately, though, after nearly a month of heavy sedation, he began to make progress, slowly recovering from his numerous injuries. At first, improvements came at a glacial pace, but eventually Bobby began to heal more quickly.

By the time the Tim Lee 3 returned to Columbus the following year, Bobby joined us on stage to play a song.

On January 19, 2013, our Atlanta friend Chris Chandler promoted a Rain Parade reunion show at the Earl, a great rock club on the east side of that city. The Tim Lee 3 opened, and the evening was billed as a benefit for Bobby to raise money to assist him during his long recovery.

The event also served as a release party for *Skrang: Sounds Like Bobby Sutliff*, an 18-song CD paying tribute to Bobby and his songs. The project was a collaboration between Jim Huie of Paisley Pop Records, Ron Sanchez of Career Records, and Susan and I, through our own Cool Dog Sound imprint. The idea was to raise a few bucks and try to lift Bobby's spirits during his time of mending.

The limited edition disc, which quickly sold out, included contributions from a variety of artists, including Velvet Crush, Peter Holsapple, Don Dixon, Donovan's Brain, and members of the Rain Parade, Dumptruck, Long Ryders, and Wilco. Bobby's long-time Jackson friends John Thomas, Jeff Lewis, and David Minchew also provided their versions of his songs.

The Atlanta show was a beautiful thing, filled with good music and great friends. By then, Bobby was strong enough to make the trip down. Robin Sutliff and his wife Jennifer were on hand as well. Even our old friend Greg Ellis came in from Texas. Along with Robin, Susan, and I, Greg lived in the house in midtown Jackson that hosted the birth of the Windbreakers in its basement in 1981. As always, it was grand to see my Rain Parade brothers Matt Piucci and Steven Roback. Plus, nearly every person we knew in Atlanta was on hand.

I was thrilled, too, to see Gil Ray, my old pal and former Game Theory drummer. When Matt and Steven first put Rain Parade back together, Matt, who lives in Oakland, contacted me and asked if I knew any drummers in the Bay Area that they could consider.

Gil lived in San Francisco, but had recently battled cancer, so I reached out to him to see if he might be willing, able, and interested in the gig before I passed his name along.

He was excited at the prospect, and I helped connect him with the band. Matt, Steven, and the rest of guys were immediately taken by Gil and it was a perfect fit. He drummed with the Rain Parade for several years until his health began to fade again.

That night in Atlanta, Bobby joined my band on stage for a couple songs, as did Linda and Ruthie from Magnapop, and then he and I played "Glory" with the Rain Parade. It was another example of that kind of musical night I live for, when the spontaneity opens the doors of the imagination and special moments occur.

It was early in the morning when we finally all made it back to the Highland Inn, where both bands were staying after the Earl show.

I remember walking in the front door to see an obviously tipsy Gil in the lobby, swaying on his heels and grinning sublimely.

We hugged and he said, "Thank you so much, Tim."

Gil succumbed to cancer on January 24, 2017.

In August of 2018, the Windbreakers played a show in Jackson, our first in more than a decade. The event was another benefit, this one for our old pal James Patterson, an accomplished photographer who had been Bobby's first roommate, as well as a housemate of mine and Susan's in the late 1980s. James had recently been diagnosed with stage IV cancer, and many of us who loved him gathered to pay tribute with an event dubbed "With Friends Like These...".

Most of the Jackson bands of our generation played. In addition to the Windbreakers, there was Beat Temptation, Radio London, the Oral Sox (with guest Webb Wilder), and the Used Goods, as well as Bark and singer/songwriter/visual artists Lee Barber and Wyatt Waters. We even produced a limited-edition CD version of *Familiarity Breeds Contempt* to sell at the merch table.

It was a hell of a bash, and despite the somber nature of the event, it had the feel of a high school reunion, particularly the couple days prior to the show as everyone drifted back into town and together for quick rehearsals and casual hangs.

Most of the Jackson crew, circa 1979-1989, was there: Susan, Bobby, Sherry Cothren, Bruce Golden, Robin Sutliff, Jeff Lewis, David Minchew, Joe Partridge, Robert Crook, Joe Bennett, John Thomas and Larry Taylor from the Sox, Randy Everett, John Hicks, Lee, Wyatt, and others.

In the general spirit of a by-gone era, there was a lot of sharing of band members during the evening. Bruce and Joe Partridge played drums with three bands each. Sherry played bass with Beat Temptation and Wyatt, and sat in on guitar with the Windbreakers on "Run," a song she and I co-wrote. Bobby was part of both the Windbreakers and Oral Sox's sets, while John Hicks pulled triple bass duty with Lee, Radio London, and the Windbreakers.

The whole experience was like an episode of "This Is Your Life" starring everyone and based on each of our lives. Again, it's the friends you make along the way that make the trip worthwhile.

As per my usual modus operandi, I was deeply involved in the planning and coordinating, so I was busy the night of the show, stage managing and keeping seven acts on schedule, while playing with four of the bands. Thus, for me, the weekend was largely a blur.

They say hindsight is 20/20, and I have to say they are generally correct. In retrospect, I should have been more in the moment for "With Friends Like These…". Oh, we had a fabulous time during those three days, and I got to hang out with many of my favorite people, not the least of whom was James himself (I would make a subsequent trip to Jackson to visit him one more time before he passed that October). The event was quite successful and raised a lot of money between the show and the adjacent silent auction.

It was a gift to be among so many people with whom you've shared so much in the past. And it is not likely that something like this will happen again. But my primary concern that night was making sure everybody was on and off stage in a timely manner.

I Saw A Dozen Faces…

In some ways, I think that's the story of my life. I bust my ass to facilitate cool things as they happen and then miss out on much of the inherent coolness because of the blinders I convince myself are necessary to accomplish anything.

Gotta run, you know. Things to do.

When all is said and done, nights like "With Friends Like These..." are exactly why this guy starts bands. The nights of joyous racket that start with some organized agenda and then unfold into some other explosive musical event. When the unexpected actually happens. Like when a semi-famous rock star sits in with your high school band, when you share a small stage with one of your favorite bands, when like-minded people get together to show their support for an ailing comrade, when a friend makes an impromptu appearance in your set, like those nights when the gloves come off and the rock and roll gets down and dirty. When anything can happen, and often does.

Or when you find yourself surrounded by nearly all the people you knew when you began this journey.

Like that night we gathered for James.

It has nothing to do with glory, applause, or attention. It has everything to do with that feeling, that vibe, the magic that happens when the stars align, chemistry is ignited, and a joyous racket ensues.

Like the first time you played rock and roll with other folks.

32. THIS WORLD JUST WANTS TO BREAK MY HEART

"Where do you think you're going? Man, the show's about to begin."

August of 2017 was a particularly tough month for Susan and me. On the 18th of that month, her dad, Fred Bauer, died in his sleep from acute onset dementia after suffering declining health for several months. Susan had been there with her mom Yvonne in Corinth, Mississippi, for most of that time, coming home only when we had shows booked.

Ten days later on the 29th, I got a call from my sister Kaye informing me that our mom, Dot, had died suddenly from congestive heart failure. She'd had a hard time getting up that morning, and my father called on my brother Jack to come help him. They'd managed to get her out of bed en route to fulfilling her wish to make it to the couch, but she didn't make it and died in their arms.

After a whirlwind of funerals and family gatherings, despite our shell-shocked state, Susan and I began preparations for the first Bark tour of the Northeast in late September. Before that could happen, though, we were surprised by our friends at Lost & Found Records, who hosted an outdoor rock and roll show in our honor in their parking lot with live bands, food booths, beer trailers, and a silent auction. Susan and I have been involved in a lot of events at Lost & Found, working with owners Maria and Mike Armstrong and long-time employee Nathan Moses, along with a host of their other friends and supporters. Their gesture was particularly sweet and moving, and the day was a lot of fun with many of our friends and favorite bands taking the porch stage to fill the afternoon with music and good vibes.

It was a kind gesture, and the day was perfect on every level. It reminded us that, although we both have a tendency to feel like perpetual outsiders, we had made a home in Knoxville.

And yeah, as would be expected, Susan and I both sat in with some of the bands.

Our East Coast tour kicked off as we set out on the road to support our recently released *Year of the Dog* album with shows from the D.C. area to Boston. Along the way, we hung out and played gigs with friends around the Northeast before winding up with a raucous time at Dan and Liz Ferguson's Roots Hoot House Concert series in Peacedale, Rhode Island.

One highlight of the trip was a Monday night show at the Spotty Dog, a combination book store and bar in Hudson, New York. Our friend Amy Rigby works part time at the shop, and her husband Wreckless Eric offered to run sound for us. We've known Amy since she was touring with her first band the Last Roundup in the 1980s, and we'd met Eric through her, although I'd been a fan of his work since the late 1970s. They're two of the coolest folks you'll ever meet.

We drove up to Hudson that afternoon, following a live noontime appearance on Joe Belock's excellent Three Chord Monte radio show on WFMU in Jersey City. Upon our arrival and load in, we helped the store employees move the shelves around in order to make space for us to set up. We crammed our gear into a small area, after which Susan found herself more or less trapped behind her drum kit. Never mind, though, as Eric took it upon himself to pull up a chair and keep her entertained until time for us to play. Eric is unbelievably funny and kept Susan in stitches for the duration.

One of his funniest bits is his description of Susan and me and our status as deep Southerners. "They're a happy people," Eric intones in his British accent, as if narrating a *National Geographic* documentary. "Apt to break into song at a moment's notice.

"Word is that indoor plumbing will soon be coming to their neighborhood."

Oh, and the show was just as cool as the hanging out with old friends. I even reconnected with my old pal Spike Priggen, who I hadn't seen since his late-1980s stint as bass player in Dumptruck.

by Tim Lee

The week-and-a-half trek was an enjoyable break from the heavy aftermath of the previous month's events. Back home, though, there was still grieving to be done. My mother and I had become particularly close in her later years, and it was hard to believe I couldn't call her up for our occasional phone conversations any more. Susan's relationship with her father had been pretty rocky, but that didn't make things any easier for her.

We did the only thing we knew to do: get back to work. Making art from loss and heartbreak is a time-honored tradition, but it was a new thing for the two of us. Over the course of the next year, we plowed ahead, crafting the songs that eventually made up the next Bark album, *Terminal Everything*. We put a lot of effort into the arrangements, taking our time to let the songs find their own way.

The spirits of lost loved ones loomed large in songs like "Walk Small," "This World," "The Good Part," and "Home." We spent a lot more time than usual with them in development. At times, it was hard to sing through the tears but we persevered with our work, which was intensely personal in a way that we probably couldn't have accomplished with other band members in the mix.

By the fall of 2018, we felt like we had most of the pieces in place to make plans for recording the next album.

The personal hits kept coming that autumn, though. On Sunday, October 21, just a week after our 15-year-old basset hound Scooter passed away, we were preparing to attend a wake for Knoxville artist Eric Sublett at the recently-reopened Corner Lounge when I got a text from Sherry Cothren with three simple words, "James is gone." Our old friend James Patterson had succumbed to his battle with cancer.

Feeling the weight of all that loss, words started to pour out. It had to happen. But we'd had enough of sad songs. We didn't have any more in us:

> There's been a lotta loss here lately.
> It's getting kinda hard to take.
> You know, we oughta throw a big ol' party.
> We oughta do it before it's too late.

Based on a simple Hill Country-inspired riff, the song "Big Ol' Party" took shape quickly, providing us with the exclamation mark for our upcoming record, a celebration of and joyous commitment to the memory of all our loved ones who'd passed:

> *Yeah, we oughta throw a big ol' party.*
> *Oughta show 'em just how we feel.*
> *Oughta tell 'em how much we love 'em.*
> *Oughta make 'em out to be a big deal.*

The song mentions good dogs and dive bars in heaven where the artists gather for happy hour. It was the final piece in the puzzle, the tune we needed in order to feel ready to move forward with the project at hand.

In December of 2018, we moved in with John and Mary at Top Hat Studio for a long weekend of recording. Taking advantage of their large studio and home, we staked out a new sonic space, one both familiar and forward looking.

Drawing from the Knoxville music community, we collaborated with good friends on a trio of songs. Josh Wright of Big Bad Oven and Whole Wizard played his homemade baritone lap steel on "Big Ol' Party," while Black Atticus brought his mad lyrical and rapping skills to "Apocalypse Shimmy," a cover of a song by our friends Liver Mousse and 5th Child from Mississippi. The record closes with "Chimneyville," a song we recorded live in the studio before turning it over to Mike Baggetta, who added his own soundscapes to the piece.

As we wrapped up mixing and mastering, Susan was busy developing the artwork for the package with help from Bryan Baker and Sarah Shebaro at Striped Light, a letterpress operation associated with the record label of the same name. Successfully taking on a medium she'd never tried before, Susan made a three-color linoleum cut that we hand-printed on the album covers. She also set the type for the back cover.

It was a big undertaking but, with Bryan and Sarah's assistance, we managed to pull it off, providing the album with a nice handmade touch that complimented the personal nature of the material.

The physical task of running the press to print the jacket was grueling at times, but added to the cathartic feeling we experienced once the total package was in hand.

by Tim Lee

As part of the lead up to the album's release, Susan asked our friend Kristi Larkin Havens, a lecturer and professor who taught a class on punk rock at the University of Tennessee, to write a "one-sheet" promo page. Kristi and I talked about the songs and their origins, and she delivered an excellent treatise on **Terminal Everything.**

Kristi died unexpectedly on April 29, 2019, two weeks after delivering the one-sheet to us. It was a brutal blow.

Terminal Everything *is dedicated to the memory of Dot Lee, Fred P. Bauer, James Patterson, and Kristi Larkin Havens.*

We released *Terminal Everything* in the summer of 2019 to good reviews, and stayed pretty busy the rest of that year, playing shows and expanding our travel range.

In 2020, *Terminal Everything* won the prestigious Mississippi Institute of Arts and Letters award for Contemporary Music. It was extremely humbling and gratifying to be chosen among the impressive list of nominees that included the North Mississippi All Stars, Christone "Kingfish" Ingram, Molly Thomas, and my old friend George Cartwright.

It's not every day that a rock and roll duo gets rewarded for its contributions to the arts.

After spending the winter laying low and working on new material, Susan and I were just getting our road legs back under us in early 2020 when the pandemic hit, forcing us (and everyone else) to cancel all upcoming shows.

Our final pre-pandemic road trek was a Valentine's Day weekend mini-tour. Kicking off on that Thursday in Nashville with a show at Douglas Corner with Tommy Womack, we then headed to Champaign, Illinois, for a gig at the Sandwich Life House Concert series in the home of Cynthia Voelkl and Ernest Blackwelder, and a Saturday night at Mary's Place in Rockford, Illinois, where we were hosted by locals the Blue Healers.

Originally, we were to share the Nashville bill with the great singer-songwriter David Olney, with whom we'd become friends in recent years. But during a songwriter's festival the previous month in Florida, David collapsed and died on stage. His manager, our good friend Mary Sack, arranged for Tommy to join the show with his new band, the Crime Family, that featured David's long-time bassist Daniel Seymour. During our set, we

debuted an Olney cover, "James Robertson Must Turn Right,"
a song he'd played for an internet broadcast the afternoon of
his passing. For their part, Tommy and Family added a rocking
version of "Wait Here for the Cops," an old David Olney & the X
Rays tune.

The following night in Champaign, the specter of David
Olney continued to hover over the festivities, as Cynthia and
Ernest had hosted him on several occasions, and many of the
folks on hand were familiar with David and his work. The
evening was a joyous affair, though, and we all had a great time.
And as per usual, we left with new friends.

Mary's Place in Rockford was my kind of joint, an older bar
with a low stage in the back corner. We met up with Blue Healer
Michael Whyte for pizza before the show, and then loaded in
and got settled to watch his band. Before the show, we met
Michael's wife, Kathy Benton, and his brother, Dan, who had
seen the Windbreakers in Chicago some many moons prior.
Again, more new friends to carry forward.

It was a great weekend, and it provided a high note to go
out on since we were going to be sidelined from playing out for
a while.

Of course, none of us knew it at the time.

33. WHAT MAKES A MAN START BANDS

"Have a piece of cake," Mary said, pointing to the full-size confectionary replica of my Fender Bass VI.

Susan and I were gathered with friends at the Pilot Light, our favorite Knoxville rock club, to celebrate my 60th birthday on February 28, 2020. It was one of the last gigs we played before the pandemic hit.

We'd invited several of my favorite local artists to join Bark for the festivities, including the Roacheaters, consisting of our friends Elizabeth Wright, Harold Hefner, and Will Fist, and solo sets from Palatheda (Jason Boardman), and Criswell Collective (Brad Fowler). Whole Wizard, the other band I'm in with Will, Brad, and Josh Wright, also played a set. So did my pal Steve Gigante, who under the guise of Old Man Fuck You, debuted a new piece entitled "The Ballad of Ol' Tim Lee," in which he'd lined up various folks to take turns offering up rhymed roasts of yours truly in a musical setting.

Steve's bit was simultaneously one of the most hilarious and endearing things I've ever witnessed. I had no idea this was being planned behind my back. Nearly everybody in the room took a turn offering up their verses.

Among the highlights were these gems:

Don't buy him too many Pabst Blue Ribbons,
or he'll talk your ear off about ol' Billy Gibbons
(courtesy of Kevin Abernathy as recited by Mike Baggetta)

I Saw A Dozen Faces...

Twinkle, twinkle, old man Tim,
wonder if I'll be like him,
rocking out with furious rage,
even at a feeble age.
(Chris Rusk of ex-Gold, Caps, and Royal Bangs)

He can keep his when ya get on his nerves,
but he'll lose his shit if u request Free Bird!
(Black Atticus)

Of course, Susan provided my favorite of the lot:

You are my favorite iconoclast,
one of those good guys always picked last.
But if they gave out awards for being steadfast,
you'd have a room full of Grammys and a plaster cast.
(get yer minds outta the gutter)
At 60, yer as punk as when we first met,
way back when we were both brunette.
Thru vinyl, CDs, and even cassettes,
we're not the jet set,
More like Jones and Wynette.

It was flattering to have your friends go to the trouble to pen a few words and share them. I've never laughed so hard, or been so touched, in my life.

Frankly, after decades of this music stuff, it was all the validation I'll ever need.

The whole night was a blast, from the aforementioned guitar cake, courtesy of Mary Podio, through the nonstop music. It was my idea of a perfect evening. I got to celebrate with friends, dig some live music, and play sets with Bark (my favorite band I've ever been in) and Whole Wizard (the loudest, fastest band I've ever been in).

It was magic, like so many nights I've had the privilege to experience in the past, and it provided great memories, which in this case would have to carry us through the coronavirus pandemic until we and our friends could get out and safely commandeer a few stages for the purposes of rock and roll again.

It was a great reminder of why one does this. It's the friends, the joy, and those evenings of pure magic that make this guy climb in the van well past my sell-by date.

It's what makes a man start bands.

Never was or not, I've been a lucky man to have experienced all the fun, the love, and the music of this life. I wouldn't trade a minute of it for anything.

I'm an old guy now, an adult for all practical purposes. I can hold down a job, pay bills, shop, dress myself, be a productive member of society. Hell, I'm not a half-bad cook.

But when it comes to playing music, I have no interest in growing up. Even if I am a never-was who has surpassed his "sell-by" date, I have no interest in being a musician's musician and, no, I don't want to be a star. I just want to chase that initial buzz that I got from playing in the garage with a couple pals when I was 14 years old.

As long as I am physically able, I'll no doubt keep at it. There are more songs to be sung, records to be made, gigs to be played, and memories to collect.

Besides, there's always a dozen faces somewhere, and they aren't going to rock themselves.

Me and Susan on one of her first times on stage for a Windbreakers' reunion set at Sparklefest 2002, Raleigh, North Carolina. Mitch Easter played drums with us that night and claimed he kept up by watching the consistent tapping of Susan's foot.

I Saw A Dozen Faces...

Susan and me at Proud Larry's, Oxford, Mississippi, 2003. At one point in the set, a three-foot flame shot out of the center wedge monitor mid-song. Photo by Bruce Newman (from of the author's collection)

Don Coffey Jr. (left) and me, listening back to tracks from *Concrete Dog* at Money Shot Studio, Water Valley, Mississippi, 2005. He and I spent a lot of time together in studios during the early early-naughts. Photo by Susan Bauer Lee

by Tim Lee

The original line-up of the Tim Lee 3 at the Corner Lounge, Knoxville, 2007 (left to right): Susan, me, Rodney Cash. Photo by Jody Collins (from the author's collection)

Trading solos with Indigo Girl Amy Ray on Neil Young's "Cortez the Killer." Amy joined the TL3 for a song during a benefit at the Earl, Atlanta, Georgia, 2009. Photo by Jim Johnson (from the author's collection)

Susan and Black Atticus during the WUTK *Redistilled* compilation release show at the Electric Ballroom, Knoxville, 2008. Atticus is a long-time friend and collaborator of ours. Photo by Todd Reinerio (from the author's collection)

I Saw A Dozen Faces...

Listening to playbacks at WaveLab, Tucson, Arizona, circa 2012 (left to right): me, Susan, Craig Schumacher. We spent a lot of time on that couch over the years. Photo by Chris Bratta (from the author's collection)

Susan and guest Linda Hopper with Gravel Truck, Club 529, Atlanta, Georgia, 2009 (left to right): Linda, drummer Chris Garges, Susan, Mitch Easter. Photo by Jim Johnson (from the author's collection)

by Tim Lee

A rock and roll band in its natural habitat, the rock and roll club. The Tim Lee 3 at Knoxville's Pilot Light, October 10, 2013, (left to right): Susan, Chris Bratta, and me. (Photo by Bill Foster)

Susan and me, James Patterson Studio, Jackson, Mississippi, 2012. Photo by James Patterson

I Saw A Dozen Faces...

Tim Lee 3 at the Tennessee Theater, Knoxville, October 8, 2014 (left to right, Susan, me, Chris Bratta), rocking the rare large stage, opening for Cheap Trick. Photo by Saul Young (from the author's collection)

The Quake Orphans at WDVX Studios, Knoxville, 2013 (left to right): Cecilia Wright Miller, me, Susan, Greg Horne. Just jumping up and down on a song to test its strength. Photo by Beto Cumming (from the author's collection)

RB Morris leading the prayer service on one of those magic nights that makes rock and roll so special at the Pilot Light, Knoxville, Tennessee, 2017 (left to right): Greg Horne, Jon Dee Graham, RB Morris, Chris Bratta's sunglasses, me, and Black Atticus. (Photo by Bill Foster)

Bark at the Pilot Light, July 10, 2016. Susan and me at our favorite rock and roll club. Photo by Kristi Larkin Havens

I Saw A Dozen Faces...

Bark on the porch, April 2018. Susan and I play at Lost & Found Records for Record Store Day.

With friends like these … the Windbreakers rip through a song at a benefit for our friend James Patterson, Duling Hall, Jackson, Mississippi, 2018 (left to right): me, Sherry Cothren, John Hicks, Bobby Sutliff, Joe Partridge on drums. Photo by Reid Horn (from Sherry Cothren's collection)

by Tim Lee

ADDENDA

WE DIDN'T GET FAMOUS, BUT ...

Today, well into the 21st century, interest has picked up a bit for the American indie scene of the 1980s.

In 2012, Camilla Ann Aiken completed *We Didn't Get Famous: The Story of the Southern Music Underground 1978-1990* as part of her Masters Thesis in Southern Studies at the University of Mississippi.

It was a cool documentary that included interviews with plenty of the folks of our time and place, including me and Sherry Cothren, along with Mitch Easter, Peter Holsapple, Vanessa Hay of Pylon, and the late Mark Reynolds of Carnival Season (an alum of the final Windbreakers tour in 1990).

According to the film's promo spiel, "The Southern bands making what we'd now call 'indie' music in the 1980s were as equally in debt to punk rock, new wave, and Big Star, as they were to Southern culture and traditions. The bands of the Southern underground scene were fearless, innovative, original, and are enduringly influential and relevant in today's musical climate."

I tried to tell you we were pretty cool.

Camilla did a great job, and the film is as much fun as it is informative. Look it up on YouTube if you've not already seen it.

More recently, in 2021, record label Captured Tracks released the more broad-ranging **Strum & Thrum: The American Jangle Underground 1983-1987**, a double album compilation including the Windbreakers, Primitons, Great Plains, Absolute Grey, Holiday, and many of our friends and contemporaries.

It's cool to see that scene get the pro compilation treatment, with colored vinyl pressings and an 80-page booklet filled with stories, quotes, artwork, and photographs.

by Tim Lee

Surprisingly, both vinyl pressings, the black one and the orange one, sold out in less than a week after *Strum & Thrum*'s initial release.

And thanks to the work of the folks at Captured Tracks, the Windbreakers song "All That Stuff" wound up in an episode of the short-lived Netflix show, "I Am Not Okay With This."

Over the years, there have been remasters and repressings of records of that era, but recent years have seen a spate of reissues of bands from that scene, including updated versions of the Game Theory catalog from Omnivore Records and remastered pressings of the Great Plains canon from St. Louis' Rerun Records. Prior to that, Arena Rock Recordings compiled the Primitons and Carnival Season (including the demos I produced) collections into great comprehensive CD issues.

Even the Windbreakers were able to get in on the new old wave of 1980s nostalgia with an Italian CD reissue of *Terminal* on the Mark label, complete with a handful of live recordings from the era. As of this writing, Mark was preparing a similar version for *Run*. Jim Huie's Paisley Pop label released a WBs compilation, *Time Machine 1982-2002,* in 2003 that featured two new songs that Bobby and I recorded with Mitch.

Terminal enjoys some standing among the other indie releases of the 1980s. One-time London record store Plastic Passion ran their "Top 100 Albums of the '80s" poll results in UK zine *Bucketfull of Brains* at the end of that decade, and *Terminal* ranked 56th overall on the list (among 1,239 albums that received votes). Our pals the Rain Parade topped the list with their debut LP *Emergency Third Rail Power Trip*. Those who participated in the poll also listed the Windbreakers at 38th (tied with the Lyres) on the "Top 50 Groups" of the decade listing.

In 1990, Jim Testa's *Jersey Beat* fanzine published a retrospective of the previous decade, naming *Terminal* the top album of 1985 and among the "Top Ten Records of the 1980s" alongside Bruce Springsteen, the Clash, the Feelies, the dB's, R.E.M., Minor Threat, Hüsker Dü, the Replacements, and Squirrel Bait.

Speaking of Springsteen, the Boss played both a Bobby Sutliff solo tune and the Windbreakers' "Girl from Washington" on his satellite radio show in early 2021. In talking about the songs, he referred to us as a "great band." Thanks for the unintended blurb, dude!

In 2018, the Windbreakers were recognized by the Jackson Indie Music Week organization with a Jackson Icon award at a ceremony during their annual event. The Icon designation serves to "honor vanguards and trailblazers who have paved the way for independent music in central Mississippi."

*To prove that there's maybe a little more to this old dog than a few old tricks, Bark's album **Terminal Everything** was awarded the Mississippi Institute of Arts and Letter's 2020 award for contemporary music. It's pretty nice to receive such a prestigious honor at what is supposed to be well beyond our sell-by date.*

Remember me talking about the Divine Horsemen way back a bunch of chapters ago? Here's a cool thing: they reformed in recent years, still led by Chris D. and Julie Christensen. They recorded a new album, ***Hot Rise of an Ice Cream Phoenix***, which came out in 2021 and includes their version of the Tim Lee 3 song, "Any Day Now," for which they made a happening music video that was released this past September. Pretty slick, huh? We thought so.

Although my obsessions generally deal more with the present and the future than the past, it's been gratifying to see a little bit of light shone on the tiny corner of the music world that my friends and I occupied in that time and place.

It was a cool time, an era of endless possibilities, until it wasn't any more. But many of us have survived with life-long friendships intact and fond memories of those who are no longer with us.

I'll go out with a line I spoke in Camilla's film, from which her documentary got its name.

"We didn't get famous, but we had a lot of fun."

DISCOGRAPHY

Bark
Terminal Everything (Striped Light) 2019
A Single Bark 7" (Cool Dog Sound) 2018
Year of the Dog (Striped Light) 2018
Bark 8-song EP (Cool Dog Sound) 2015

Tim Lee 3
Tin, Man (Cool Dog Sound) 2016
33-1/3 (Cool Dog Sound) 2015
Live from Armory Sound Boston (Cool Dog Sound) 2015
Devil's Rope (Cool Dog Sound) 2013
Live at the Pilot Light (Cool Dog Sound) 2013
Raucous Americanus (Cool Dog Sound) 2010
good2b3 (Paisley Pop) 2008
In the Meantime ... EP (Paisley Pop) 2008

Tim Lee
Concrete Dog (Fundamental) 2005
No Discretion (Paisley Pop) 2004
Under the House (Paisley Pop) 2002
All That Stuff 1983-1993 (Fundamental) 1995
The New Thrill Parade (Blue Rose/France) 1991
Crawdad (DB Recs) 1991
What Time Will Tell (Coyote) 1988

The Windbreakers

Terminal CD Reissue w/live tracks (Mark/Italy) 2017

Time Machine 1982-2002 (Paisley Pop) 2003

Boxing Day Live (Paisley Pop) 2003

Electric Landlady (DB) 1990

At Home with Bobby and Tim (DB) 1989

A Different Sort (DB) 1987

A Different Sort (Zippo/UK) 1987

Run (DB) 1986

Run (Zippo/UK) 1986

"I'll Be Back" 12" single + 2 (DB) 1986

Disciples of Agriculture (Closer/France) 1985

Terminal (Homestead) 1985

Any Monkey With a Typewriter EP (Big Monkey) 1983

Meet the Windbreakers EP (Big Monkey) 1982

Beat Temptation
(Tim Lee, Bruce Golden, Sherry Cothren, Robin Sutliff)

Concerned About Rock Music (Homestead) 1986

Beat Temptation EP (Big Monkey) 1984

Quake Orphans
(Tim Lee, Susan Bauer Lee, Cecilia Wright, Greg Horne)

Quake Orphans (Cool Dog) 2013

The Gimmecaps
(John Stirratt, Tim Lee, Charles David Overton)

The Gimmecaps (Black Dog Records) 1997

Gone Fishin'
(Tim Lee, Matt Piucci)

Can't Get Lost if You're Going Nowhere (Restless) 1986

Howard & Tim's Paid Vacation
(Tim Lee, Howard Wuelfing)

I Never Met a Girl I Didn't Like (Midnight) 1986

Various Artists
Just One More: A Musical Tribute to Larry Brown, A Great American Author (Bloodshot Records) 2008, Produced and compiled by Tim Lee

Compilations/Tribute Appearances
Strum & Thrum: The American Jangle Underground: 1983-1987 (Captured Tracks) 2020, The Windbreakers, "All That Stuff"

Let Me Turn You On! (Easy Action/UK) 2013, The Windbreakers, "Never Too Soon"

My Hometown: A Tribute to New Jersey, (FDR Label) 2013, Tim Lee 3 "The Bulrushes" (Bongos cover)

Skrang: Sounds Like Bobby Sutliff, (Cool Dog/Paisley Pop/Career) 2013, Tim Lee 3 "I Thought You Knew"

Rave On: A Tribute to the Reducers, Vol. 1, (Good Sponge) 2012, Tim Lee 3 "Don't You Wanna"

Just One More: A Tribute to Larry Brown (Bloodshot) 2008, Tim Lee & Susan Bauer Lee, "The Bridge"

Bear Family Records 35th Anniversary, (Bear Family Records) 2010, Tim Lee 3 "Ursa Major"

Oxford American 11th Edition *Southern Music* (OA) 2010, The Windbreakers, "So Much"

ReDistilled: 25 Years of Knoxville Rock, (WUTK) 2008, Tim Lee 3 with Black Atticus, Starr, and Mercedes, "Distillery" (RB Morris cover)

PotLuck Audio Conference 2008 Sampler (WaveLab) 2008 Tim Lee 3 "Saving Gracie"

5 Way Street: a Tribute to Buffalo Springfield (Not Lame) 2005, The Windbreakers, "Expecting to Fly"

Stand-Ins for Decibels: A Tribute to the dB's (Paisley Pop) 2005, Tim Lee, "Molly Says"

Sensitive Guy's Guide to Groovy Music (Paisley Pop) 2004, Tim Lee, "Keep It True" / The Windbreakers, "Girl From Washington"

A Bucketful of Possibilities (BoB/UK) 2004, The Windbreakers, "Don't Wanna Know"

Pop Culture Press Sampler (PCP) 2003, Tim Lee, "Keep it True"

I Saw A Dozen Faces...

Hit the Hay Vol. 5 (Sound Asleep/Sweden) 2001, Tim Lee, "King and Queen of Uptown"

Pop Culture Press Sampler (PCP) 2000, Tim Lee, "Without Action (electric version)"

Every Word: Tribute to Let's Active (Laughing Outlaw/Australia) 2003, Failed Energy Giants, "Blue Pipeline"

Mississippi's Dreaming (Fishtone) 1993, Tim Lee, "So Cold" 1991

Squares Blot Out the Sun (DB Recs) 1990, Tim Lee, "Talked About It (acoustic version)"

20th Anniversary of the Summer of Love (Shimmy-Disc) 1987, George Cartwright, "I Remember it All"

Acres for Cents (Zippo/UK) 1987, The Windbreakers, "Run"

Ghost Snake Monster Friend (Mustang) 1987, Tim Lee, "Just Like Amazing Grace"

Hanging Out at Midnight (Midnight) 1986, Paid Vacation, "That Won't Make You Love Me"

Jericho Go! (Stiff/UK) 1985, The Windbreakers, "Nation of Two"

Familiarity Breeds Contempt (Big Monkey) 1985, The Windbreakers, "You Never Give Up" "Don't Say No" / Beat Temptation, "On Your Mark" "Bad Sermonette"

Studio Work

Mark Coram, *Black Cloud Umbrella* (self-release) 2019 (guitar)

Brian Paddock, *Under New Management* (self-release) 2018 (guitar on one song)

Hudson K, *Hudson K* (self-release) 2017 (guitar on one song)

Barstool Romeos, *Last Call for Heroes* (self-release) 2017 (guitar)

Jon Dee Graham, *Knoxville Skyline* (self-release) 2016 (guitar)

Greg Horne, *Working on Engines* (self-release) 2016 (guitar on one song)

Heiskell, *Arriving* (self-release) 2015 (guitar)

Kevin Abernathy, *Ain't Learned Yet* (Life Socket) 2015 (guitar/vocals/production)

Beth McKee, *Sugarcane Revival* (self-release) 2015 (guitar)

Barstool Romeos, *Twisted Steel & Sex Appeal* (self-release) 2015 (guitar)

Matt Woods, *With Love From Brushy Mountain* (Lonely Ones Records) 2014 (guitar)

Primitons, *Don't Go Away: Collected Works* (Arena Rock Recordings) 2012 (guitar, backing vocals)

Carnival Season, *Misguided Promise: Carnival Season Complete 84-89* (Arena Rock Recordings) 2010 (produced two songs)

Matt Woods, *The Manifesto* (Lonely Ones Records) 2011 (guitar, baritone guitar)

Plainclothes Tracy, *Plainclothes Tracy* EP (self-release) 2010 (guitar on one song)

Kevin Abernathy, *A Beautiful Thing* (Life Socket) 2009 (stunt guitar)

Kevin Hyfantis & the Bishop's Band, *Kevin Hyfantis & the Bishop's Band* EP (self-release) 2009 (guitar)

Heiskell, *Clip-On Nose Ring* (Jeff Heiskell Music) 2008 (co-produced, guitar, bass, keyboard)

John T. Baker, *Flirting with Azrael* (self-released) 2008 (guitar on one song)

Daniel Miller, *Backporch* (Daniel Miller) 2007 (co-produced, guitar, bass)

Angel & the Love Mongers, *Humanist Queen* (Rock Snob Records) 2007 (guitar)

John T. Baker, *Man in the Street* (Disgraceland) 2006 (guitar)

Mark Coram, *Garageacana* (self-release) 2006 (guitar)

Todd Steed, *Heartbreaks and Duct Tape* (Apeville 2005) (guitar)

Misery Loves Company, *Misery Loves Company* (Neverending 2005) (guitar)

Daniel Miller, *Southbound* (Daniel Miller 2005) (guitar, bass, keyboards)

Hoover's G-String, *Elephant Parts* (Red Tide 2005) (guitar)

Angel & the Love Mongers, *Angel & the Love Mongers* (Disgraceland) 2005 (guitar, keyboards)

Dogma Dogs, *Songs of Catholicism for Kids* (Liturgical Grooves) 2005 (guitar, bass)

John T. Baker, *Rough Skeleton* (Disgraceland) 2004 (guitar)

Invisible Mind Circus, *Look Inside* (Never Too Late) 2004 (guitar, organ)

Plan A, *The View Through These Words* (My One Plan) 2004 (guitar)

Sci-Fi Love Story, *Songs from the Planet's Surface* (SFL Records) 2004 (guitar)

Dutch Rub, *Somewhere in Summertime* (SFL Records) 2004 (guitar)

Leslie Woods,*The Luxury of Sin* (Cultstar) 2004 (guitar)

Todd Steed & the Suns of Phere, *Knoxville Tells* (Disgraceland) 2003 (guitar)

Swimming Pool Q's, *The Deep End* reissue (DB Recs) 2001 (bass on one song)

George Cartwright, *Dot* (Cuneiform) 1994 (bass on one song)

Primitons, *Happy All the Time* (Caroline) 1987 (guitar, backing vocals)

The Skeeters, *Wine, Women & Walleye* (DB Recs) 1988 (produced, keyboards)

Bobby Sutliff, *Only Ghosts Remain* (JEM) 1987 (guitar on one song)

Will & the Bushmen, *Gawk* (Mustang) 1987 (co-produced)

Even Greenland, *Another Place to Hide* single (Big Monkey) 1986 (produced)

Absolute Grey, *What Remains* (Midnight) 1986 (produced)

Bobby Sutliff, *Another Jangly Mess* (Tambourine/UK) 1986 (guitar on one song)

Used Goods, *Runaround/Drive-In* single (Big Monkey) 1983 (produced)

Podcasts

Play Dead: The Jackson, MS, Music Scene of the '80s and '90s, (podcasts. apple.com/ie/podcast/play-dead/id1487549945), December 20, 2019

The Watt from Pedro Show (www.twfps.com), April 8, 2020

Campfire Songs (www.buzzsprout.com/1460920/7728802-episode-5) February 7, 2021

In Loving Recollection (www.podbean.com/media/share/pb-tdgtj-d6717b), March 18, 2020

Paisley Stage, Raspberry & Rhyme (paisleystageraspberryandrhyme. podbean.com/e/episode-88-our-conversation-with-matt-piucci-and-tim-lee-gone-fishin/), July 24, 2020

Songs Covered by Other Artists

"Kiss Me Goodbye," recorded by Bobby Sutliff. *Perfect Dream* (Not Lame Recordings) 2002

"Any Day Now" recorded by Divine Horsemen. *Hot Rise of an Ice Cream Phoenix* (In the Red) 2021

ACKNOWLEDGEMENTS ...

As pointed out previously, it takes a village to raise a just-past-middle-age rocker, so I'd like to acknowledge a few individuals from that vast population.

First of all, Ron Rice, who I've never met in person, inadvertently lit the fuse on this firecracker in September of 2020 when he replied to one of my lengthy Facebook posts with "when you're ready to write a book, you let me know. I'll proof it." Thanks for the kick in the pants.

Big thanks to Edward Whitelock, who broke one of his own rules (and that of wise English professors everywhere) and got involved with a friend who said, "I wrote a book." Ed was a helpful advisor and offered wise counsel during the process. I owe you a couple rounds, buddy.

To Kevin Abernathy and RB Morris, two great pals who were always game to sit outside during the pandemic with a beer (or two or three) and talk about books, the act of writing, music, and art in general. Thanks, guys. Let's do it again. I've got this idea, you see...

My heartfelt appreciation goes out to Joe Partridge, Robin Sutliff, Bruce Golden, Mark Wyatt, Bobby Sutliff, Jon Byrd, and anybody else I pestered for their memories, usually with the vague disclaimer, "You see, I'm working on this project." Extra big thanks to Sherry Cothren for allowing me to comb through her archives for supporting artwork.

Much gratitude to my friend Carl Clements, who has kept me employed the last few years. I've long said that I go to work every day to pay my bills so that I have the freedom to play whatever music I want to play, how I want to play it, and when I want to play it. That same freedom applies to writing a book during a pandemic. Thank you, Carl.

Of course, nobody deserves more thanks than Susan, my muse and my love. She encouraged me from the start, insisted I was doing something good, and admonished me to stop referring to this as my "dumb book project." She also provided the excellent design. Thank you, thank you, thank you.

And a final thanks to anybody who joined me on stage, in a van, or in the studio along the way, anyone who ever bought a record or paid a cover charge when I played (that's right, all twelve of you deserve a pat on the back), and anyone who ever let me sleep on their couch, drink their coffee, or borrow a functioning amplifier.

Thanks for ignoring my mother's plea when she implored, "don't encourage him."

INDEX

I Saw A Dozen Faces...

by Tim Lee

American Author: 201, 203, 204, 205, 206, 260

by Tim Lee

I Saw A Dozen Faces...

by Tim Lee

I Saw A Dozen Faces...

by Tim Lee